Ron

Hope this go...

Uncle John's
Bathroom
Reader

TEES OFF
ON GOLF

By the
Bathroom Readers'
Institute

Bathroom Readers' Press
Ashland, Oregon

OUR "REGULAR" READERS RAVE!

"Love the books! I've learned more in the can than I ever learned in school."

—*Julie R.*

"My boyfriend gave your book to me for my father. I liked it so much, I kept it for *my* bathroom and got another one for him."

—*Angela O.*

"My sister-in-law sent me one of your *Readers* for Christmas a couple of years ago, and I became an instant devotee! Not only does the BRI provide essential tranquility and entertainment during a vital part of each person's day, but many of the facts and factoids absorbed during those now blessed respites can liven up conversation and impress the masses with the breadth of knowledge and wit of the reader! I am truly a grateful reader!"

—*Alex M.*

"My husband and I are huge fans of your books. I can't imagine how we were able to live without them as long as we did."

—*Nora P.*

"Your books are consistently gaining popularity in my workplace. I always have at least one *Bathroom Reader* in the classroom and read out of it at least once a day. Thanks again!"

—*Michael L.*

"I absolutely love your books. Your book has everything…facts, humor, silly stuff, and even things that make you go 'hmmm…'. I take my book everywhere. I just can't seem to put it down."

—*Ted Q.*

"Hey Uncle John and Co. I must say, your book series is one of my favorite things in world—other than golf. If you guys were to make a *Bathroom Reader* all about golf, well…it would be the best thing ever as far as I'm concerned!"

—*Philip B.*

UNCLE JOHN'S BATHROOM READER
TEES OFF ON GOLF®

For information, write
The Bathroom Readers' Institute,
P.O. Box 1117, Ashland, OR 97520
www.bathroomreader.com
888-488-4642

Cover design by Michael Brunsfeld,
San Rafael, CA (*Brunsfeldo@comcast.net*)
Uncle John's Bathroom Reader Tees Off On Golf®
by The Bathroom Readers' Institute
ISBN-13: 978-1-59223-382-3
ISBN-10: 1-59223-382-1

Library of Congress Catalog Card Number:
2005922735

Printed in the United States of America

Second Printing 2005
11 10 9 8 7 6 5 4 3 2 05 06 07 08 09

*   *   *

Congratulations to Joel Horowitz on winning the
2007 Tranquility Invitational.

Hiya Sam! Hiya Gideon!

THANK YOU!

The Bathroom Readers' Institute sincerely thanks the people whose advice and assistance made this book possible.

Gordon Javna
Thom Little
Jay Newman
John Dollison
Brian Boone
Julia Papps
Jeff Altemus
Jef Fretwell
John Gaffey
Jack Mingo
Erin Barrett
Michael Brunsfeld
Angela Kern
Amy Briggs
Jennifer Thornton
Dan Mansfield
JoAnn Padgett
Jennifer Browning
Lori Larson
Sydney Stanley
Joe "Ketchup" Diehl
Rain Thering
Sharilyn Hovind (WSLY)
Steven Style Group
Debi Taylor

Allen Orso
Scarab Media
Christine Degeuron
Tom Mustard
Banta Book Group
Paul Stanley
Kristine Hemp
Nancy Toeppler
Barb Porshe
Jenny Baldwin
Mana "Mayo" Manzavi
Barbi Pecenco
Raincoast Books
Allan MacDougal
James Broadhurst
Paula Leith
Leah Thom
Chris Olsen
Bil Leonhart
Adam Zoldan
Oak Knoll Golf Course
Joel Horowitz
Maggie "Salsa" Javna
Porter the Wonder Dog
Thomas Crapper

*　　*　　*

...AND BEST FLUSHES

to the millions of bathroom readers out there.

"I play golf because my sole ambition is to do well enough to give it up." —David Feherty

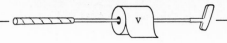

CONTENTS

Because the BRI understands your reading needs, we've
divided the contents by length as well as subject.

Short—a quick read
Medium—2 to 3 pages
Long—for those extended visits, when something
a little more involved is required
* Extended—for those leg-numbing experiences

*   *   *

HOW TO WIN AND LOSE AT THE SAME TIME

• Roger Maltbie pocketed $40,000 for taking first place in the 1975 Pleasant Valley Classic. That night he went to a bar to celebrate and took the check with him so he could show it off. When Maltbie awoke the next morning…the check was gone. He had to stop payment on it. (It's unknown if ever he got a replacement check.)

• Gary Player won the 1965 U.S. Open at Bellerive Country Club with first place winnings of $26,000, yet he managed to lose money on the deal. At the trophy presentation, Player donated $5,000 of the pot to a cancer research charity and $20,000 to the USGA to promote junior golf. He still had to pay his caddie $2,000 for his week's worth of work. That adds up to $27,000, leaving Player $1,000 in the red.

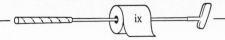

THE LITTLE WHITE BOWL…er…BALL

I f you're new to the world of *Uncle John's Bathroom Reader*…
Welcome!
The Bathroom Readers' Institute has been creating compendiums for the commode since 1988, right here in the sleepy little Rogue Valley in southern Oregon (home of six golf courses).

Our books usually cover a range of topics, but in the last few years we've started making "Little Johns" about single subjects. This is our first foray into the world of sports…and what better sport to start with then golf? It's got such a long and fascinating history, not mention so many characters, traditions, and idiosyncrasies that we could barely fit it all in this book. Bear in mind that we're not claiming this is *the* comprehensive book on golf, though—it's just the most fun book on golf.

We packed everything we could into *Uncle John Tees Off On Golf*, and we would have needed about 300 more pages to include all the fascinating information we found. But here's some of what we were able to fit:

• **The origins.** Even though the modern game of golf is over 500 years old, it's still evolving today. We begin the story from ancient times and take you through golf's royal upbringing and the formation of the golf course (there's a reason there are 18 holes).

• **The majors.** The stories behind the great tournaments, the PGA, the R&A, the sport's exodus from Great Britain to America, and what lies ahead.

• **The courses.** We've got the inside info on the most famous courses such as Augusta, St. Andrews, and Pebble Beach, but we also take a walk on the wild side, journeying from courses that have alligators in their water hazards to links that lie in a volcanic crater—or in one case, the entire country of Mongolia.

• **The equipment.** This game is also about the many instruments we use in our vain attempts to master it. You'll find the history of golf clubs, balls, carts, fashions, shoes, tees... We've also got some tips on what clubs to use and how to swing them (like that's what you need...*more* advice).

• **The strange language of golf.** From doglegs to niblicks to Captain Kirks. (We make no guarantee that this book will make you a good golfer. But at least you'll be able to *sound* like a good golfer.)

• **The basics.** If you can handle it, we give you a guide to deciphering the handicap system, what you need to do to get on the PGA Tour, as well as how to *stay* on the PGA Tour.

• **The best, worst, and weirdest.** Golf can put you on top of the world or make you want to hide your head in a sand bunker. From amazing holes in one to a hole in 161...to a hole haunted by a headless horseman—this book examines *every* side of golf.

• **But most of all, the people.** You'll meet a host of eccentric characters that have been in the center of this sport, from the days of Mary, Queen of Scots to Old Tom Morris to 20th-century greats such as Jack Nicklaus, Walter Hagen, and Arnold Palmer. And don't forget the modern phenoms—Vijay Singh, Anika Sorenstam, Michelle Wie, and Tiger Woods. If they're any indication, then golf is assured a future of new records and amazing stories.

In the end, no amount of words can adequately describe the feeling a golfer gets when he hits the sweet spot and sends the ball flying down the middle of the fairway. But perhaps that is golf's allure—to be able to stand in the sunshine and lose yourself in the moment. And when you can't be out on the links, we hope this book will be a good partner that keeps you entertained and amused...and understands what drives you to play this great game.

See you out there.

And, as always, remember,

Go with the flow!

—Uncle John and the BRI staff

GOLF IS...

*It means different things to different
people. Here are some of them.*

"...a game whose aim it is to hit a very small ball into an even smaller hole, with weapons singularly ill designed for that purpose."
—**Winston Churchill**

"...the most fun you can have without taking your clothes off."
—**Chi Chi Rodriguez**

"...an awkward set of bodily contortions designed to produce a graceful result."
—**Tommy Armour**

"...a fascinating game. It has taken me nearly forty years to discover that I can't play it."
—**Ted Ray**

"...a game in which you yell 'fore,' shoot six, and write down five."
—**Paul Harvey**

"...an open exhibition of overweening ambition, courage deflated by stupidity, skill scoured by a whiff of arrogance."
—**Alistair Cooke**

"...so popular simply because it is the best game in the world at which to be bad."
—**A. A. Milne**

"...a game where guts and blind devotion will always net you absolutely nothing but an ulcer."
—**Tommy Bolt**

"...like a love affair. If you don't take it seriously, it's no fun; if you do take it seriously, it breaks your heart."
—**Arthur Daley**

"...a game to teach you about the messages from within, about the subtle voices of the body-mind. And once you understand them you can more clearly see your 'hamartia,' the ways in which your approach to the game reflects your entire life. Nowhere does a man go so naked."
—**Michael Murphy,**
Golf in the Kingdom

"...deceptively simple and endlessly complicated."
—**Arnold Palmer**

At the 1914 Bamberger Trophy tournament, 100 caddies went on strike, starting a riot.

WORD ORIGINS

Here are the etymologies of some common words used in golf.

GRAND SLAM

Meaning: A sweeping victory

Origin: "Comes from whist and related card games—notably bridge, where it means the winning of all 13 tricks by one side. It was commandeered by baseball to mean a bases-loaded homer, for four runs. Golf (and tennis) adopted it to refer to winning all four of the sport's major pro competitions in a single season. In golf it's the British Open, the U.S. Open, the PGA Championship, and the Masters." (From *Southpaws and Sunday Punches*, by Christine Ammer)

HANDICAP

Meaning: A system that rates a golfer's play and allows golfers of different abilities to compete on an equal basis

Origin: "From an obsolete English expression, *hand in cap*. It referred to a betting game in which two players put money in a cap and exchanged items of different value, the money being forfeited if the contestants rejected the decision of a third person—an umpire—regarding the value of the exchange. The broad sense that developed from this spread to the sporting world—at first horse racing—in which advantages or disadvantages of time, weight, distance, etc. were given to contestants to equalize their chances of winning." (From *Jesse's Word of the Day*, by Jesse Sheidlsower)

MULLIGAN

Meaning: Informal rule permitting a player to retake a bad shot

Origin: Uncertain, but may have come from one of three places:
• Buddy Mulligan, 1920s New Jersey golfer notorious for do-overs.
• David Mulligan, a Canadian hotel owner (and bad golfer) in the early 20th century.
• An ethnic slur from the late 1800s. The common Irish surname Mulligan was a derogatory term for unwelcome golfers who wanted to join fancy country clubs, but presumably didn't know the proper rules of golf. (As in, "Hey, Mulligan! No do-overs!")

Billie Fries, Jr., hit a 90-yard drive...at the age of 19 months.

OFF COURSE

Weird golf in the weird world news.

AROUND MONGOLIA IN 18 HOLES

"Andre Tolme has just finished a round with an eagle on the 18th hole. But his score was 506. That's because Tolme's course is the entire length of Mongolia. After nine months of traversing the Mongolian steppe with nothing but a Jeep, a tent, and a three-iron, Tolme has completed his golf journey across the land once ruled by Genghis Khan.

Tolme, 35, is an American civil engineer. Dividing the Mongolian countryside into 18 holes, he has completed an expedition of 1,234 miles—a course he estimated with a par of 11,880.

"His final scorecard: 290 over par—and 509 lost balls. 'It was a pretty exhausting round of golf,' Tolme said from Ulaanbaatar, the capital of Mongolia."

—Associated Press

THE CADDYSHACK SCHOOL OF GREENSKEEPING

"Police in Kent, New York, responding to reports of gunfire at Sedgewood Golf Course, found a member of the course's maintenance crew, 36-year-old Christopher Lehan, roaming the fairways in a golf cart with a flashlight and 20-gauge shotgun. Lehan told officers he was hunting for skunks. 'The skunks damage the course, and he said he had shot a couple,' said Lt. Alex DiVernieri of the Kent police. 'He didn't realize he needed a hunting license.' Police said they would charge Lehan with a variety of offenses, including hunting out of season and possessing a loaded firearm in a motor vehicle."

—Golf Digest

ELVIS HAS LEFT THE COURSE

"A five-foot-long alligator nicknamed Elvis who lived in a Sarasota, Florida, golf course's pond was found dying in October with a hunting knife in his head. A $1,000 reward for information was posted and an anonymous tip led the Florida Fish and Wildlife Conservation Commission to Rick Allen Burns, 49, a local fisherman. Burns, who insists he stabbed the reptile in self-defense, now faces up to 60 days in jail and a $500 fine. Golf course staff said Elvis first showed up at their pond about 18 months ago, and had never hurt anyone—not even the ducks living nearby."

—*Miami Herald*

CADDIE CRASH DIET

"More than 400 caddies from a renowned Thai golf course rallied at the Labor Ministry on Wednesday to protest a threat by their manager to fire them for being 'too fat, short, and old.' The manager of the Pinehurst Golf Course—where Prime Minister Thaksin Shinawatra and his Cabinet play regularly—ordered overweight caddies to lose at least 11 pounds within two weeks or face dismissal, said one caddy, who identified herself only as Umporn. The manager 'told us that the bosses (golfers) do not want old, fat, and short caddies anymore,' Umporn told reporters. 'We can manage to lose weight, but what can we do about being short and old?'"

—ABC News

THE GOLFER OF THE MILLENNIUM

"A New Zealand doctor has been dubbed 'wacky' after teeing off at midnight for the second year in a row in a bid to become the first person in the world to complete a round of golf in the new Millennium. Armed with a three-iron, a luminous golf ball, and a light strapped to his head, Ant Gear dashed around the course at North Island Manawatu Golf Club in 114—eight shots better than his previous New Year's effort. He told the *Manawatu Evening Standard*: 'I wanted to make sure I had both years covered in case someone gets picky about which is the true Millennium.' The doctor had a little help from his wife, Rosemary, who stood in the middle of each fairway shining a torch to give her husband something to aim at."

—**Reuters**

*   *   *

"Golf combines two favorite American pastimes: taking long walks and hitting things with a stick."

—P. J. O'Rourke

In 2004, Maj. John McBrearty created "Operation Iraqi Putting Green"...

THE GOLDEN BEAR

In 1940 Grantland Rice wrote a prediction in The
Saturday Evening Post: *"There is no more chance that golf
will give the world another [Bobby] Jones than there is that
literature will produce another Shakespeare." But
that was before he saw Jack Nicklaus play.*

CHAMPION: Jack Nicklaus

BACKGROUND: Born in Columbus, Ohio, on January 21, 1940.

STORY: When he was ten, his father, a pharmacist, started playing golf as therapy for an ankle injury…and Jack joined him. By
the time he was 13, Nicklaus had shot his first round under 70,
and he knew what he wanted to do with his life. His first big win
came in 1959 when, as a student at Ohio State University, he
became the youngest golfer since 1909 to win the U.S. Amateur.
In 1960 the 20-year-old entered the U.S. Open. He not only qualified for the event—he came in second. He would go on to win
the U.S. Amateur again in 1961.

The "Golden Bear" turned pro in 1962 and that year won the
U.S. Open, his first major. Arnold Palmer, who had won the
event in 1960, said after Nicklaus's win: "Now that the big guy's
out of the cage, everybody better run for cover."

Everybody probably wanted to. By 1966, at the age of 26,
Nicklaus had won each of the four majors at least once. He won
113 tournaments over the course of his career, 73 on the PGA
Tour, 10 on the Champions Tour, and 30 more unofficial events.
He holds countless world golfing records: 66 of them at the Mas-
ters alone.

CAREER HIGHLIGHTS

• At his first pro tournament, the 1962 Los Angeles Open, he
finished 21 strokes off the lead and earned $33.33.

• Nicklaus won 18 majors. The next closest is Walter Hagen with
11.

• He won three British Opens (1966, 1970, 1978), four U.S.
Opens (1962, 1967, 1972, 1980), five PGA Championships

(1963, 1971, 1973, 1975, 1980), and six Masters (1963, 1965, 1966, 1972, 1975, 1986). He also finished second in major tournaments 19 times.

• He's won six Australian Opens.

• Nicklaus was always a bit on the heavy side. Some of the nicknames he's had throughout his life: Ohio Fats, Fat Jack, Blob-o, and Whaleman. His wife, Barbara "Babs" Nicklaus, called him Fat Boy. And in 1960 *Sports Illustrated* put Nicklaus on the cover of the magazine with the headline: "One Whale of a Golfer."

• Nicklaus holds the record for most consecutive years with at least one win: 17 years (1962 to 1978).

• He was inducted into the World Golf Hall of Fame in 1974.

• In 1988 *Golf* magazine voted him "Golfer of the Century."

• He was voted Golf Course Architect of the Year in 1993 by *Golf World* magazine. Today he is one of the leading designers in the business, with over 200 courses built all over the world.

• In 2000 *Golf Digest* ranked Nicklaus the top golfer in the history of the game.

CLASSIC NICKLAUS

A week before the 1986 Masters tournament, the *Atlanta Journal-Constitution* wrote that Nicklaus was "done, washed up, through." His numbers had dropped dramatically in recent years, as might be expected for a golfer in his forties (he had only won twice since 1980), but the insult got him riled up. He taped the article to his refrigerator. "All week I kept thinking, 'Through,' 'washed up,' huh?" On the last day of the tournament, which he started in seventh place, Nicklaus shot a 65—with a blistering 30 on the back nine—and won by one stroke. The 65 is still two strokes off the record for the best round in Masters history, and at 46 he became (and still is) the oldest Masters winner ever. It was his 18th major…and it was his last victory on the PGA Tour.

*   *   *

"It's hard not to play up to Jack Nicklaus's standards when you're Jack Nicklaus."

—Jack Nicklaus

Actual rule at a course in India: "Balls eaten by sacred cows may be replaced with no penalty."

ANCIENT ORIGINS OF GOLF, PART I

*You might not think of golf as being similar to baseball,
hockey, or polo, but many historians think they are. In fact,
all these stick-and-ball games may have a single ancestor.*

SCOTLAND'S GAME?

Most sports historians agree that an early form of golf
was being played in Scotland by the 15th century. But games
that involved the hitting of a small object—a stone or a carved
piece of wood or bone—with a bent stick have been played all
over the world for thousands of years. So why do the Scots get the
credit? Because they added a simple signature ingredient to the
already existing games: the hole. Earlier games had targets—a pole,
a doorway, a tree—but historians say the Scots added the cup and
made golf the unique game it is today.

And that's not all they added. They built the world's first golf
courses, developed the basic rules and equipment that are still in
use today, and started many of golf's traditions, including the 18-
hole course, the yelling of "Fore!", and probably even the tradition
of the visit to the "19th hole."

But what were the ancient games that the Scots took for their
own when they created "Scotland's game"?

THE CRADLE OF SPORT

Experts say that golf shares its origins with games that developed in
Europe and Asia. Some theorize that the games go all the way back
to the cradle of civilization—the city-states of the Sumerians in
Mesopotamia (present-day Iraq). As far back as 3000 B.C., they say,
the Sumerians played a game known as *pukku-mikku*, a ritual, reli-
gious-themed game that was representational of their creation myth.
It was played with a stick, the *mikku*, and a hoop or ball, the *pukku*.
(The pukku and the mikku are mentioned in the *Epic of Gilgamesh*,
the world's oldest known written story, from about 2100 B.C.)

Is it going too far to say this game could be the origin of most
of the stick-and-ball games that exist today? Consider this: the

Sumerians invented the wheel. They also created the 12-month calendar and the world's first writing system. As Sumerian technology spread throughout the ancient world, other aspects of their culture—including their games—probably did, too.

PHARAOH'S FIELD HOCKEY

The oldest known depiction of a stick-and-ball game comes from the ancient Egyptians (who were themselves greatly influenced by the Sumerians). Hieroglyphic scenes in Egyptian tombs depict people engaged in a variety of sports, such as gymnastics, swimming, juggling, and wrestling. In one famous scene carved into a wall in the burial chamber of Prince Kheti in Beni Hassan in the Nile valley, two men are shown facing each other, bent at the waist and poised over a ball (or possibly a small hoop), holding long sticks with curved ends. Put gloves, helmets, and skates on them and it's a picture of a hockey face-off...made more than 4,000 years ago.

ASIAN GAMES

Some games that may trace their roots to the Sumerians:

• **Chogan.** This game was played on horseback and is believed to be polo's precursor. It was developed by Persian tribes around the sixth century B.C. and was probably first played without horses. An inscription on a stone tablet found in the Persian city of Gilgit (in modern day Iran) describes the importance of chogan:

> Let other people play at other things.
> The king of games is still the game of kings.

• **Sagol kangjei.** Another pololike game, it was played by the Manipuri people in India as early as 30 B.C. *Sagol* means "pony" or "horse," *kang* means "ball" or "round object," and a *jei* is the stick used for hitting the *kang*. (The Manipuri claim that this is the real ancestor of polo.)

• **Dakyu.** Played in Japan for more than a thousand years, dakyu may be a descendant of chogan, brought to Japan through China. It looks like a cross between polo and lacrosse, with players on horseback using pouch-fitted sticks to hurl a ball toward a goal. Dakyu is still played in Japan today.

THE ROMAN ROAD TO ABERDEEN

A marble sculpture from ancient Greece dating to around 514

Jack Nicklaus and Sean Connery once teamed up to design a golf course in France.

B.C. shows young men playing field hockey, a game the Greeks called *keritizin*. It is very likely that they inherited the game from the Egyptians, whom they had conquered. The Romans were greatly influenced by the Greeks and many believe that they took keritizin and developed their own game—*paganica*—from it. It was played on streets or in the countryside and involved hitting a feather- or wool-stuffed leather ball with a specially-made stick.

The Romans took paganica with them as they conquered nearly all of Europe. Historians believe that paganica would develop into different games all over the continent... including the one (or ones) that eventually made it to Scotland and became golf. There are many different theories as to exactly how that happened, although spotty historical records make it almost impossible to know with certainty. Every modern region of Europe and many parts of Asia have their own distinct versions of the stick-and-ball game and most claim to be the basis for golf. But which one is the true ancestor?

*To find out more about the Roman games and
the origins of golf, slice on over to page 83.*

...the origins of golf, slice on over to page 83.

*   *   *

ANCIENT WORLD OF SPORTS

*Not all stick-and-ball games were direct predecessors of
golf—15th-century Europeans never heard of these:*

• The Mapuche peoples in the southern part of South America played a field hockey–like game called *chueca*. It was highly developed, with organized rules such as the number of players and the size of the playing field, and it was popular for centuries before the Spanish arrived in the 1500s.

• North American natives played many different kinds of organized stick-and-ball games at least 700 years ago and probably much earlier. One of the better known examples was played in various forms from eastern Canada to the southeastern United States and is the origin of lacrosse. It was a particularly brutal game, played as ritualistic training for war. The Hurons called it *baggataway*, which means "little brother of war."

The Rolling Hills Country Club in Florida was the setting for the movie *Caddyshack*.

BIG SHOTS

One of the best tournament finishes ever.

TAKE THAT! NO, TAKE THAT...
Players: Ernie Els and Tiger Woods
Event: The 2000 Mercedes Championship at Kapalua's Plantation Course in Hawaii.

Big Shot 1: Els and Woods were locked in a great duel. Coming up to the 18th hole of the final round, they were at 14 under, four ahead of their closest competitor. It's hard to get on the green in two shots at a PGA par-5—a lot of pros don't even try—and this one was the hardest. The 18th at Kapalua measured 663 yards that year—the longest hole on the entire PGA Tour. But Woods and Els are two of the longest hitters in the game—and there was a tournament on the line. They were going for it. Both were perfect off the tee and were looking at "only" 290 yards to the green for their approach shots. Tiger took out his three-wood and blasted the ball—to about 15 feet from the hole. The crowd went wild.

Big Shot 2: Ernie "Big Easy" Els wasn't intimidated. He took out his two-iron, hit the ball cleanly, and when it stopped rolling it was inside Tiger's—just 12 feet from the hole. The crowd went wild again.

Big Shot 3: Tiger was away (farthest from the pin), so he putted first. The putt was perfect, and Tiger's trademark fist pump sent the gallery into hysterics again as he dropped the eagle.

Big Shot 4: Els had no room for error—he had to match the eagle just to tie and force a playoff, and amazingly...he dropped the putt. Regulation play was over; the sudden-death playoff was on.

Big Shot 5: Both golfers birdied the first playoff hole (the 18th again). On the next hole Tiger had a 40-foot putt for a birdie; Els had a 35-footer. The crowd waited to see who would win.

Big Finish: Tiger's went in, Els's didn't—Tiger won the tournament. His eagle-birdie-birdie was one of the greatest PGA Tour finishes ever. It was also the 24-year-old's fifth-consecutive victory, the most since Ben Hogan won five in a row in 1953.

"Golf is not a funeral, although both can be very sad affairs." —Bernard Darwin

CHILI DIPS AND ALBATROSSES

How to talk like a golfer.

A bnormal ground conditions: An official term for unintended conditions, such as gopher holes or rain puddles, which entitle players to relief (moving the ball without penalty).

Above (or below) the hole: The position of the ball on a sloping green in relation to the cup.

Ace: A hole in one.

Address: A golfer is "at address" when standing over the ball and has grounded his club behind it (except in a hazard, where the club may not touch the ground during address).

Air presses: Bets called while a ball is in the air.

Air shot: Swinging the club and missing the ball completely.

Albatross: The rarest score in golf—a double eagle, or three under par on one hole. More commonly used in the U.K.

All square: A tie score in match play.

Approach shot: A shot intended to get the ball from the fairway onto the green.

Apron: The area of slightly-taller grass bordering the green. (Also called a *collar*.)

Army golf: Insulting term for bad play, as in hitting the ball "left-right, left-right..."

Attend the flag: To hold and then remove the flagstick while another player putts.

Away: If you're "away," your ball is farthest from the hole. It's always played first.

B ack door: When a ball circles the lip of the cup and drops in from the opposite side.

Back nine: The last nine holes of an 18-hole course.

Baffie: (Also *baffy*.) A 4-wood.

Bail out: To shoot away from the hole in order to avoid a hazard. Some courses have designated bail-out areas.

Ball marker: Any small object, usually a coin, used to mark a ball's position on the green.

Banana ball: Slicing the ball in a banana-shaped trajectory.

Beach: A sand bunker.

Bent grass: A thin, densely growing grass species favored for putting greens.

Shaquille O'Neal has a putting green in his front yard.

Bermuda grass: A coarse grass used in warmer climates where bent grass can't grow.

Biarritz: A green that has a deep gully running through it.

Big dog: A driver.

Birdie: One stroke under par for a hole.

Bite: Backspin that prevents a ball from bouncing forward after it lands on the green.

Blade shot: To hit the ball above its center with the edge of an iron, making it fly low or bounce along the ground. Also called "hitting it thin."

Blast: Type of shot from a sand trap, as when a ball is deeply buried, that throws a lot of sand out of the bunker.

Bogey: One over par.

Brassie: A two-wood.

Break: The curved path of a putted ball, or the slope of the green that causes the curve.

Bump and run: A long-distance chip shot.

Bunker: A hazard. A pit of sand or grass next to a fairway or green.

Burn: A Scottish term for a creek or stream on a golf course.

Casual water: Any water on a golf course that's *not* a water hazard, such as rain puddles.

Chicken stick: A safe club chosen over a risky one, i.e., using an iron instead of a driver. (Used insultingly, but it's often the smart choice.)

Chili dip: A muffed shot, where the clubhead hits the ground behind the ball. (Also called a *pooper-scooper* or *hitting it fat*.)

Chip: A very short, low-flying shot onto the green, usually with a pitching wedge.

Cleek: A two-iron.

Closed face: Turning the clubface slightly inward to correct a slice or to cause a desired hook.

Clubface: The part of the clubhead that hits the ball.

Compression: The density of a golf ball. (90 compression is soft, 100 is hard.)

Conceded putt: A short putt "given" to an opponent without his having to play it. (Only allowed in match play.)

Cup: The target in golf; the hole.

Cut: A tournament's "elimination line." For example, the PGA typically eliminates half the players after two days of a four-day event, based on the midline of all players' scores. A player strives to *make the cut*.

THE SKYWATCHERS

Statistically, you are more likely to be struck by lightning on a golf course than any other place. Who keeps golf's biggest stars safe every weekend during the PGA season? Why, the PGA meteorologist, of course.

WHEN LIGHTNING STRIKES

Remember the scene in *Caddyshack* where the guy plays the best golf of his life in the rain...only to be struck by lightning as he holds his putter aloft in triumph? Well, it's not as uncommon as you might think: a 1997 study by the National Oceanic and Atmospheric Administration found that 159 people were killed by lightning on golf courses during the preceding 35 years. That's 5 percent of all lightning fatalities in the United States in that time. And those are just the ones who died—dozens more are struck and injured each year.

The most famous lightning strike in golf occurred at the 1975 Western Open in Chicago when Lee Trevino, Jerry Heard, and Bobby Nichols were all struck by the same bolt as they waited out a weather delay. All three survived, but the incident drew attention to the need for safety precautions on the golf course. Insurance companies began to require course managers to provide lightning shelters and issue severe weather warnings to their customers.

THE PGA METEOROLOGIST

Even with added safety measures, lightning remains a very real threat to golfers, as well as to spectators in the gallery. A large, open field with isolated trees and ponds is just about the worst place to be in a lightning storm. During the 1991 U.S. Open in Minneapolis, 12 fans were struck as they huddled together under a tree during a rain delay. One of them died.

To prevent further tragedy—and to help officials plan events *around* bad weather—the PGA Tour now contracts traveling meteorologists to monitor the weather at every event. The PGA meteorologist can usually be found in a trailer in the parking lot, using a bank of computers to tap into National Weather Service

---

Golfer Craig Parry is known as "Popeye."

and Doppler radar satellite feeds. And on the roof of the trailer: a "Thor Guard" lightning detector.

Although it looks like a prop from a cheap science-fiction movie, the Thor Guard actually measures static electricity in the atmosphere and can accurately predict the percentage chance of lightning strikes within 12 miles. PGA meteorologists can also watch the National Lightning Detection Service's satellite map of the United States, which shows the location of every lightning strike in the country 15 seconds after it hits.

In addition to protecting golfers and fans, the meteorologist is responsible for tracking all weather patterns relative to the tournament. He gives PGA Tour officials the information they need to determine tee times and to work around weather delays. Heavy rain, wind, or fog can cause play to be suspended, and officials need to know that bad weather is coming well before it arrives.

METEOROLOGY FOR THE COMMON GOLFER

If you aren't a member of the PGA Tour, you can still get satellite information about weather conditions around courses in your area. The Weather Channel, a PGA Tour sponsor and supplier of PGA Tour meteorologists nationwide, maintains an online golf course weather service. Just type in your zip code for a ten-day forecast and storm alert for each of your local courses.

And if you don't have Thor Guard to keep you safe, remember these lightning safety tips:

• When caught on a golf course during a thunderstorm, remove metal-spiked golf shoes and put down your golf clubs.

• Stay away from your golf cart.

• Avoid open water, wet sand, and anything metal, such as fences, pipes, tractors, or equipment sheds.

• Do not hide under a tree!

• If possible, seek shelter in a permanent building or in a vehicle. If your only option is a vehicle, close the windows and keep your hands in your lap. Don't touch any metal.

• If you can't find shelter, crouch down with your feet together and your hands over your ears, and try to stay at least 15 feet away from any other person.

The worst playoff record in the PGA belongs to Ben Crenshaw, with a lifetime record of 0-8.

GOLF GUFFAWS

Golfing necessities: Clubs, balls, beer, and some good jokes to tell while looking for your ball (again).

The golfer stood over his tee shot for what seemed like an eternity, looking up, looking down, measuring the distance, figuring the wind direction and speed. Generally, he was driving his partner nuts.

Finally his exasperated partner said, "What the heck is taking so long? Hit the ball!"

"My wife is up there watching me from the clubhouse," the guy answered, "and I want to make this a perfect shot."

His partner pondered this for a moment and then replied, "Forget it, man, you'll never hit her from here."

Golfer: Notice any improvement since last year?
Caddie: Polished your clubs, did you?

A retiree is given a set of golf clubs by his coworkers. He goes to the local pro for lessons, explaining that he knows nothing about the game.

So the pro shows him the stance and swing, then says, "Just hit the ball toward the flag on the first green."

The novice tees up and smacks the ball straight down the fairway and onto the green, where it stops inches from the hole.

"Now what?" the fellow asks the speechless pro.

"Uh...you're supposed to hit it into the cup," the pro finally says.

"Oh great!" says the beginner, disgustedly. "*Now* you tell me!"

A man was stranded alone on a desert island for ten years. One day, he sees a speck on the horizon. He watches and waits as the speck gets closer and closer until out of the surf emerges a gorgeous woman wearing a wet suit and scuba gear. She calmly walks up to the man and asks, "How long has it been since you've had a cigarette?"

"Ten years!" he says.

She unzips a pocket on her left sleeve and pulls out a pack of cigarettes.

He takes one, lights it, takes a long drag, and says,

The R&A Rules Committee chastised Alan Shepard for not replacing his divot on the moon.

"Man, that's good!"

Then she asks, "How long has it been since you've had a beer?"

"Ten years!" he replies.

She unzips a pocket on her right sleeve, pulls out a bottle of beer, and gives it to him. He takes a long swig and says, "Wow, that's fantastic!"

Then she starts unzipping the longer zipper that runs down the front of her wet suit and says to him, "And how long has it been since you've had some *real* fun?"

And the man replies, "Wow! Don't tell me that you've got a set of golf clubs in there!"

Two friends play a round of golf together. One has a little dog with him and on the first green, when he holes out a 20-foot putt, the little dog starts to yip and stands up on its hind legs.

His friend says, "Wow! That dog's really talented! What does he do if you miss a putt?"

"Somersaults," says the man.

"Somersaults?!" says his friend. "That's incredible! How many does he do?"

"That depends on how hard I kick him."

The pope met with the college of cardinals to discuss a proposal from the prime minister of Israel. "Your Holiness," said one of them, "The prime minister wants to determine who's better—Jews or Catholics—by challenging you to a game of golf!" The pope was greatly disturbed, as he had never played golf in his life.

"Don't worry," said the cardinal, "we'll call America and talk to Jack Nicklaus. We'll make him a cardinal, and *he* can play for us. We can't lose!"

Everyone agreed it was a good idea, so the call was made and Nicklaus agreed to play.

The day after the game, Nicklaus reported back to the Vatican.

"Your Holiness," he said sheepishly, "I came in second."

"Second?" shouted the pope. "Jack Nicklaus came in second to the prime minister of Israel?"

"No," said Nicklaus, "second to Rabbi Woods!"

Q: What are the four worst words you can hear on a golf course?
A: "It's still your turn."

Attention Bob Jones: To enter the Bob Jones Open, you must be named Bob Jones.

HOW'D YOU GET YOUR NICKNAME?

Golfers' nicknames are part of the history of the game. Here's how some of them came to be.

The Mechanic: Spaniard Miguel Angel Jimenez got the name for his methodical and efficient style of play (and some say for his love of fast cars).

• **Fuzzy:** Most fans don't even know his real name: it's Frank Urban Zoeller. "Fuzzy" comes from his initials: FUZ.

• **The Squire:** Gene Sarazen got the name because he lived on a farm during his playing days in the 1920s, 30s, and 40s.

• **The Shark:** Savvy golfer Greg Norman got the name from the American media in 1981 because of his aggressive style of play, his pearly white smile, and because he is Australian, where great whites are common.

• **The Slammer:** Hard-hitting Sam Snead was also known as Slammin' Sammy and the King of Swing.

• **The Black Knight:** Gary Player always dressed in black—and even painted his putter black.

• **The Hawk:** Ben Hogan was an intense player—with an intense glare. "Those steel-gray eyes of his," a friend once said. "He looks at you like a landlord asking for next month's rent."

• **Super Mex:** Golfing legend Lee Trevino is of Mexican-American heritage.

• **Boom Boom:** Fred Couples got the name for his driving distance. (In 2004 he was still ranked 35th in the PGA—at age 44.)

• **The Big Easy:** South African Ernie Els got the name from the American media in the 1990s. It refers to his size (he's 6'3"), his ultra-smooth swing, and his easygoing manner.

• **The Welsh Wizard:** 1991 Masters champ Ian Woosnam calls Wales his home. He's also known as Woosie (or Boozie) because he's known to tip a pint or two.

• **The King:** Arnold Palmer, for obvious reasons (and he never really liked the name).

Katharine Hepburn, a lifelong golfer, started playing at the age of five.

THE HISTORY OF THE USGA

Here's how a golfing scandal got the United States its first national golfing organization.

THE GREAT DISPUTE

In 1894, a golfing scandal broke out in the United States. It wasn't a huge scandal—golf wasn't a very popular sport yet—but its ramifications would be far-reaching.

Two prestigious clubs, the Newport Golf Club in Rhode Island and St. Andrew's Golf Club in New York, held invitational tournaments to determine the country's best amateur player. W. G. Lawrence won the Newport tournament and Laurence Stoddard won at St. Andrew's. The only problem: both winners were members of the clubs at which the matches had been held and each club had declared *its* winner the "National Amateur Champion." The dispute had actually been brewing for some time. As golf was gaining a greater foothold in the United States, many different clubs around the country were claiming to be "the best." The 1894 dual champions were the final straw. Something had to be done.

THE GREAT SOLUTION

On December 22, 1894, representatives from five prominent golf clubs—St. Andrew's, Newport, Shinnecock (New York), The Country Club (Brookline, Massachusetts), and Chicago Golf Club (Illinois), met in New York City to find a solution. There they formed the Amateur Golf Association of the United States, which would soon become the United States Golf Association (USGA). Within one year, the organization had written national rules for the game, set up legitimate men's and women's amateur championships, and created an "open" championship for amateurs and professionals—the U.S. Open. Almost instantly, the popularity of the game soared.

Today the USGA remains golf's governing body in the United States and Mexico, working in cooperation with their Scottish counterpart, the R&A (the Royal and Ancient Golf Club of St.

Howard Twitty let Burger King put its logo on his golf bag. His price: 500 Whoppers.

Andrews), golf's governors everywhere else it is played. Under their guidance, the game has grown into the powerhouse that it is today. Some important USGA rulings through the years:

• **1909:** In its position as protectors of the amateur game, the USGA makes a controversial ruling: caddies, caddiemasters, and greenskeepers over the age of 16 are henceforth considered professionals—and therefore may not play in the U.S. Amateur. The rule would stand until 1963.

• **1910:** The R&A bans center-shafted putters, but the USGA allows them to remain legal, differing with the Scottish about golf equipment for the first time…but not the last.

• **1911:** The USGA institutes the "par" system with set yardages for the different holes: par-3 is up to 225 yards; par-4 is 225 to 425 yards; par-5 is 426 to 600 yards; and par-6 (which no longer exists) is over 601 yards.

• **1912:** The Handicap Index system is introduced (see page 101). The USGA requires a minimum six-handicap or better to qualify for playing the U.S. Amateur.

• **1920:** After a deluge of complaints about the greens at the U.S. Open at Inverness in Ohio, the USGA creates the Green Section, a committee that will study the science of grasses in order to improve course conditions. Also, the USGA and R&A agree to a standard ball size—1.62 inches in diameter and 1.62 ounces.

• **1924:** Steel-shafted clubs are allowed in the United States for the first time. The R&A won't allow them until 1929.

• **1931:** The USGA decreases the maximum weight for golf balls to 1.55 ounces and increases the minimum size to 1.68 inches in diameter. This "balloon ball" is not popular, so after one year the weight goes back to 1.62 ounces, but the size stays at 1.68 inches. The R&A sticks with the 1920 standard, leading to a rule controversy that would last 59 years.

• **1938:** The USGA limits players to 14 clubs (some had carried as many as 25). They claim the rule is designed "to restore shot-making skill."

• **1947:** The rules of golf are simplified, going from 61 rules to 21. The R&A does not agree to the change.

• **1951:** The USGA and R&A finally agree on uniform rules of

According to experts, it's about 10 times easier to shoot a hole in one while golfing…

golf. The only rule they disagree on: the size of the ball (the R&A's is still slightly smaller). Golf is now nearly standardized worldwide.

• **1956:** Par yardage is changed to current levels. Par-3 is up to 250 yards; par-4 from 251 to 470 yards; and par-5 is 471 yards and over.

• **1968:** Croquet-style putting (between the legs), used most notably by Sam Snead, is made illegal.

• **1985:** The slope system is introduced to adjust handicaps according to the difficulty of different golf courses.

• **1990:** The R&A adopts the USGA ball dimensions.

TODAY'S USGA

The USGA of the 21st century is a multimillion-dollar nonprofit organization based in Far Hills, New Jersey. Together with the R&A, they "write and interpret the rules of golf to guard the tradition and integrity of the game."

Have they been successful? They now conduct three national open championships (the U.S. Open, the U.S. Women's Open, and the U.S. Senior Open), as well as ten national and four international amateur championships. When they started in 1894, there were fewer than 60 golf courses in the United States. By 2004, there were more than 17,000 courses and more than 24 million golfers playing on them. And no more controversy over who is the true champion.

*   *   *

REAL NAMES OF ACTUAL GOLF COURSES

• Bloody Point Club (Dafuskie Island, South Carolina)

• Nutcracker Golf Club (Granbury, Texas)

• Dub's Dread Golf Club (Lawrence, Kansas)

• Predator Ridge Golf Resort (Vernon, British Columbia)

• Potholes Golf Club (Othello, Washington)

• Humpty Doo Golf Club (Northern Territory, Australia)

FREE ADVICE

*Some helpful tips on how to be a better
golfer from golfers who are most
likely better than you are.*

ON PRACTICING...

"No golfer can ever become
too good to practice."
—**May Hezlet**

"Practice puts brains in your
muscles."
—**Sam Snead**

HITTING THE BALL...

"Reverse every natural instinct
and do the opposite of what
you are inclined to do, and you
will probably come very close
to having a perfect golf swing."
—**Ben Hogan**

"A golf ball is like a clock.
Always hit it at 6 o'clock and
make it go toward 12 o'clock.
But make sure you're in the
same time zone."
—**Chi Chi Rodriguez**

"Hit 'em hard. They'll land
somewhere."
—**Stewart Maiden**

TALKING TO THE BALL

"You can talk to a fade but a
hook won't listen."
—**Lee Trevino**

HEAD UP OR DOWN?

"Nobody ever looked up and
saw a good shot."
—**Don Herold**

"The worst advice in golf is
'keep your head down.'"
—**Patty Sheehan**

ON GOLF ETIQUETTE...

"If your opponent is playing
several shots in vain attempts
to extricate himself from a
bunker, do not stand near him
and audibly count his strokes.
It would be justifiable homi-
cide if he wound up his
pitiable exhibition by applying
his niblick to your head."
—**Harry Vardon**

ON PATIENCE...

"Don't be in such a hurry.
That little white ball isn't
going to run away from you."
—**Patty Berg**

"It is nothing new or original
to say that golf is played one
stroke at a time. But it took
me many years to realize it."
—**Bobby Jones**

"Be the ball." —**Chevy Chase, Caddyshack**

THE COMEBACK KID

Never give up. Never surrender.

SKIP

Stewart "Skip" Alexander was a golfer from North Carolina. A star of the Duke golf team, he won the Southern Conference Championship three times. He was the North Carolina state amateur champion in 1941 and, after a four-year stint in the military, made it to the PGA in 1947.

Alexander quickly established himself as a great player. In his first three years in the pros, he finished first three times and was in the top ten 38 times. Then, in 1950, disaster struck: Alexander was in a plane crash in Indiana. Of the four people on board, he was the only survivor. Both of his ankles were broken, he had severe burns over his entire body, he was hospitalized for three months, and needed plastic surgery for another five months.

RISING FROM THE ASHES

Doctors told him that playing golf again would be impossible, especially since his left hand had been severely burned and contracted into a permanent fist. Undaunted, Alexander had the hand operated on, forming it into a permanent "grip"—that would securely fit around a golf club. After more than 75 operations, Skip made it back to the course—and even to the PGA Tour. He didn't do as well after that, but he had one major golf moment left in him.

He had already been picked for the 1951 Ryder Cup team because of how well he'd played before the crash. He was only expected to be a sub, but when the match came up, one of the players got sick and captain Sam Snead called on Alexander, who told him, "Yes, I can play," (but didn't tell Snead he was all bandaged up—his hands were bleeding).

Less than a year after the crash, Alexander beat the British team's best player, John Panton, 8 and 7, meaning with seven holes left to play he had already won 8 holes and there was no way Panton could catch him. The American team won 9 ½ to 2 ½. And the icing on the cake for Alexander: the match was held at Pinehurst in his home state of North Carolina.

That's a hazard: Richard Blackman was once chased off the course by an escaped circus lion.

ARMCHAIR OFFICIALS

A knowledgeable fan can be a pro golfer's worst nightmare. Golf fanatics know the rules, they've got telephones, and apparently they're not afraid to use them when they spot mistakes on TV.

REAL GOLFER: Lee Janzen

THE STORY: During the 1998 NEC World Series of Golf, Janzen attempted a birdie putt on the 17th green. The ball stopped right at the very lip of the cup, almost hanging over the edge, but didn't drop in. Janzen stared at it in disbelief. Even his playing partner, Vijay Singh, bent over and stared at it. It seemed impossible that it didn't fall in. And then, just as Janzen finally stepped up to tap the ball in, it dropped into the hole. Janzen cracked up—hey, it was his birthday, he deserved a gift— and the crowd roared its approval.

ARMCHAIR GOLFER: A fan watching at home called the tournament and said that Janzen had broken Rule 16-2, which states that "when any part of the ball overhangs the lip of the hole, the player is allowed enough time to reach the hole without reasonable delay and an additional ten seconds to determine whether the ball is at rest." The officials watched the tape and timed it. Their ruling: Janzen had waited 20 seconds; it was a one-stroke penalty. But by this time Janzen had already turned in his scorecard—without a penalty. That's a big no-no. He was disqualified from the tournament. "Strange things happen on the course sometimes," said the disappointed birthday boy, "and this was one of them."

REAL GOLFER: Paul Azinger

THE STORY: It was the 18th hole of the second round of the 1991 Doral Ryder Open. Azinger hit his tee shot just barely into a lake near the fairway. He decided to try and play it. He plopped the ball out onto the fairway and finished with a 65...one stroke off the lead.

ARMCHAIR GOLFER: A fan called the PGA and pointed out that when Azinger stepped into the water, he had inadvertently moved some rocks, violating Rule 13-4, which says a player may not move loose impediments inside a hazard. The officials decided the fan was right. Since it was the 18th hole, Azinger had already filled out his scorecard without assessing himself a penalty and was disqualified. Azinger, always known as a gentleman, viewed the tape, agreed with the ruling, and went home. But it wouldn't be the last time a fan got him in trouble. (See next entry.)

REAL GOLFER: Paul Azinger (again)
THE STORY: During the 2003 Bell Canadian Open, Azinger waited as his playing partner, Fred Funk, chipped onto the 13th green. The ball stopped a few feet past the hole and Azinger's caddie grabbed the flagstick. The two men putted out and continued on.
ARMCHAIR GOLFER: A fan watching the tournament called the PGA's office and said that Azinger's caddie had pulled the flagstick out before Funk's ball had stopped rolling, a violation of Rule 17-2b. The officials viewed the tape and agreed. Nobody said (or noticed) anything at the time, but when Azinger got to the scorer's table, they told him to add two strokes to his scorecard… which dropped him from second to tenth place.

REAL GOLFER: Craig Stadler
THE STORY: During the third round of the 1987 Andy Williams Open in San Diego, Stadler hit a tee shot into the trees and his ball came to rest under some low branches. He had to get down on his knees to play the shot, and since the ground was damp, he put a towel down so his pants wouldn't get wet. In the final round, as he got to the 18th green—in second place—an official said there was a problem. They had to talk.
ARMCHAIR GOLFER: A handful of viewers had seen a replay of Stadler's Saturday shot and called the PGA. Stadler, they said, had violated Rule 13-3: "a player is entitled to place his feet firmly in taking his stance, but he shall not build a stance." Using the towel, said the fans, was building a stance, and they were right. The rules had been changed to include towels just that year. That meant that the previous day's scorecard was incorrect. Stadler was disqualified and lost out on the $37,333 in second-place money.
REVENGE: In 1995 Stadler was back at the Open when he learned that that same tree had become diseased and was going to be removed. Tournament officials offered Stadler the honors—and he happily chainsawed it to the ground.

One course in Florida tried using goats to trim the rough…

BINGO-BANGO-BONGO

Going down to the course for some weekend fun? Here are a few popular betting games and side bets. Just set a dollar amount beforehand (make sure it's one you can afford!) and swing away.

NASSAU. The "$2 Nassau" is probably the most common betting game in golf. It can be played between individuals or teams in match or stroke play. The format consists of three separate bets: one bet on the best score on the front nine, one bet on the back nine, and one bet on all 18 holes.

THE PRESS. This is a popular side bet used in Nassau. Say that, after the 6th hole, you're way behind your opponent and in danger of losing the front nine bet. At this point you can "press" the original bet, meaning make another bet that will start at the 7th hole and also finish on the 9th—so it's a new three-hole bet. If you win that one, but lose the other one, at least you break even. Note: you don't have to accept a press if you're the leader, but it's frowned upon not to.

BINGO-BANGO-BONGO. This game has three different bets per hole and gives less-talented players a chance to win. Separate bets are made on *bingo*, the first ball on the green; *bango*, the closest to the pin once everyone is on the green; and *bongo*, the first ball in the hole.

SCRAMBLE. This is a popular tournament format for teams of two, three, or four players. Each player tees off, then everybody moves their ball to where the best ball landed. They all hit again, and they all move to the best location again. That repeats until someone holes out. The team with the lowest score for the round (or rounds) wins.

GRUESOMES. This is for two two-person teams. Both team members tee off, but only one ball will be played to finish the hole. The fun part: the opposing team decides which ball you play. Obviously, it's going to be the more "gruesome" of the two shots. Whoever hit the gruesome tee shot goes second; teammates alternate after that.

CHAIRMAN. This is a points game for three or more players. The first player to win a hole becomes the "chairman." If the chairman wins the next hole, he collects one point from the other players. If it's a tie, there are no points, but still the same chairman. If someone else wins, they become chairman, and so on.

WOLF. This is for four players. Set a teeing-off order and rotate through it so that a new player tees off first on every hole. Whoever tees off first on the first hole is the "wolf." After the second player tees off, the wolf must either select or reject that player as a partner before the next player tees off. Same with the third player. After the fourth player tees off, the wolf must either select that player as a partner or play against *all three* players. To win, the wolf and his partner (if one has been chosen) must have a lower "better ball" score than the other team—the "hunters." Bonus: if the wolf plays alone, he wins double; if he loses, he pays double. Variation: the wolf can declare "lone wolf" before teeing off, thereby immediately declaring his intention to play against the other three.

NINES. In this three- or four-player point game, each hole has a total value of 9 points. Best score—5 points; second best—3; last—1. If two players tie for best, they split the first- and second-place points—they each get 4, and last place gets 1. If the worst two scores tie, the winner gets 5 points and the other two get 2 each. Three-way tie: 3 points each.

JUNK (or GARBAGE) is the name golfers give to a collection of side bets that can be made regardless of what game you're playing. Maybe you'll win a…

• **Barkie.** Also called a "Seve" (after Seve Ballesteros): if you hit a tree with your ball and still finish in par, you've won the barkie.

• **Cousteau (or shark).** Making par after landing in the water.

• **Sandie.** Making par from a greenside bunker.

• **Greenie.** First player on the green.

• **Nasty (or ugly).** Sinking a shot from off the green to make par.

• **Arnie.** Named after Arnold Palmer, for his ability to get out of trouble. This bet is making par on a par-4 or par-5 without driving on the fairway or reaching the green in regulation.

#$-%&*@!
(FLUBBED IT!)

Had a bad day on the links? Hey—it happens to the best of us, as these stories about some of golf's most famous goofs prove. (And even if it doesn't make up for a bad round, at least you can feel superior for a few minutes.)

TAPPED OUT

At the 1983 British Open, two-time U.S. Open champ Hale Irwin had an easy, two-inch tap-in putt to make during the third round. He walked up to the ball and made a casual one-handed swat at the ball…and missed it completely. The putter had hit the ground in front of the ball and bounced over it. And that counts as a stroke. "It was an unintended sword fight with the ground," he explained. The next day Irwin lost the Open to Tom Watson—by one stroke.

IN THE BAG

Ian Woosnam was off to a great start in the final round of the 2001 British Open: he birdied the first hole to go into a tie for the lead. But the good feeling didn't last long. At the second tee, his caddie informed him that they were carrying 15 clubs—one more than the rules allowed. They had been on the driving range before the round and the caddie had forgotten to take Woosnam's practice driver out of the bag. Result: Woosnam was penalized two strokes. How costly were those two strokes? He finished in a six-way tie for third instead of alone in second, a prize-money difference of $312,216. (It also cost the caddie his job.)

"V" AIN'T FOR VICTORY

Jean Van de Velde arrived at the final hole of the 1999 British Open with a three-stroke lead. He needed only a double bogey or better on the par-4 hole to win the prestigious event—the first time since 1907 that a French golfer would win it. The official Claret Jug engraver was already putting Van de Velde's name on the trophy. What happened next was agony, not just for Van de

---

Sad but true: the putting stroke accounts for about 43% of all swings made.

Velde, but for thousands of fans in the gallery and millions watching on TV.

Inexplicably, Van de Velde went with a driver off the tee (the prudent choice would've been an iron)…and missed the fairway, landing the ball in the rough. Then, instead of going with a safe shot, he went for the green…and bounced the ball off the grandstand and into rough again. He was still okay—it was only his third shot—so he hit it into the creek in front of the green. He took off his shoes and socks and waded into the creek with a club in his hand, but then came to his senses and took a drop and the penalty. Next he hit into a bunker, blasted out of the bunker to five feet from the pin, then (finally) put the ball in the hole. Result: a triple bogey 7 and a tie for the lead with Paul Lawrie (who started out the day 10 strokes behind Van de Velde) and Justin Leonard. Everything after that was an afterthought as Van de Velde had lost all his confidence. Lawrie won the four-hole playoff by three strokes. It remains the biggest collapse in major championship history.

SWEDISH GOLF BALLS

One of Sweden's top golfers, Anders Forsbrand, had one of the most embarrassing rounds…ever. At the 2002 French Open, he was having trouble off the tee and kept hitting shots into the trees—and losing balls. By the 16th hole, he already had 91 strokes on his scorecard and had run out of balls. According to the rules, golfers are not permitted to go back to the clubhouse to get more balls, so (possibly to his relief) Forsbrand was disqualified.

LOSING COUNT

At the 2003 Wachovia Championship in Charlotte, North Carolina, David Toms came to the 72nd hole with a six-shot lead and the victory almost wrapped up. Then he teed off. His drive sliced nearly 50 yards right and went into the trees. He chipped out from there…and landed in a fairway bunker. He needed two more strokes to reach the green, but still had plenty of wiggle room to win the event. Then he putted. Then he putted again. Then he putted again. (Have you lost count?) His next putt went into the hole—and he still managed to win the tournament by two strokes with a quadruple bogey 8. (Some flubs don't hurt as much as others.)

U.S. president Warren G. Harding golfed in his cowboy hat.

THE COLOR BARRIER

*When Tiger Woods won the Masters in 1997, he thanked golfers
like Teddy Rhodes, Charlie Sifford, and Lee Elder for opening the
doors of professional golf to black Americans. Never heard of
them? Here's a look at some of golf's unsung heroes.*

CHANGING TIMES

If you ask a person, "Who is Tiger Woods?" how do you
think they'd answer the question? They'd probably say
something like, "He's the greatest golfer in the world." His African
American heritage (Woods also claims Asian, American Indian,
and European ancestry), if it was mentioned at all, would probably
be a point of pride. But the fact that it doesn't get him thrown off
the pro circuit is a measure of just how far professional golf has
come in a fairly short period of time. Just 45 years ago, blacks were
banned from professional golf.

ON THE JOB

That's not to say that blacks didn't play golf. Even with discrimination, golf was probably *more* accessible to blacks than it is now.
Before the days of golf carts, courses employed large numbers of
caddies—most of them minorities. Caddies spent more time on
the golf course than anyone else, observing how experienced
golfers played the game and often sneaking in rounds of their own
before and after work. One day a week, usually Monday, was "caddie day"—the course was closed to the public and caddies could
play as much golf as they wanted. Many caddies developed into
some of the finest golfers in the country.

If a caddie was white, he could go as far as his talent could take
him—he could give golf lessons, become the club pro, or even play
on the PGA Tour. Golf legends such as Lee Trevino, Ben Hogan,
and Gene Sarazen, for example, all got their start as caddies.

If a caddie was black, that was a different story. No matter how
good they became at golf, blacks rarely got the chance to advance
beyond the status of caddies. Playing on the PGA Tour was out of
the question: the PGA had discriminated against blacks since its
founding in 1916, and in 1943 it made the policy official by

An average pro golfer uses 5 to 8 balls per round.

amending its constitution to restrict membership to "professional golfers of the Caucasian race." The amateur USGA wasn't much better—it didn't have an anti-black clause, but it deferred to golf clubs that discriminated against blacks. Nearly all of them did.

KEEP OUT

Frustrated with not being able to compete and earn money in the growing professional sport, a group of black golfers got together and formed the United States Colored Golfers Association (soon changed to the United Golfers Association)—a black golfing circuit. Their first tournament was in 1925 at the Shady Rest Golf Club in Westfield, New Jersey. In the final round, Harry Jackson defeated John Shippen by three shots. His prize for the victory: $25. The first National Colored Golf Championship, or "the National," was held the following year at the Mapledale in Stow, Massachussetts.

The National became the black golfers' "major," and the UGA grew, expanding to weekly pro tournaments with packed rosters by the 1950s, as well as men's and women's amateur championships. And they were all "open" events—even to whites, who often showed up to play. "We knew what it was like to be excluded," said former UGA president Norris Horton, "and we didn't want to do the same thing to anybody else, so whites, blacks, anybody who qualified and paid the entry fee, could play."

But it wasn't the PGA. First-place money on the UGA tour in the 1950s: about $500...in the PGA: about $20,000. If they wanted to earn a living as pros, black golfers would have to break in.

OPENING THE DOORS

In 1942 seven black golfers tried to enter a USGA-affiliated golf tournament in Chicago and were turned away. When they complained to the USGA, the association refused to do anything about it. That prompted a sympathetic Chicago alderman to write to George S. May, owner of a Chicago country club called the Tam O'Shanter, and ask him to invite black golfers to his upcoming All-American tournament. This was during World War II; May figured that if blacks were fighting in the war just like everyone else, they should be able to play golf like everyone else, too.

By the late 1940s, both the Tam O'Shanter and the Los Angeles

---

Bad luck? At the 1978 Masters, Tommy Nakajima shot a 13 on the 13th hole.

Open were flouting the PGA's caucasians-only clause and allowing blacks to compete in their tournaments. In 1948 two black golfers named Bill Spiller and Teddy Rhodes, both stars of the UGA, scored well enough in the Los Angeles Open to qualify for the upcoming Richmond Open in northern California. Well enough, that is, if they had been white.

Tournament rules stated that the top sixty finishers in the Los Angeles Open were eligible to play in the Richmond Open, but the PGA's rules said that blacks were not allowed to play at all. (Guess which rule the PGA decided to enforce.) Spiller and Rhodes were shooting a practice round of golf at the Richmond Golf Club a few days before the tournament when a PGA official walked up and told them they would not be allowed to play in the tournament. Spiller, Rhodes, and a third golfer named Madison Gunter decided to sue the PGA for discrimination and asked for $315,000 in damages.

One week before it went to trial, the case was settled out of court after the PGA promised not to discriminate against blacks in the future. But then it weaseled out of the deal by switching most of its tournaments from "open" tournaments, for which anyone could qualify, to "invitationals," which were by invitation only.

The Caucasians-only clause stayed in place—and the PGA saw to it that no blacks received invitations to its invitationals.

THE BROWN BOMBER

One PGA tournament that kept its open format was the San Diego Open in California, and that's where the next big blowup came, in 1952. That year, the tournament's sponsor, the San Diego County Chevrolet Association, asked retired heavyweight champion Joe Louis, the "Brown Bomber," to play in the tournament. Bill Spiller also qualified for the tournament by scoring well in two qualifying rounds.

Louis still hadn't decided whether to go or not when Horton Smith, the president of the PGA, contacted the organizers of the San Diego tournament and told them that the rules forbade blacks from playing in PGA-sponsored events. That's when the San Diego tournament withdrew its invitation to Joe Louis...and that's when the Brown Bomber decided he was going after all.

Part II of "The Color Barrier" is on page 208.

FOR THE LOVE OF GOLF

You either love this game or you hate it. These folks love it.

"Indeed, the highest pleasure of golf may be that on the fairways and far from all the pressures of commerce and rationality, we can feel immortal for a few hours."
—**Colman McCarthy**

"It is almost impossible to remember how tragic a place this world is when one is playing golf."
—**Robert Lynd**

"I'd play every day if I could. It's cheaper than a shrink and there are no telephones on my golf cart."
—**Brent Musburger**

"One of the most fascinating things about golf is how it reflects the cycle of life. No matter what you shoot, the next day you have to go back to the first tee and begin all over again and make yourself into something."
—**Peter Jacobsen**

"It is more satisfying to be a bad golfer. The worse you play, the better you remember the occasional good shot."
—**Nubar Gulbenkian**

"What other people find in poetry or art museums, I find in the flight of a good drive."
—**Arnold Palmer**

"Playing golf I have learned the meaning of humility. It has given me an understanding of futility of the human effort."
—**Abba Eban**

"I'm a golfaholic, no question about that. Counseling wouldn't help me. They'd have to put me in prison, and then I'd talk the warden into building a hole or two and teach him how to play."
—**Lee Trevino**

"When I play, I feel as if I'm in a fog, standing back watching the Earth in orbit with a golf club in my hands."
—**Mickey Wright**

"Happiness is a long walk with a putter."
—**Greg Norman**

"As you walk down the fairway of life you must smell the roses, for you only get to play one round."
—**Ben Hogan**

At Bear Valley Golf Course in Alaska, bears have the right to play through.

UNCLE JOHN'S PAGE OF LISTS

Random bits of information from the BRI's golf files.

3 Highest Golf Courses
1. La Paz Golf Club, Bolivia (10,800 ft.)
2. Jade Dragon Snow Mountain Golf Course, China (10,000 ft.)
3. Copper Creek Golf Club, Colorado (9,700 ft.)

3 Songs on Brad Belt's Country Album *Golf Is a Cussin' Game*
1. "Smart Aleck Caddie"
2. "I Don't Go Golfin' With My Wife"
3. "It Don't Take Brains to Play This Game"

6 Tiger Woods Endorsements
1. Nike
2. Titleist
3. American Express
4. Buick
5. NetJets (planes)
6. Wonda—Coffee in a Can (Japan)

5 Defunct Tournaments
1. Hardscrabble Open
2. Girl Talk Classic
3. Gasparilla Open
4. Rubber City Open
5. Iron Lung Open

13 Original World Golf Hall of Fame Inductees (1974)
1. Patty Berg
2. Walter Hagen
3. Ben Hogan
4. Bobby Jones
5. Byron Nelson
6. Jack Nicklaus
7. Francis Ouimet
8. Arnold Palmer
9. Gary Player
10. Gene Sarazen
11. Sam Snead
12. Harry Vardon
13. Babe Didrikson Zaharias

5 States with the Most Golf Courses
1. Florida (1,261)
2. California (1,007)
3. Michigan (971)
4. Texas (906)
5. New York (886)

18 Holes at Augusta National
1. Tea Olive
2. Pink Dogwood
3. Flowering Peach
4. Flowering Crabapple
5. Magnolia
6. Juniper
7. Pampas
8. Yellow Jasmine
9. Carolina Cherry
10. Camelia
11. White Dogwood
12. Golden Bell
13. Azalea
14. Chinese Fir
15. Fire Thorn
16. Red Bud
17. Nandina
18. Holly

5 Worst U.S. Cities for Golf (*Golf Digest*)
1. New York
2. Boston
3. Los Angeles
4. Oakland
5. Philadelphia

"Hillcrest" is the most popular name for country clubs in the United States.

LAND MINES
AND CROCODILES

*Think auto racing or mountain climbing are the most
dangerous sports? Try golfing these courses.*

COURSE: The Hans Merensky Golf Course, South Africa
DANGER! This course is in the town of Phalaborwa, and
borders one of Africa's largest game preserves. There's a
fence, but it won't stop the antelope, giraffes, impalas, and monkeys from sharing the course with you. Don't worry, though;
they're not really a danger—it's the warthogs, hyenas, water
buffalo, cheetahs, leopards, crocodiles, and lions you have to
watch out for. And the elephants. In 1988 a visitor was trampled
to death when she frightened an elephant with her camera.

COURSE: Singapore Island Country Club, Singapore
DANGER! The course has unusual hazards: poisonous snakes.
During the 1982 Singapore Open, golfer Jim Stewart encountered
a 10-foot cobra on the course. (He killed it with his club.)

COURSE: Lost City Golf Course, Sun City, South Africa
DANGER! The par-3 13th at this beautiful course is one of the
most dangerous in the world. There are nine bunkers and water
hazards around the hole—and 38 Nile crocodiles live in the water,
some up to 15 feet long.

COURSE: The Scott Base Golf Course
DANGER! What's so dangerous about this course? Geography:
it's in Antarctica, where the average summer temperature is –20°F
and there's no dirt, just snow and ice. And you have to use pink
golf balls (because you can't see the white ones in the snow, of
course).

COURSE: Henderson Golf Club, Savannah, Georgia
DANGER! In 2003 Roy Williamson was playing at this club
when he hit his ball into the deep rough. "I saw my ball pretty

much in plain view," he said. "Unfortunately, it was being tended to by a rattlesnake that I *didn't* see." When he went to pick the ball up (naughty, naughty), the six-foot-long snake bit him on the right temple. Williamson, severely poisoned, woke up in the hospital three days later. He said he would be golfing again soon, but added, "If I go out now and hit a ball off of the fairway in any fashion or form, I will not go after it."

COURSE: Camp Bonifas Country Club, the DMZ
DANGER! The DMZ is the demilitarized zone between North Korea and South Korea. American soldiers stationed there at Camp Bonifas wanted to play golf, so they built themselves a one-hole, 192-yard, par-3 course. But they have to play very carefully. A sign on the course reads: "Danger! Do Not Retrieve Balls From The Rough. Live Mine Fields!"

COURSE: Elephant Hills Country Club, Zimbabwe
DANGER! This course was designed by South African PGA legend Gary Player. It boasts the largest water hazard in the world—Victoria Falls, which is right next to the course. Another feature is the wildlife, of which you must remain constantly aware. One of the club's many unique rules: "Players may take a free drop with any ball that lands in a hippopotamus print."

COURSE: Pelham Bay Golf Course and Split Rock Golf Course, Bronx, New York
DANGER! These two courses are among New York's finest—but they also have a creepy reputation…as dumping grounds for dead bodies. Thirteen corpses have been found on the two courses in the last 20 years.

COURSE: Scholl Canyon Golf Course, Glendale, California
DANGER! The course was built on an unused section of the massive Scholl Canyon Landfill in Los Angeles County—atop three million tons of garbage. And if that seems a little ripe for your golfing pleasure, consider this: other sections of the landfill are still in use. So golf away, but you may want to wear a gas mask. According to some reports, methane gas occasionally escapes from divots.

Pro golfer Ky Laffoon once punished his putters by dragging them behind his car.

GOLF 101: ETIQUETTE

*Rules of golf etiquette were developed to keep the game safe,
fun, and fair. Here are some of the more important ones.*

• Don't talk, laugh, yawn, fart, or make any noise or move during another player's swing.

• Don't throw clubs. You may want to, but consider the risk to the people around you.

• Never stand directly behind another golfer in the act of hitting. Stand even to the ball to the left or the right.

• Don't dawdle—you don't want to wait all day for the group in front of you, so don't do it to the group behind you. And if you are playing particularly slowly and making the group behind you wait, let them "play through," so that you end up behind them.

• Always replace the flag and leave the putting green as soon as your group has finished putting.

• Repair all divots that you make and never take divots on practice swings.

• Don't take practice swings toward another person—many a bystander has been accidentally whacked by flying dirt or pebbles.

• Repair any dent your ball makes when it lands on the green.

• After hitting out of a sand trap, use the rake provided to smooth out whatever footprints or ball and club marks you've made.

• Never walk through someone's putting line. The slightest mark can alter the roll of their putt.

• Don't let your shadow fall across another player's putting line.

• Don't hit your ball until you're certain that the group ahead of you is out of range.

• If your ball appears to be headed toward another player, group, or anybody, yell "Fore!" loud enough to warn them.

• Most important, learn the rules...and follow them.

STRANGE LAWSUITS

It seems like the nation's two most popular participatory sports are playing golf and filing lawsuits. So why not combine the two?

THE PLAINTIFF: The Kellogg Company
THE DEFENDANT: Toucan Gold golf equipment
THE LAWSUIT: The cereal giant sued the small sporting goods company in 2003, claiming that their name and the company logo (which featured a drawing of a toucan) would fool breakfast consumers into thinking that Kellogg now made golf equipment.
THE VERDICT: The judge found that Kellogg's suit was a bit flaky. Case dismissed.

THE PLAINTIFF: Wilbur Coblentz
THE DEFENDANT: Wilbur Coblentz's playing partner
THE LAWSUIT: In 2005 Coblentz was run over by a golf cart that was being driven by his playing partner. The defendant's lawyer argued that golf carts are an intrinsic part of the game, so anyone out on the course should know to watch out for them, just as they would watch out for wayward golf balls.
THE VERDICT: After much deliberation, the judge ruled that golf carts were *not* an intrinsic part of the game. Getting hit by a ball or a backswing may be an inherent risk, he said, but getting hit by a bowling ball or a tire iron…or a golf cart, are not forseeable risks. Coblentz won the suit.

THE PLAINTIFF: Tom Stafford, a recreational golfer
THE DEFENDANT: A golf course in Mission Viejo, California
THE LAWSUIT: In 1994 Stafford's drive went wide and the ball ricocheted off a steel pole and hit him on the head. He sued the golf course "for not preventing that possibility."
THE VERDICT: Amazingly, Stafford won $8,500.

THE PLAINTIFF: Karsten Manufacturing Company
THE DEFENDANT: Walt Disney Entertainment
THE LAWSUIT: In the Disney movie *Mulan*, there is a charac-

Evolution? Charles Darwin's grandson Bernard Darwin was a famous golf writer.

ter named Ping. Karsten has been making PING golf clubs since 1959, so they sued Disney for trademark infringement.

THE VERDICT: The case was settled out of court. Disney agreed—among other things—to not manufacture any golf equipment bearing the name (or likeness) of Ping. Fortunately for Disney, they had no plans to manufacture golf equipment.

THE PLAINTIFF: The Florida Club golf course

THE DEFENDANT: Paul Thompson, a pig farmer

THE LAWSUIT: Paul Thompson has been raising Yorkshire pigs in Martin County, Florida, since 1957. He plays loud country music near their stalls because, he claims, "It makes 'em grow fatter." In 1997 the Florida Club bought the adjacent land and built a golf course on it. The 15th hole ended up right next to Farmer Thompson's pigs.

The Florida Club sued, claiming that the awful smell and blaring music was disturbing golfers. "They knew I was here and they chose to build anyway," Thompson steamed. "They're just a bunch of rich, arrogant people who come in and take over by suing." The Florida Club's lawyers claimed in return that Thompson was generating extra noise and stench in the hope of being bought out.

THE VERDICT: The Florida Club dropped the suit in 2000 and decided to capitalize on all the press it got by adding "Pig Crossing" signs at the 15th. Some of the more "cultured" golfers reportedly wear ear and nose plugs on the infamous hole.

THE PLAINTIFF: Dale Larson, a recreational golfer

THE DEFENDANT: A golf course in Wausau, Wisconsin

THE LAWSUIT: In 1997 Larson was walking down a brick path on the course and fell flat on his face, causing injuries that required major dental work. He sued, claiming that if the path had been made of concrete instead of brick, his spikes would not have gotten caught in the cracks and he wouldn't have fallen.

THE VERDICT: The judge agreed with Larson, claiming that the course was 51 percent responsible for his injuries, and that Larson was only 49 percent responsible—despite having consumed 13 cocktails that evening (90 minutes after the fall, his blood-alcohol level had been measured at 0.28, more than twice the legal limit in Wisconsin). Larson's award: $41,000.

Pennsylvania has a golf club called the Double Dam.

SLAMMIN' SAMMY

The man with the golden swing.

CHAMPION: Sam Snead
BACKGROUND: Born Samuel Jackson Snead in 1912 to a farming family in backwoods Virginia.

HIS STORY: Like Gene Sarazen and Byron Nelson, as a boy Snead caddied to help supplement his family's income and learned that he had a knack for the game. He was an outstanding high school athlete and his first love was football, but when an injury halted his football hopes, he turned his attention to golf. In his trademark outfit—plus-fours (knickers) and straw hat—with his backwoods charm, his folksy sense of humor, and what is still described as the smoothest swing ever seen in the game, Snead would go on to become one of the most famous athletes of his time, and the winningest golfer in the sport's history.

CAREER HIGHLIGHTS

• He was known as "Slammin' Sammy" Snead because of his power off the tee—he was able to drive well over 300 yards…in the days when woods were really made of wood.

• Snead amassed 82 PGA victories, the most ever. The next closest: Jack Nicklaus with 73 and Ben Hogan with 64. He also won six PGA Senior tournaments, five World Seniors Championships, and 80 more international events.

• He joined the PGA Tour in 1937, winning five times in his first year. In 1938 he won eight times and claimed the money title.

• He won seven majors: the Masters in 1949, 1952, and 1954; the PGA in 1942, 1949, and 1951; and the British Open in 1946.

• He was a member of eight U.S. Ryder Cup teams and was captain three times.

• He won the Greater Greensboro Open for the first time in 1938 at the age of 26—and the last in 1965 when he was 52, making him the oldest player to win a PGA Tour event. (He won the Greensboro Open eight times in all.)

Sam Snead practiced golfing barefoot.

- In 1950 alone he won 11 tournaments, the last player to win ten or more in a single year.

- At the 1974 PGA Championship, he tied for third. He was 62 years old.

- In 1979 he became the first player known to score his age, shooting a 67 at the Quad Cities Open at the age of 67. In 1983, at 71 years of age, he shot a 60 at his home course, the Homestead, in Virginia (the same course he caddied at as a boy).

- He was inducted into the World Golf Hall of Fame in 1974.

RAVE REVIEWS

Tom Watson: "The first time I went to the Masters, my father told me, 'Sit in the bleachers behind the practice area and watch Sam Snead swing.'"

Jack Nicklaus: "He brought so much to the game with his great swing and the most fluid motion ever to grace a golf course."

USGA president William Campbell: "He was the best natural player ever. He had the eye of an eagle, the grace of a leopard, and the strength of a lion."

Curtis Strange: "It was a gift, something you can't teach. His hands looked like they were born to have a golf club in them."

Phil Mickelson: "I don't think there's ever been a golf swing as aesthetically pleasing as Sam Snead's."

John Schlee, runner-up at the 1973 U.S. Open: "Watching Sam Snead practice hitting golf balls is like watching a fish practice swimming."

*   *   *

WORDS OF WISDOM FROM SAM SNEAD

"Practice puts brains in your muscles."

"The only reason I played golf was so that I could afford to go hunting and fishing."

There are 36 "Royal" golf clubs in the British Isles.

RAGS TO RICHES

*Some folks who started in the sand trap of
life and made it to the 18th green.*

GOLFER: Harry Vardon

RAGS: Vardon was born to a poor family in Jersey, one of England's Channel Islands, in 1870. They were so poor that they couldn't afford to raise Harry and gave the youngster to a rich doctor to be a houseboy. Vardon did not earn his freedom until he was 17 years old. He then started playing golf, turning pro in 1890 at the age of 20.

RICHES: Vardon won the British Open in 1896 and went on to win it five more times. At the turn of the century he was the world's most famous golfer, even touring the U.S. in 1900 and playing in more than 80 tournament and exhibition matches. He earned more than $20,000—about $400,000 in today's dollars—that year alone. Over his career he won 62 professional tournaments, including seven majors. No career earnings records were kept in those days, but it's clear that the former houseboy earned (when converted to today's value) millions of dollars.

GOLFER: Gene Sarazen

RAGS: The son of poor Italian immigrants, Sarazen was born in Harrison, New York, in 1902. He had to start working at age 6; he picked fruit, sold newspapers, and did whatever else he could to help his carpenter father make ends meet. He also caddied. He became so good at golf that he became a pro…at the age of 16.

RICHES: After a couple hard years, Sarazen won the 1922 U.S. Open at the age of 20, and a second major, the PGA Championship, the same year. In 1932 he earned $42,000, making him the highest-paid sportsman of any kind. He went on to win 39 tournaments, seven of them majors, and became one of the most famous—and wealthiest—golfers of his era. (For more, see page 170.)

GOLFER: Lee Trevino

RAGS: The Mexican-American Trevino was born on the outskirts of Dallas, Texas, in 1939. He was raised by his mother, a housecleaner, and his grandfather, a grave digger. They lived in a

---

Tee taboo: golfers believe it is bad luck to borrow a pencil.

shack with no electricity, no running water—and not even any windows. Luckily for him, the 7th fairway of the Dallas Athletic Club golf course was less than 100 yards from their front door. He quit school after the seventh grade and went to work full-time on the greens crew at the club.

RICHES: Trevino joined the PGA Tour in 1966 at the age of 26. He stunned the sports world when the self-taught golfer won the U.S. Open just two years later. By the time he retired from the PGA Tour in 1985 (he still plays on the Champions Tour), he had won 32 tournaments—seven of them majors—and had earned nearly $4 million (not counting endorsement deals), making him—at the time—the second-leading money winner ever.

GOLFER: Rich Beem

RAGS: In 1995 Beem, the 1993 New Mexico state amateur champion, quit the semipro golf circuit because he wasn't making enough money to survive. He moved to Seattle with his girlfriend and got a job at Magnolia Hi-Fi selling cell phones for $7 an hour.

RICHES: In late 1996 Beem decided to give golf another try. By 1999 he had qualified for the PGA Tour and on just his 12th start won the Kemper Open, where they handed him a check for $450,000. Beem's career has been up and down since then, but one of the ups was a big one: he won the 2002 PGA Championship (and $810,000). The former cell phone salesman won $2,938,365 that year alone, and since 1999 has earned more than $5 million (and he still carries his identification card from Magnolia Hi-Fi).

GOLFER: Vijay Singh

RAGS: Singh dropped out of high school in his native Fiji and tried to make a living playing golf. In 1985, after being thrown off the Asian Tour for allegedly cheating, he worked as a club golf pro in Borneo, making barely enough to feed his family. In 1987 the 24-year-old went to Scotland to try to qualify for the British Open. He didn't make it. He stayed in Edinburgh, though, and worked as a bouncer in a nightclub while he tried to make a living on the European Tour.

RICHES: In 2004 Singh won nine tournaments and became the first golfer to earn $10 million in a single season. The former golf teacher and bar bouncer has now earned more than $30 million (not counting millions more in endorsements).

Down in the dumps: in 1954, Harry Leach hit a shot into a moving garbage truck.

FANTASTIC FINISHES

Some more super shots to finish off a tournament.

WHO'S PUKING NOW?

Setup: At the 2004 Ford Championship at Doral, Craig Parry finished in a tie with Scott Verplank. They went back to the 18th hole for a sudden-death playoff. Parry was a bit miffed. During the tournament, commentator Johnny Miller had said on TV that Parry's golf swing looked like that of a 15 handicapper and was so bad that it would "make Ben Hogan puke."

Fantastic finish: Parry wanted nothing more than to put Miller in his place. From 176 yards out on the 18th—the second hardest-rated hole on the PGA Tour that year—he knocked a six-iron to about 13 feet in front of the hole...and it ran straight into the cup. He had eagled the first playoff hole and won the tournament. "Sure," Parry said afterward, "my swing mightn't be that pretty, but I get the job done."

SHOOTING BLIND

Setup: Forty-four-year-old Dan Forsman arrived at the 18th hole at the 2002 SEI Pennsylvania Classic one stroke behind Billy Andrade and Robert Allenby. He proceeded to knock his tee shot into the rough, but then ripped a three-wood to get on the green, 22 feet from the hole. Now all he had to do was get close and birdie the hole to force a playoff—but he didn't know that. "I didn't look at the leaderboard," he said later. "I knew I was keeping pace with the leaders. I felt if I could knock it on the green, maybe something crazy could happen."

Fantastic finish: Something crazy did happen. Instead of getting the birdie, he holed the eagle putt and won the tournament. It was his first win in ten years.

SHAKIN' ALL OVER

Setup: At the 2004 Kraft Nabisco Championship at Rancho Mirage in California, the first women's major of the year, 17-year-old Aree Song sank a 30-foot eagle putt on the last hole to pull into a tie with Grace Park. Park's six-foot birdie putt suddenly looked a lot longer. The 25-year-old had come close on many occasions, but in ten tries she had never won a major. She waited for the roar of the crowd after Song's eagle to die down and stepped up to the ball...then stepped away. "My knees, my arms, my whole body was shaking," she said. "I didn't know if I could start the club."

Fantastic finish: She stepped up again, stepped back again, then stepped up to the ball...and drained the birdie for the win. She and her caddie then performed the traditional Rancho Mirage celebration: they jumped into the pond beside the green. She happily received her trophy (and her check) wrapped in a white bathrobe.

ROYAL PAIN

Setup: At the 1991 Australian Open, it looked like Robert Allenby, a 19-year-old amateur, was going to win. This was against the likes of Greg Norman and an international list of golf superstars. It would have been one of the greatest moments in the long history of the event, but then Australian star Wayne Riley birdied the 16th to pull within one stroke of the unknown amateur. At the 17th, things were looking up for Allenby again as Riley faced a 30-foot birdie putt—until he sank it to pull into a tie. At the final hole, Allenby breathed a sigh of relief and got ready for a playoff. Why? Riley had just hit a bad approach shot and was now 40 feet from the hole on the long, undulating green.

Fantastic finish: But there would be no playoff. Riley stroked the long putt and three years later (okay, it was only about five seconds), it dropped into the hole. Riley had won by one stroke. The last two birdies of 30 and 40 feet made for one of the best finishes the event has ever seen.

ALOHA

Setup: At the 1983 Hawaiian Open, Jack Renner could taste victory. With a two-stroke lead, he stood at the 18th green waiting for Isao Aoki to finish up so he could collect his trophy and winner's check. From 176 yards out on the par-5, Aoki would have to make a pretty good shot to get a chance for a birdie and force a playoff.

Fantastic finish: Aoki didn't make a good shot—he made a brilliant one. Renner could only watch, stunned, as the crowd exploded when Aoki's rocket dropped into the hole for an eagle...and the win.

PERKS FOR PERKS

Setup: At the 2002 Players Championship at TPC in Florida, Craig Perks bogeyed the 14th and 15th holes to fall one stroke off the lead. If he was going to get back into contention, he was going to have to do it on three of the hardest finishing holes in the game.

Fantastic finish: Perks shanked his second shot on the 16th into the deep rough at the side of the green, then proceeded to right himself in what Tiger Woods called an "unbelievable" finish. Perks chipped in out of the rough from 20 feet for an eagle. Then he birdied the 17th. And then he chipped in on 18 for a crucial par...and won the tournament by one stroke. Stephen Ames, the second-place finisher, said it was "miracle stuff." It was Perks's first-ever win on the PGA Tour, and it earned him a guaranteed PGA Tour card for five years—as well as over $1 million in prize money. (His previous win had been on the Hooters Tour, for which he'd won $11,000.)

*　　*　　*

GOLF BUMPER STICKERS

When I die, bury me on the golf course
so my husband will visit.

I WON'T SAY MY GOLF GAME IS BAD, BUT IF I GREW
TOMATOES THEY'D COME UP SLICED.

I have spent most of my life golfing...
the rest I have just wasted.

*I am hitting the woods just great...but having
a terrible time getting out of them!*

A golfer's diet: live on greens as much as possible

My body is here, but my mind has already teed off

MAY THY BALL LIE IN GREEN PASTURES...AND NOT IN STILL WATERS.

**If I hit it right, it's a slice. If I hit it left, it's a
hook. If I hit it straight, it's a miracle.**

Golf is a game invented by the same people
who think music comes out of a bagpipe.

Bobby Jones won Georgia's amateur title at age 14.

PAR FOR THE CURSE

*As if golf pros don't already have enough obstacles
hindering them from playing well, some tournaments
may harbor an additional, unseen hazard…*

THE MASTERS PAR-3 JINX

On the Wednesday before the start of the Masters, golfers can take part in a nine-hole, par-3 competition. Yet many of golf's fiercest competitors don't even bother to compete in the par-3 contest. Why? They say it's cursed. Since the friendly competition was first held in 1960, not a single winner has ever gone on to win the Masters in the same year.

THE RYDER CUP CAPTAIN'S DOWNFALL

Most American pros would be honored to lead the Ryder Cup team against Europe's best, but golfers in the know keep their distance. Since 1993, every team captain followed up the event with one of his worst seasons ever. A few examples: Tom Watson (1993) sank to 43rd place in 1994. Tom Kite (1997) finished 159th the next year. Ben Crenshaw (1999) was 240th in 2000. Hal Sutton (2003) played in only a handful of tournaments in 2004, and barely made the cut in most of them.

CHIEF LEATHERLIPS'S REVENGE

The Wyandot tribe once thrived in what is now Dublin, Ohio. White settlers called the chief "Leatherlips" because he always told the truth. But although they respected him, they settled on land stolen from the Wyandots. In 1810 Leatherlips's own tribe executed him for allowing the settlers to move in without a fight.

A century and a half later, Jack Nicklaus built Muirfield Village on the Wyandots' sacred burial grounds, and according to local legend, this angered Chief Leatherlips. The proof: over its 25-year run, the Memorial Tournament held each May has been dumped on by torrential rains more than half of the times it has been held. Normally, May is a dry month in central Ohio with only a 3 percent chance of heavy rain on any given day. Inexplicably, that increases to more than 50 percent when the pros are there. Could the spirit of Chief Leatherlips be drowning out the Muirfield Memorial Tournament?

THE BAGMEN

Here's the story of how lowly servants helped make golf what is today—and in some ways, took over the game.

MARY, QUEEN OF CADDIES
One popular story says that the word "caddie" was brought into use by Scotland's golf-loving monarch, Mary, Queen of Scots. Mary spent much of her childhood in France during the mid-1500s, and while golfing she was provided with military cadets to carry her clubs and protect her. When she returned to Scotland, the story goes, she brought the word with her—and over the years the French pronunciation "ca-day" was Scotticized to "cah-die."

Another version says that the word came from the Scottish *cawdy*, for servant (although some records say that that word came from Queen Mary as well). Cawdys were lower-class young men who begged on street corners for any sort of work they could find. When wealthy golfers tired of carrying their own clubs, the story goes, the cawdys were ready to go to work.

But whatever the true origin of the word, the status of the caddies as lower-class servants had been established and, in many ways, remains to this day.

MEN OF MANY TALENTS

The first recorded caddie in history was a man named Andrew Dickson, a club and ball maker who in 1681 carried clubs for the Duke of York (who would later become King James VII of Scotland) in a match against two English noblemen. Once the duke's opponents saw that he had a servant carrying his clubs for him, they wanted one, too. And as the 1700s rolled in, the caddie became as important to golf as clubs and balls.

It soon became evident that the caddie could be more than just a servant who carried clubs, but also the golfer's confidant and adviser...and sometimes partner in crime. That was the case of a legendary St. Andrews caddie known was Willie "Trapdoor" Johnson. Because one of his legs was shorter than the other, he wore a large, extended hollowed-out sole on one of his shoes. But late in Johnson's life, the real truth came out: his legs were the same size—the large shoe was a ruse. He could carry up to six balls inside it, using the hiding place either to miraculously "find" his master's lost ball, or if he felt like it, to scoop a ball up while no one was looking and sell it back to a ball maker or golfers.

Johnson was just one of many resourceful men out on the links in the early days of golf. And just as golfers learned that their games could improve with the aid of a competent caddie, caddies found that golfers had a lot to offer them, as well.

WATCH AND LEARN

In what other sport can someone go out onto the playing field and observe the best players in action? Not only that, but help them through the process? (Imagine standing next to Roger Clemens on the pitcher's mound.) But caddies are in that unique position as apprentices to golfers, good and bad. It's no accident, then, that some of the best golfers in the history of the sport came from the ranks of former caddies.

The man known as the first professional golfer, Allen Robertson, was a caddie as a boy. So, too, were Willie Park, Old Tom Morris, and his son Young Tom Morris. They collectively won twelve British Opens (four each). Some other former bagmen: Francis Ouimet (who at 20 years old won the 1913 U.S. Open), Walter Hagen, Sam Snead, Byron Nelson, Tommy Bolt, Charlie Sifford, Lee Elder, Roberto de Vicenzo, Seve Ballesteros, Bernhard Langer, Jim Thorpe, and Vijay Singh.

As caddies, they were out on the links almost every day, observing everything about the game, growing up with it. Most important, they usually had a free pass to play on slow or off days.

ENDANGERED SPECIES

Two major changes have led to fewer caddies: 1) the golf cart offered an alternate means of transporting equipment; and 2) golf became more of a middle-class game, meaning fewer recreational players could afford caddies. But that doesn't mean that the bagmen are gone.

For more about caddie lore, go to page 205.

GOOFY GOLF GADGETS

Almost since the beginning of golf, people have been coming up with inventions "guaranteed" to turn anyone into a world-class golfer.

Product: Golf Swing Glasses
Purpose: Makes you keep your eyes on the ball
Pitch: Mimicking the blinders worn by racehorses to prevent being distracted by other horses, these glasses force the golfer to keep his eyes on the ball by staring through two "eye tunnels." Result: if your head moves too far to one side, the ball disappears from view behind the thick, opaque ridges that surround the eye-holes.

Product: Golfer's Crotch Hook
Purpose: Keeps your head down during a swing
Pitch: The golfer wears a tight-fitting headband attached by an elastic cord to a massive, seven-inch fishhook fitted into the crotch of the golfer's pants. If the wearer lifts his head up too high during the swing, he is instantly—and uncomfortably—notified.

Product: Floating Magnetic Ball Bearing
Purpose: Helps you swing with the proper amount of force
Pitch: A six-inch cylinder is screwed onto the club's shaft, just above the head. If the golfer exerts the correct amount of power on the downswing, a ball bearing inside the tube audibly clicks into place.

Product: Golf Coach
Purpose: Provides expert on-course advice
Pitch: This pocket-sized dial helps a golfer overcome every dilemma: sand traps, rough, etc. Just turn the dial to the golfing problem and up pops step-by-step instructions on how to make the perfect shot for that situation.

Product: Power Putty
Purpose: Improves hand strength and gripping power
Pitch: This gelatinous Silly Putty–like glob of silicon was developed

---

The 7th hole at Satsuki Golf Course in Japan is the world's longest: a par-7 of 964 yards.

by a health food magnate. If golfers regularly squeeze it in their hands, it's supposed to make them stronger.

Product: Putt Teacher
Purpose: Helps improve your putting
Pitch: It's a putter attached to a belt on rollers (it looks sort of like a combination golf club and belt sander). If your swing is crooked, the belt will twist into a mess, telling you what you probably already know: your putting needs work.

Product: Putt-Caster
Purpose: Practice putting...without having to retrieve your ball
Pitch: Essentially a fishing reel, the Putt-Caster clamps onto the club and dangles a golf ball attached to a fishing line. Press the trigger as you putt and the tethered ball moves freely. Then just reel it in and putt again.

Product: "Talking" Golf Ball
Purpose: Locates a lost ball
Pitch: Someone invented a golf ball that made a high-pitched squeak, which made it easy to find in the rough. How did it work? Inside the solid rubber core was one-fiftieth of a gram of *radioactive plutonium*. Bonus: golfers were supposed to be able to use a hand-held Geiger counter to locate the ball anywhere on the course, but it didn't work as advertised. Reason: the manufacturer used such a small amount of plutonium (for safety reasons) that the ball only registered if the Geiger counter was within four feet of the ball.

Product: Applauding Club
Purpose: Helps develop the perfect swing
Pitch: Amateur golfer George Carney figured the best way for golfers to improve was through positive reinforcement. So he concocted a club attachment that "applauded" a perfect swing. Since voice chip technology had not yet been invented, the applause was simulated by the teeth of a metal roller vibrating against a brass plate. If the club traveled 16 inches along the ground before liftoff (Carney's idea of a perfect swing), there was applause. Any variations and the golfer was greeted with shameful silence.

Jimmy Carter is an avid fan of Putt-Putt golf.

TEED OFF

*Have you ever cursed a blue streak or thrown a club after a
bad shot? It's not unusual for people to lose their tempers
on the golf course, but these folks took it to extremes.*

Golfer: Harry Wagner, a golfer from New York City (in some news reports his name is given as Cyril Wagner)

Incident: In December 2000, Wagner was golfing at the Trump International Golf Club in West Palm Beach, Florida, as the guest of a member. When their golfing party, which included two children, ages 6 and 12, got to the 16th hole, one of four exotic black swans that lived on the course hissed at them and behaved aggressively; then when they got to the 17th hole it did it again.

Teed Off: Wagner took out his titanium driver and swung it at the swan, killing it with one blow. Wagner said he acted in self-defense and wanted to protect the children. No matter: he was charged with a single misdemeanor count of animal cruelty, which is punishable by up to a year in jail and a $5,000 fine.

Aftermath: The charges were later dropped after Wagner agreed to perform 30 hours of community service at an animal shelter in New York, and to donate $2,500 to another animal shelter near the golf course in Florida. He also had to reimburse the county sheriff $800 to cover the cost of investigating the case. And there's one more thing: Donald Trump has banned Wagner from all Trump properties—the casinos, the hotels, the golf courses, and everything else—for life. "I don't care if it was self-defense or not," Trump said. "The actions seemed excessive. Swans are not alligators or crocodiles."

Golfers: Graham Rusk, Reginald Dove, and John Buckingham, all members of England's Sherwood Forest Golf Club

Incident: Rusk and Dove accused Buckingham of cheating during a 1990 golf tournament. They claimed he had moved the ball with his foot twice near the 7th hole, then replaced "lost" balls at the 12th and 13th holes by secretly dropping them down his inside pant leg through a hole in his pocket. They accused him of cheating in other matches, too.

Teed Off: A club disciplinary hearing found that the charges hadn't been proven. But Rusk and Dove refused to reimburse Buckingham's expenses or even to apologize, so Buckingham sued them for libel. He probably wishes he'd just taken a swing at them with his clubs: after nearly four years in the courts, a jury sided with Rusk and Dove, ruling that while their cheating charges were still unproven, they had not acted with malice and thus were not guilty of libeling Buckingham.

Aftermath: Buckingham ended up with $520,000 worth of legal bills, which he hopes to defray by charging admirers $2,500 to play a round of golf with him. "It's a minimal fee. It won't pay my costs," he said. "But every little bit helps."

(Non) Golfer: Imran Hashmi, 24, of West London, England

Incident: Who says you have to play golf to be a victim of golf rage? Hashmi, 24, was *driving* past the Camberly Heath Golf Club in Surrey when someone in a foursome of golfers on the 12th hole hit a slice that nearly hit his car. Hashmi "gestured" at them in response.

Teed Off: It must have been a pretty nasty gesture, because all four golfers ran up to the car and started attacking it with their clubs, denting the body and smashing the windows and windshield before Hashmi was able to turn the car around and drive off. He drove to his sister's house—only about 100 yards away—and ran inside. When the golfers continued to pursue him, he came out of the house brandishing a fake army pistol. The fight ended there, but someone called the cops. Hashmi was arrested and taken to jail on a weapons charge—and the golfers were not charged.

Aftermath: Hashmi pleaded self-defense and beat the rap; not only that, the judge called for an inquiry into "why no police action was taken against the four golfers."

*　　*　　*

"I'll take a two-shot penalty, but I'll be damned if I'm going to play the ball where it lies."

—Elaine Johnson,
*after her tee shot hit a tree
and caromed into her bra*

15% of the general population is left-handed. Only 5.5% of golfers are.

MUTINY ON THE GOLF TEE

*Many people think of the PGA as one unified
golfing organization—but it's not. Here's the story
of the PGA of America, and the splinter group
that broke from them—the PGA Tour.*

ROUND ONE

On January 16, 1916, a group of golfers, both professionals and amateurs, met for a luncheon at the Taplow Club in New York City. It was hosted by department store magnate (and golfing fanatic) Rodman Wanamaker. Wanamaker thought it was time for professional golfers in the United States to become organized. The British already had their own professional organization, the British PGA, and Wanamaker believed that if the Americans did the same, they could increase the popularity of the sport all across the nation—and sell a lot more golfing equipment in his stores.

On April 10, Wanamaker's wish came true: with 35 charter members, the Professional Golfers Association of America was founded in New York City. At that time golf professionals worked at golf clubs, mostly giving lessons to amateur players, and played in the few pro tournaments that existed—there was no national ranking and no tour. So the first real job of the PGA: organize a big tournament to determine the best club pro in the country, and, hopefully, get some good publicity for professional golf.

THE CLUB CHAMPIONSHIP

That October the PGA held the country's first-ever exclusively professional golf championship at the Siwanoy Country Club in Bronxville, New York. Wanamaker donated the purse: $2,580, a generous prize at the time, and a large silver trophy. The first winner of the Wanamaker Trophy: Long Jim Barnes from England, who defeated Scotsman Jock Hutchison 1-up in the final round of the tournament. In 1921 Walter Hagen, one of the founding members of the PGA, became the first American to win the

---

A score of 8 on a single hole is called "making a snowman."

event. The flamboyant Hagen's popularity—on and off the course—would be a huge boon for the PGA Championship. He would go on to win it five times in the 1920s, helping to make it one of the most popular golfing events in the country.

Today, the PGA of America has more than 28,000 members. They operate through a network of 41 sections, and hold more than 30 tournaments a year for professional and apprentice golfers, including the Senior PGA Championship, the PGA Club Professional Championship, and the biennial Ryder Cup matches. But the PGA Championship remains their most prestigious event: it is one of golf's four majors and winning the Wanamaker Trophy is still considered one of the highest honors in the world of golf.

THE TOUR

In the early years of the PGA, there were very few professional tournaments and most golfers either couldn't make a living just playing golf or they weren't willing to take the risk. As the game became more and more popular, more courses were built around the country and more people came to see the show. By 1925 PGA tournaments were offering about $77,000 in total prize money—more than $770,000 in today's money—and by 1930 it was up to $130,000.

In 1930 the PGA first raised the idea of a year-round tournament circuit for the game and created the "Tournament Bureau" to study the idea; two years later they formed the "Playing Pros" organization. Over the next few decades, with the founding of events such as the Masters Tournament and the Crosby Clambake, the rise of American golfing legends like Ben Hogan and Arnold Palmer, along with the rise of television, golf's popularity soared. There were now tournaments to play all over the country, all year round, and they were offering huge sums of money in prizes. But trouble was brewing in the PGA.

REBELLION

In August 1968, a group of professional golfers met at Firestone Country Club in Akron, Ohio, before the American Golf Classic. By now, there was serious contention growing between the two distinct kinds of pro golfers that made up the membership of the PGA of America: the touring pros and the club pros. Even though

If a sand shot is done correctly, the clubhead never touches the ball.

they could now make a living traveling and playing golf, most PGA pros didn't. They were still club pros. That made the touring pros a minority, and they felt that those "stay-at-home" golfers didn't understand them or represent them well in the organization. Something had to change.

The day before the American Golf Classic, 100 touring pros issued a list of demands to the PGA. They wanted their own commissioner, their own public relations department, their own offices, and they wanted to be run by their own autonomous organization inside the PGA of America. And they didn't just issue demands, they threatened to boycott PGA events if the demands weren't met. This group included the likes of such stars as Arnold Palmer and Jack Nicklaus—the PGA had no choice.

THE GREAT DIVIDE

Within months, the Tournament Players Division of the PGA was formed. In 1975 they became the PGA Tour Inc., and under the watch of their very savvy commissioner, Deane Beman, became the behemoth that it is today. When Beman took the job in 1974, the total purses for a PGA year added up to $730,000. When he left in 1994, it was well over $200 million. But the PGA Tour has an odd feature, especially for such a lucrative professional sports organization: it's nonprofit—and they don't pay taxes. They get that nonprofit status because a portion of all PGA Tour profits goes to charity. Since the PGA made its first charitable donation in 1938—$10,000 from the Palm Beach Invitational—they've donated nearly $1 billion.

And they've expanded. Today there are three official PGA Tours: the PGA Tour that is the men's "big league" tour; the Senior PGA Tour (now the Champions Tour), created in 1980 and a very successful tour in its own right; and the Ben Hogan Tour (now the Nationwide Tour), golf's "minor league," which was formed in 1990. The PGA Tour runs more than 100 professional tournaments every year for those three circuits and a championship for each of them. The Players Championship is the main event and has the largest purse in the U.S.—more than $8 million in 2005. And as far as the PGA Tour is concerned, it is the "fifth major" in the sport.

Average depth of a golf ball dimple: one hundredth of an inch.

CHI CHI RODRIGUEZ

He not only has a funny first name, but he's a pretty funny guy as well. (And he's a pretty good golfer, to boot.)

"The first time I played the Masters, I was so nervous I drank a bottle of rum before I teed off. I shot the happiest 83 of my life."

"I don't exaggerate—I just remember big."

"If I could have putted like this years ago, I'd own a jet instead of a Toyota."
—On playing the Senior Tour

"The best wood in most amateurs' bags is the pencil."

"When Lee and Jack win, it is good for golf. When I win, it is better."

"You could put horse manure on an ice-cream cone with whipped cream and a cherry on top, and some people will buy it just because a top-30 Tour pro is selling it."

"Golf is the only sport that a professional can enjoy playing with his friends. Can Larry Holmes enjoy fighting one of his friends?"

"When you're having trouble and topping the ball, it means the ground is moving on you."

"We must always be humble in victory and cocky in losing."

"When a man retires, his wife gets twice the husband but only half the income."

"I never pray to God to make a putt. I pray to God to help me react good if I miss a putt."

"I'm playing like Tarzan and scoring like Jane."

"I do not fear death...but I sure do hate those 3-footers for par."

"I am a millionaire today and my wife deserves all of the credit. Before I met her I was a multimillionaire."

"After all these years, it's still embarrassing. Like the time I asked my caddie for a sand wedge and he came back ten minutes later with a ham on rye."
—On his Puerto Rican accent

Water hazard: Chi Chi Rodriguez once made his caddie carry him across a river.

DOGLEGS AND FROG HAIRS

The not-so-pro's guide to talking like a golfer, D–F.

Deuce: A score of 2 on a hole.

Dew sweepers: In the third and fourth rounds of a tournament, the poorest scorers start their round first, often very early, when the dew is still on the ground.

Dimple pattern: The way the dimples are arranged on a golf ball. The patterns vary among brands and can affect distance and accuracy.

Divot: A piece of turf lifted when a club strikes the ground. Also the scar on the ground where the turf was.

Dogleg: A left or right bend in the fairway. Two bends on one hole is a *double dogleg*.

Double bogey: Two over par on one hole.

Double D: Using a driver on the fairway after using it off the tee.

Double eagle: Three under par on one hole. (*See* albatross.)

Double green: A very large green that serves two different holes, with two cups, two flagsticks, and room for two groups to play simultaneously.

Downhill lie: When the ball rests on a hill, below the golfer's feet as he swings.

Draw: A ball intentionally struck in such a way as to make it fly slightly right to left (for a right-hander).

Driver: A one-wood.

Driving iron: A one- or two-iron.

Drop: To put a ball back into play (when it goes into a water hazard, for example) by dropping it from an outstretched arm at shoulder height.

Duffer: Slang for bad golfer.

Eagle: Two under par for one hole.

Even (or even par): To have a score that is at par.

Executive course: A small golf course with mostly par-3 and short par-4 holes.

Fade: A ball intentionally struck in such a way as to make it fly slightly left to right (for a right-hander)—opposite of a draw.

Fairway: The closely-mowed

playing area between the tee and the green.

False front: The front part of any green that slopes back toward the fairway. It can trick players into thinking they're safely on the green—until the ball rolls off again.

Fat (also heavy or thick): To hit a ball fat means hitting the ground before the ball, greatly reducing distance.

Ferrule: The plastic ring that covers the joint between the shaft and head on an iron club.

Fescue: A fine-bladed grass commonly used on putting greens (especially on British links courses).

First cut (or first cut of rough): The strip of grass between the fairway and the rough, cut slightly higher than the fairway.

Five-minute rule: *See* lost ball.

Flat stick: Slang for putter.

Flex: Flexibility rating of a golf club's shaft. Examples: L (Ladies), A (Senior), R (Regular), S (Stiff).

Flop shot: A high, soft-landing shot from close to the green, usually made with a sand or lob wedge.

Fluffy lie: When the ball comes to rest on or near the top of high grass. (Sitting off the ground is advantageous for some shots, risky for others).

Flush: Making perfect contact with the ball. "He caught it flush."

Forecaddie: A "spotter" situated ahead of a golfer to watch where the ball lands. Forecaddies were used in the 18th and 19th centuries when balls were very expensive.

"Fore!": A "heads up" cry to warn people that your ball might hit them. (In the old days, golfers yelled "forecaddie!" to warn of an errant shot and "Fore!" is believed to be a shortened version of that word.)

Forward press: A slight forward movement of the arms and hands just before the backswing.

Fried egg: A ball that's half-buried in a sand bunker (and looks kind of like a fried egg).

Frog hair: Slang for "apron," the slightly taller grass that surrounds the putting green.

Front nine: The first nine holes of an 18-hole golf course.

Full-finger grip (or baseball grip): A less-common grip in which the club is held with all ten fingers on the grip and none overlap or interlock.

Q: What was the first American-produced golf ball? A: The Spalding Wizard.

REVENGE OF THE RULE BOOK

The most important rule of golf: Know the rules.

PEE, AS IN PENALTY

During the first round of the 2003 Sony Open in Hawaii, Australian Scott Laycock had to go...to the bathroom. He couldn't find one close by, so when a man in a golf cart offered to drive him to one, he accepted. Laycock knew that riding in a cart was against the rules, but hoped that since it wasn't to get to his ball, it would be all right. After the fact, Laycock told an official what he'd done and asked if it was a violation. The official asked if it had been an emergency. Laycock asked him to define "emergency." "Diarrhea," said the official. The good news: Laycock wasn't afflicted with that condition. The bad news: he got a two-stroke penalty for his cart ride. "That," he said later, "did give me the s***s."

TRADING PLACES

During the 2003 British Open at Royal St. George's in Sandwich, English golfer Mark Roe and Sweden's Jesper Parnévik played the third round together. The eccentric Swede, known for his bizarre, brightly colored outfits, had a terrible day, shooting an 81. But Roe did great, shooting a 4-under 67 to put him at one over par, just three strokes off the leader, Thomas Bjorn. After the round they turned in their scorecards at the scorer's trailer and minutes later were informed that they'd both been disqualified.

What went wrong? At the beginning of the round, the golfers were handed each other's scorecards by officials, which they were then supposed to exchange (it's an old tradition). But they didn't trade cards; they simply forgot. So all day they were marking their scores on the wrong cards. When they signed them at the end of the round, they had signed cards with someone else's name printed on top—a violation of the rules.

Parnevik was incensed for his friend. "It's not like he tried to put down for a 64 and hope no one noticed," he said, adding, "It's the dumbest rule I have ever heard of."

Roe, however, kept his sense of humor. "To be perfectly honest," he said, "I was distracted by Jesper's outfit once again."

THE WINNER IS—NOT!

At the 1957 U.S. Women's Open, Jackie Pung finished with a score of 298 for the 72 holes and was declared the winner. Then officials noticed that she'd scored the 4th hole as a 5, but had actually played it in 6 strokes. Result: Although her total score was correct, her scorecard was wrong, and she was disqualified. The $1,800 prize money—the largest on the women's tour at the time—was suddenly not hers. Members of the Winged Foot Golf Club, where the Open was played, felt so bad that they raised $3,000 and gave it to her.

DEW THE RIGHT THING

It was the first round of the 2001 U.S. Open. Lee Janzen had just taken a tee shot when a horn sounded, announcing that play was being suspended because of rain. So Janzen marked his ball on the fairway and walked off the course. When play started again on Friday morning, Janzen used a towel to soak up some of the moisture around his marker, then put his ball back and continued to play. An official saw him do it and assessed Janzen a two-stroke penalty for violating Rule 13-2, which states:

> The removal of dew or frost from the area immediately behind or to the side of a player's ball is forbidden. Such action is deemed to improve the position or lie of the ball.

The only problem: the official neglected to tell Janzen. So when Janzen turned in his scorecard, he hadn't included the penalty, which meant he turned in an incorrect scorecard, which is grounds for disqualification. "Ordinarily, when a player fails to include a penalty and signs for a score lower than should have been recorded, the result is disqualification," said a USGA spokesman. "But since the committeeman failed to notify the player of the penalty, the disqualification is waived." Nice gesture, but it didn't matter; they made him add the two penalty strokes to his score, which put him over the cutline and he was knocked out of the tournament anyway.

HERE'S TO THE LADIES

The winningest golfers in the history of the LPGA…
and one that might just catch them.

MICKEY WRIGHT

In 2000 *Golf Digest* announced their list of the ten best golfers of all time. At number nine was Mickey Wright. Who's he? "He" is Mary Kathryn "Mickey" Wright—and the vote was for men *and* women. The Californian joined the LPGA in 1955 at the age of 20, and although her career officially lasted until 1981, foot and hand injuries limited her most competitive play to one decade. But it was an incredible decade. From 1959 to 1968, Wright won 79 tournaments—an average of almost eight wins a year. No other golfer, man or woman, has ever had such a stretch. She finished her career with 82 victories, second on the all-time list for pro golfers.

KATHY WHITWORTH

Pop quiz: Who has the most wins in the history of pro golf? If you said Sam Snead (he has 82), you're wrong. It's Kathy Whitworth, who won 88 times on the LPGA Tour. The Texan turned pro in 1958 and by 1965 was dominating the LPGA along with Mickey Wright. Between 1965 and 1973 alone, Whitworth had 56 victories. Her longevity was record-breaking, too: she had at least one win every year for 17 years (a record she shares with Jack Nicklaus and Arnold Palmer) from 1962 to 1978, and recorded her last official victory in 1985.

ANNIKA SORENSTAM

Annika Sorenstam was born in 1970 in Stockholm, Sweden. She joined the LPGA in 1994 and has dominated the women's game ever since. Her three wins in her first three starts of the 2005 season brought her victory total to 59. That puts her in fourth place on the LPGA all-time list. Can she break Whitworth's record of 88? It's possible. Whitworth needed 22 years to set the mark, and 2005 is only Sorenstam's 12th season. Another Sorenstam feat: in 2001 she became the only person in the history of the LPGA to score a 59 for a round. Only three PGA pros have accomplished that feat.

17% of sales reps who golf with clients say they let the clients win.

POETRY IN MOTION

Uncle John may never see
A thing as lovely as a tee...

Here's to the man with club in hand
Here's to the king of bogey land;
Here's to the clubs with outlandish names
And here's to golf, the game of games!
—*The Father Gander Golf Book* (1909)

Mary had a little putt,
She needed it for par.
Mary took a second putt
(The first one went too far).
—**Margaret Kennard**

This is the substance of our Plot—
For those who play the Perfect Shot,
There are ten thousand who do not.
—**Grantland Rice**

If I ever make a hole in one,
A thrill that I've never known,
I won't be believed and I'll have no fun,
For I'm sure to be playing alone.
—**Richard Armour**

The golf course being rather far,
I have an excuse to take the car.
And since the holes are far apart,
I have an excuse to use a cart.
But one thing has me still defeated—
You cannot hit the ball while seated.
—**Donna Evleth**

Some golfers lie awake at night
And brood on what went wrong;
I'd rather think of what went right.
(It doesn't take as long.)
—**Dick Emmons**

"Of all the hazards, fear is the worst." —Sam Snead

THE BRITISH OPEN

The British Open—properly known as the Open Championship—is one of golf's four major tournaments. To many fans it is the most prestigious of the four, largely because it's the oldest. In fact, it's the oldest professional golf tournament in the world, period.

OLD-TIMER

In 1860 two wealthy members of Prestwick Golf Club in Ayrshire in eastern Scotland suggested to fellow members that they all donate money for a golfing trophy. More and more "professionals" were playing all over Scotland, they argued, and it was time to decide a national champion. It was a novel idea—there were no official golf tournaments then and no prize money; pros made their living through caddying, teaching, making equipment, and gambling.

The members agreed and commissioned the Championship Challenge Belt: a wide, red, lavishly adorned leather belt with a big silver buckle. Theirs would be the first tournament to determine the "champion golfer of the world." The basics:

• Only professional golfers would be invited to play.
• They would play three rounds at Prestwick's 12-hole course.
• The winner would get to keep the belt for a year and then turn it over to the next champion.

OPENING UP

On October 17, 1860, now-legendary golfer and golf course designer Willie Park won the tournament. The next year they announced that the tournament would be "open to the world," professional and amateur alike (12 golfers entered). It's been the "Open Championship" ever since.

Old Tom Morris won the Challenge Belt in 1861. He won again in 1864 (his third time) and took home the tournament's first prize money: six pounds. From 1868 to 1870, Morris's son, "Young" Tom Morris, won the event three times in a row. According to the rules, that meant he got to *keep* the Challenge Belt—which meant the club would need a new trophy. To be able to afford a more lavish prize, Prestwick joined up with two other

---

Harpo Marx and George Burns enjoyed golfing together in their underwear.

clubs: the Royal and Ancient Golf Club of St. Andrews and the Honourable Company of Edinburgh Golfers in Musselburgh. No tournament was held in 1871, and when Young Tom Morris won again in 1872—a still-unsurpassed four times in a row—they didn't have a new prize ready, so they awarded him a medal instead.

INTRODUCING CLARET

In 1873 Mackay Cunningham & Company of Edinburgh was commissioned to create a large cup, officially named the "Championship Cup," but commonly known as the "Claret Jug." Claret is a red wine from the Bordeaux region of France that had been popular in Scotland for centuries. It was one of the favorite drinks of the wealthy golfers in Prestwick's clubhouse. They even used it as currency, by the bottle or by the case, when they gambled on rounds of golf. In honor of the tradition, the Championship Cup was made to resemble the silver jugs from which the Prestwick golfers sipped claret.

That was also the first year that the Open was held not at Prestwick but at St. Andrews. The first winner of the Claret Jug: Tom Kidd, a St. Andrews caddie. For the next 18 years, the Open would rotate between Prestwick, St. Andrews, and Musselburgh. Since then the list of host clubs has expanded, but not by much. Only 14 clubs have hosted the event—seven in Scotland, six in England, and one in Northern Ireland.

Today, more than 2,000 golfers from all over the world attempt to qualify for the event every year, hoping to be crowned Open Champion and win the immense first-prize money (Todd Hamilton won in 2004 and got $1.4 million).

BRITISH OPEN HIGHLIGHTS

• **1868:** Young Tom Morris scores the Open's first hole in one.

• **1890:** John Ball Jr. becomes the first Englishman, the first non-Scot, and the first amateur to win the Claret Jug.

• **1892:** The tournament is expanded to 72 holes played over two days to accommodate the growing number of entrants.

• **1894:** The Open is played outside of Scotland for the first

Tennis star and avid golfer Vitas Gerulaitis was buried with his 5-iron.

time, at Royal St. George's in Sandwich, England.

• **1896:** Harry Vardon wins. He will go on to win six times over the next 20 years, a record that still stands today.

• **1898:** From eight golfers in the first Open in 1860, the number has grown to 101. To keep the numbers down, the cut is introduced, eliminating the lowest scoring half of players after 36 holes.

• **1900:** J. H. Taylor, Harry Vardon, and James Braid finish 1-2-3. They become known as the "Great Triumvirate" and will win 16 British Opens in a 21-year span.

• **1907:** Frenchman Arnaud Massy becomes the first player not from the British Isles (and still the only Frenchman) to win.

• **1915–19:** The Open is suspended due to World War I.

• **1920:** The Royal and Ancient Golf Club of St. Andrews takes over the running of the British Open, although it will still rotate among different venues.

• **1921:** Jock Hutchison becomes the first American to win (though he was born in Scotland and moved to the United States as a teen).

• **1922:** Walter Hagen becomes the first American-born golfer to win. Americans will win 10 of the next 11 Opens.

• **1927:** A 36-hole qualifying round is added to further limit the growing number of golfers entering.

• **1930:** American amateur Bobby Jones wins for the third time. He also wins the U.S. Open, U.S. Amateur, and British Amateur titles. It is the first "Grand Slam," meaning a player has won all four majors in one year. (Those were the four majors at the time.)

• **1940–45:** The Open is suspended due to World War II.

• **1951:** The Open is played in Northern Ireland at Royal Portrush Golf Club. Max Faulkner wins and is the last Brit to do so for nearly two decades.

• **1953:** Ben Hogan plays in his only British Open—at Carnoustie Links—and wins.

• **1955:** The BBC first airs the event on television. Australian Peter Thomson successfully defends his title at St. Andrews. He will win the next one, too, and become the only modern golfer to win three British Opens in a row.

• **1962:** Arnold Palmer wins his second British Open title and sets a scoring record at Royal Troon with a 276 total. His participation helps revive the popularity of the event in the United States, which had fallen in recent years.

• **1963:** New Zealander Bob Charles becomes the first left-handed golfer to win.

• **1977:** Jack Nicklaus and Tom Watson compete in the Open's most epic battle, at Turnberry in Scotland. They play the last two days paired together and, battling each other shot for shot, leave the rest of the field behind. On the final hole, Nicklaus sinks a 35-footer for a birdie to tie Watson. Watson then sinks a two-foot birdie putt to win by one stroke, with a record-setting total of 268. (The legendary matchup is memorialized in Michael Corcoran's book *Duel in the Sun*.)

• **1993:** Greg Norman wins his second British Open with a record score of 267.

• **2000:** Tiger Woods wins his first British Open by an eight-stroke margin, the largest in 87 years.

• **2003:** American Ben Curtis, a 26-year-old PGA rookie with only 14 PGA tournaments under his belt, none of which included a top-10 finish, and at the time ranked 396th in the world, shocks the golf world by winning the British Open. Playing against such golfers as Ernie Els, Vijay Singh, Davis Love III, and Tiger Woods, Curtis's win has been called one of the biggest upsets in the history of sports.

*　　*　　*

SURVEY SAYS...

Two thousand U.S. golfers who play more than 25 rounds a year were surveyed by *Golf* magazine. Results:

• 8% have had sex on the course (the figure rises to 18% for low handicappers).

• 16% have broken a club in anger; 43% have thrown a club.

• 59% have improved their lie when fellow players weren't looking.

• 37% said if they could ban one thing from the golf course it would be slow players.

The trophy for the King Hassan Golf Tournament is a jewel-encrusted dagger.

VERY SUPERSTITIOUS

*Just like any athletes, golfers can be a
superstitious lot. Here are a few examples.*

LUCKY COINS

Jack Nicklaus always carries three pennies in his pocket during a round. "If I carried only one penny and lost it, I'd be without a ball marker. If I had only two pennies and lost one and a fellow player needed to borrow one to mark his ball, I'd be still out of ball markers." And he always marks his ball with the tails side up. He also won't use his own tees on par-3 holes—he finds broken ones from other players' shots and uses them.

• **Paul Azinger** also always marks his ball with a penny...with the head facing up and Lincoln facing the hole.

• **Mark Wiebe** marks his ball only with coins from the 1960s. Why? Because he wants to shoot in the 60s.

• **Fred Funk** flips a coin on the green. If it's tails he uses it to mark his ball normally, but if it's heads he makes sure the head is facing the hole.

• **Jerry Kelly** will only use dimes to mark his ball—and they can't be dated later than 1969.

• **Chi Chi Rodriguez** uses a quarter to mark his ball on birdie putts, a buffalo nickel for eagle putts, and, if the other coins aren't bringing him good luck, he uses a gold piece instead.

LUCKY FOOD

• **Adam Holden** must have a ham sandwich during a tournament, and it must be made with two pieces of bread. "It cannot be on any kind of roll." (Holden, an Australian, is superstitious about his tees, too. He brings 300 Day-Glo orange tees with him whenever he plays in the United States.)

• **Natalie Gulbis**, the LPGA's 21-year-old star who made news with her bikini calendar, has a high-calorie ritual. Before every round, she eats at McDonald's. Her favorite meal: an Egg McMuffin and hash browns.

"You know you're on the Senior Tour when your back goes out more than you do." —Bob Bruce

LUCKY BALLS

- **Karrie Webb** uses a number 4 ball on Thursday, a number 3 ball on Friday, a number 2 ball on Saturday, and a number 1 ball on Sunday. "Of course, I like to be number one on Sundays," she says.

- **Duffy Waldorf** has his wife and kids draw pictures on his golf balls before every tournament.

- **Pat Bates** writes Bible verses on his golf balls.

LUCKY CHARMS

- **Roger Maltbie** hit a bad shot in the 1976 Memorial Tournament at Muirfield Village. The ball looked like it was headed out of bounds, but then hit an out-of-bounds marker and bounced back into play. When he ended up winning the tournament, Maltbie credited the lucky marker and then carried it with him to every tournament for the next six months. What happened after six months? Maltbie had a bad round, so he abandoned the marker. (He left it under the bed in his motel room.)

- **Australian PGA golfer Peter Lonard** wore his favorite pair of red underpants on every Sunday of every tournament he played—for 15 years—until they finally wore out.

- **Tiger Woods** wears a red shirt on the final Sunday of a tournament. It's for his mother, who says that "red is a lucky color for Tiger. It brings power."

- **Doug Sanders** never uses white tees—and he has "proof" that they're bad luck. On the 18th tee of the last day of the 1970 British Open, he had the lead and needed to make par to win. He had run out of tees and had to borrow one from his playing partner; it was white. He bogeyed the hole and lost the major the next day in a playoff with Jack Nicklaus.

* * *

Golf's Most Famous (And Funniest) Urban Legend. During a televised tournament in the 1960s, a commentator told the TV audience about one of Arnold Palmer's superstitious rituals: "One of the reasons Arnie is playing so well," he said, "is that, before each tee shot, his wife takes out his balls and kisses them..." That was followed by a frozen silence, then, "Oh my God! What have I just said!?"

Heavy metal musician Alice Cooper sponsors the Annual Alice Cooper Golf Tournament.

PAR HAR HAR

*More golf jokes to tell your partner while
he's lining up his birdie putt.*

An old man and a young man are playing golf together. The young man hits his tee shot and it lands about 20 yards in front of a large pine tree blocking the green. The young man asks for advice.

"You know, sonny," says the old man, "when I was your age, I'd hit that ball right over that tree."

So the young man digs in, swings as hard as he can, and smacks the ball right into the tree. It ricochets back and lands right in front of the two golfers.

"Of course, when I was your age," says the old man, "that tree was only about ten feet tall."

Q: How is golf like taxes?
A: You drive hard to get to the green, and then you wind up in the hole.

What's the difference between a bad golfer and a bad skydiver?
A bad golfer goes: WHACK! "Damn." A bad skydiver goes: "Damn." WHACK!

A hack golfer spends a day at his posh country club and has a horrible round. At the 18th hole, he sees a lake off to the left of the fairway. He turns to his caddie and says, "I've played so badly all day; I think I'm going to go drown myself in that lake."

The caddie looks back at him and says, "I don't think you could keep your head down that long."

Pro: "Now I want you to go through the motions without actually hitting the ball."
Student: "But that's what I always do!"

Gordon was 26 over par by the 8th hole. He had landed a dozen balls in the water hazard, and dug himself into a trench fighting his way out of the rough. When his caddie coughed during a one-foot putt, Gordon exploded.

"You've got to be the worst caddie in the world!" he screamed.

"I doubt it," replied the caddie. "That would be too much of a coincidence."

IT'S A HOLE IN ONE!

It's been called the hardest thing to achieve in all of sports.

THE NUMBERS

• Your chances of getting hit by a car are 11,000 to 1. Your chances of winning a Pick Four lottery are 10,000 to 1. Your chances of hitting a hole in one are 12,600 to 1.

• Has anybody scored two holes in one in a row? Believe it or not, it's not impossible—at least 20 golfers have done it.

THE RECORD HOLDERS

• Golf pro Mancil Davis had more holes in one in his career than any other golfer—49.

• In 1942 Mrs. W. Driver became the first woman on record to achieve the feat. It happened at the Balgowla Club in Australia.

• The longest hole in one on record was made in 1965 by Bob Mitera on a course in Nebraska. He sank his tee shot from 447 yards away. The name of the course: Miracle Hill.

OLDEST AND YOUNGEST

• Scott Statler hit a hole in one on July 30, 1962, at the 7th hole of Statler's Fun Center, a par-3 golf course in Greensburg, Pennsylvania. He was only four years old.

• Brittny Andreas was playing the Jimmy Clay Golf Course in Austin, Texas, in 1991 when she became the youngest girl ever to ace a hole. She was six.

• Otto Bucher was the oldest golfer to score a hole in one. Bucher, a Swiss-born player, swung to greatness at Spain's La Manga Golf Course on January 13, 1985, at the ripe old age of 99.

• The oldest woman to make a hole in one was 95-year-old Erna Ross. She did it in 1986 on the 17th at the Everglades Golf Club in Palm Beach, Florida.

HANDICAP SHMANDICAP

• A one-armed golfer named Bill Hilsheimer went 50 years without hitting a hole in one. When he turned 68, the Floridian's luck

---

Walter Hagen and Joe Kirkwood once played downtown Tijuana as a course...

changed—he hit the first ace in his career. Then, not long after, another one. And finally, a third one…all within six months.

• At four months old, Kevin Erickson had to have a third of his brain removed because of a tumor. While life has been difficult for him, golf came easy. At the 2003 U.S. Golf National Invitational in Florida, Erickson shot a Special Olympics record 76 in the second round—including a hole in one on the sixth—and went on to take the gold medal.

EXECUTIVE OFFICERS

• The only president to hit a hole in one while in office was avid duffer Dwight Eisenhower. However, Richard Nixon and Gerald Ford both hit holes in one while out of office. Ford, it should be noted, hit not just one but three holes in one.

HOLE-Y STORIES

• Robert Trent Jones, the Frank Lloyd Wright of golf course design, was pretty good on the links as well. When a few members complained about the "impossible" 4th hole at his Balthusrol Golf Course in Springfield, New Jersey, Jones led them to the tee and took a swing. His ball flew straight to the flag, took a hop on the green, and plopped into the hole. "Gentlemen," he said, "I think this hole is imminently fair."

• Groucho Marx was one of the worst celebrity golfers ever, but even the bad ones can get lucky once in a while. While playing near Boston, he shot a hole in one, landing him on the front page of *The Globe* with golf greats Walter Hagen and Bobby Jones.

• In 1956, when Morton Shapiro hit his ball up to the lip of the 5th hole of the Indian Springs Country Club in New Jersey, a ground tremor gently shook the Earth…sending his balancing ball into the cup for a hole in one.

*   *   *

"Man blames fate for other accidents, but feels personally responsible for a hole in one."

—**Martha Beckman**

HEAD GAMES

Sure, you have to be in decent physical shape to play golf, but perhaps more than any other sport, golf is played mostly in the mind.

"Golf is a game that is played on a five-inch course—the distance between your ears."
—**Bobby Jones**

"The worst club in my bag is my brain."
—**Chris Perry**

"I look into their eyes, shake their hand, pat their back, and wish them luck…but I'm thinking, 'I am going to bury you.'"
—**Seve Ballesteros**

"I am the toughest golfer mentally."
—**Tiger Woods**

"You create your own luck by the way you play. There is no such luck as bad luck. Fate has nothing to do with success or failure, because that is a negative philosophy that indicts one's confidence, and I'll have no part of it."
—**Greg Norman**

"The harder I work, the luckier I get."
—**Gary Player**

"The mind messes up more shots than the body."
—**Tommy Bolt**

"There's an old saying: 'It's a poor craftsman who blames his tools.' It's usually the *player* who misses those three-footers, not the putter."
—**Kathy Whitworth**

"The person I fear most in the last two rounds is myself."
—**Tom Watson**

"Indecision builds nervous tension and undermines any remaining confidence."
—**Sharron Moran**

"Golf is 90% inspiration and 10% perspiration."
—**Johnny Miller**

"I've heard people say putting is 50% technique and 50% mental. I really believe it is 50% technique and 90% positive thinking. See, but that adds up to 140%, which is why nobody is 100% sure how to putt."
—**Chi Chi Rodriguez**

Hubert Green had to play the 1977 U.S. Open with an armed escort due to a death threat.

ANCIENT ORIGINS OF GOLF, PART II

(Quietly): Uncle John has just sliced terribly and his ball is now deep in the trees. Let's see if we can get a camera in there—Oh! There he is! His ball went straight into an old abandoned outhouse! But back to our story...

CLOSER TO HOME

Golf may be descended from stick and ball games of the Greeks, the Egyptians, Persians, or even the ancient Sumerians—no one knows for sure. But what is known is that the ancient Romans had a stick-and-ball game, *paganica*, and they brought it with them when they invaded and conquered nearly all of Europe, including the British Isles, which they ruled from the first through the fourth centuries A.D. Although they never conquered Scotland (they tried three times), many golf historians believe that the Romans got close enough for their game, in some form, to have made its way to Scotland over the centuries and become transformed into golf.

The following are some of the theories about how one of those games could be the exact and most recent ancestor of Scotland's golf. There are many theories and few real records—but who cares? They're all good stories and any one of them might actually be true.

HURLING: THE IRISH THEORY

Hurling is an ancient Celtic game. It was—and still is—played with a curved wooden stick, the *hurley*, or *caman* in Irish Gaelic, and a small hard ball, the *sliotar*. The object is to hit the ball down a determined field and between a set of goalposts. The age of the game is unknown. Some historians say it is an offshoot of paganica, but the Irish claim it as their own. Irish mythology mentions it numerous times, dating it all the way back to 1272 B.C. and the legendary Battle of Moytura between the native Fir Bolg peoples and the invading Tuatha De Danann. In lieu of the battle, the two sides held a hurling match. The Fir Bolg won a bloody and bone-breaking game—and then killed their opponents.

Ah, the good old days: in 1890 a complete set of golf clubs cost about $25.

Is this very ancient hitting-a-ball-with-a-stick game—played right there in the British Isles—golf's true ancestor? Very possibly. A similar game is played by the Scottish Celtic peoples. *Shinty* is very similar to hurling, and it's just as old, although it may have been brought to Scotland by the Irish.

Interesting fact: The Celtic peoples are believed to have come from Eastern Europe and northern Greece. Some believe that at one time they intermingled with the ancient Egyptians—and that the game of hurling actually comes from the same or a similar game as the one depicted on the ancient tomb of Prince Kheti.

CAMBUCA: THE ENGLISH THEORY

Cambuca is believed to have been played in England more than a thousand years ago. It is considered a direct descendant of paganica and may have even been the same game with a new name: *cambuca* is Medieval Latin—the language spoken in England at the time of the Roman occupation—for "curved stick or staff."

Cambuca became popular in Britain starting around the 12th century A.D., and it does have its similarities to modern golf: the object was to hit a wooden ball with a curved stick toward a mark in the ground. (Not much more is known about it.) In 1363 King Edward III made cambuca (along with several other games) illegal because men were playing the games instead of practicing their archery, endangering the security of the country.

The Great East Window in Gloucester Cathedral, a huge stained-glass window made in 1349, shows a man preparing to strike a ball with a club or mallet in a surprisingly golflike way. The game being played is believed to be cambuca—and the window was made 100 years before the earliest record of golf in Scotland.

COLF AND *HET KOLVEN*: THE DUTCH THEORY

Many historians say golf, and even the word "golf," comes from the Netherlands. Golf historian Steven J. H. Van Hengel says that as early as the 1300s, the Dutch played *spel metten colve*—"game with clubs." He writes that on December 26, 1297, citizens of the town of Loenen aan de Vecht celebrated a military victory by playing *colf* on their "four-hole" course (they weren't holes, but above ground targets). The fact that colf was chosen, says Hengel, shows that it must have already been around for quite a while.

Others say the game evolved from another Dutch game called *het kolven*, pointing out the similarity in the words *kolven* and "golf." This game involved driving a ball a long distance with a stick toward a goal such as a tree or a post. It was played either on ice or on land as early as the 1300s.

In any case, these historians like to point to the well-established fact that the Scottish game developed on Scotland's east coast—across the North Sea from the coast of the Netherlands. And the well-known trade routes at the time between the Netherlands and Scotland make the transfer of the Dutch games to Scotland and the evolution to "golf" easily believable.

Interesting fact: Het kolven was played in the American colonies as early as 1657.

For Part III of "Ancient Origins of Golf," blast over to page 179.

*   *   *

"STATUS QUO"
This ode came to us via the Internet—from a Longfellow of the links named Victor Biggs.

I read the column Nicklaus writes
And bought a book by Floyd,
About the things that I should do
And those I should avoid.
On TV I watch Dave Pelz
The short game noted whiz,
And listen rapt to all he tells
To make my stroke like his.
I also buy the latest gear
From folks like Orlimar,
For the promise there is clear
For drives both straight and far.
And all the while I'm thinking hard
About the mental game,
But here I am to tell you pard
My score remains the same.

Michael Jordan is a registered member of the Golf Nuts Society of America.

HOLLYWOOD HACKS

Okay, so they're not all hacks. But lots of celebrities golf. And they've got some 'splaining to do.

Samuel L. Jackson regularly golfs with ex-football star Jim Brown and former boxer Sugar Ray Leonard. Jackson reportedly enjoys hustling other celebrity golfers out of their money, including Darius Rucker (Hootie and the Blowfish) and Kenny G.

Alice Cooper has been playing golf since the early 1980s and plays 36 holes every day. His handicap is a three. Cooper says golf saved his life: it kept him busy and healthy after he kicked an alcohol addiction.

Sammy Davis, Jr. was an avid golfer and belonged to Los Angeles' Hillcrest Country Club. One morning as he started a game, someone in his playing group asked Davis his handicap. Davis replied, "My handicap? I'm black, I'm a Jew, and I have one eye."

Robert Redford had a handicap of six at one time, but it had ballooned to a 12 by 2001. His excuse: his game got rusty while he was busy directing *The Legend of Bagger Vance*—a golf movie.

Kevin Sorbo, TV's Hercules, had a handicap of two in high school. (His father managed a golf course.)

Chevy Chase and **Bill Murray**, the stars of *Caddyshack*, have high handicaps of 25 and 13, respectively. (**Kevin Costner**, star of *Tin Cup*, has a 12.6.)

Dennis Quaid's father bought him a junior set of clubs when he was nine. He hated golf and he was terrible at it. But his older brother, actor Randy Quaid, was a very talented golfer and considered going professional. Dennis didn't take up golf again until his 30s to keep busy after emerging from drug rehab. He quickly caught up with his brother: both actors now have a six handicap.

Christina Aguilera met Tiger Woods in the late 1990s. Woods told Aguilera he was a big fan of her music. Aguilera's reply: "Sorry, I don't follow tennis, so I don't know much about you."

Fork! Las Vegas hosts a tournament for maître d's only.

O. J. Simpson used to bet hundreds of dollars on golf games. He often lost, but rarely paid up, invoking his special "off the premises" rule. The rule: the bet was invalid if the loser left the course before the winner could collect. So, after the game, Simpson would tell a long-winded football story to his opponent, who would eventually need to use the restroom. And by the time he returned, Simpson was peeling out of the parking lot.

Fred Astaire's 1938 movie *Carefree* included a sequence in which Astaire danced onto a golf course and hit 12 golf balls consecutively—in time to music—while dancing. When the crew went to retrieve the balls after the take, they found that all 12 balls had hit the green—all within eight feet of each other.

Donald Trump showed off his Trump International course by hosting the LPGA's 2001 ADT Championship. Throughout the event, Trump repeatedly pestered golfers, asking them if it was the toughest course they'd ever played. He had a real reason for asking: prior to the tournament, Trump had ordered the mounds in front of water hazards be mowed at a slant so that balls would roll into the water. Even more annoying: inmates from the adjacent Palm Beach County Criminal Justice Complex screamed profanities at the female golfers. (Trump denies this happened, but he later spent $1 million on a barrier of 200 palm trees between the prison and the course.)

Groucho Marx. One day he was playing against Ed Sullivan at Cypress Point in California. On the 16th hole, which runs along the top of a cliff above the Pacific, Groucho shanked five tee shots into the water, then put his driver into his bag, carried it over to the edge of the cliff...and threw every piece of golfing equipment he owned into the sea. "It's not that I'm a poor loser," he explained, "but I figured if I couldn't beat a guy with no neck [Sullivan], then I've got to be the world's worst golfer and I have no right to be on a course at all." That was the last time Marx ever played golf.

*   *   *

"Golf is the cruelest game, because eventually it will drag you out in front of the whole school, slap you around, and take your lunch money."

—Rick Reilly

At his first appearance at the Masters in 1979, Larry Nelson forgot his clubs.

A BETTER GOLF BOOK?

*Do you find most golf instruction books boring? Here's
a fake Table of Contents that we found on the Internet for
the kind of golf book that Uncle John would buy.*

PART I: BEFORE YOU PLAY—BE PREPARED

Chapter 1.............Which No-Smudge Pencil Eraser Is Best for You
Chapter 2.....................................How to Regrip Your Ball Retriever
Chapter 3..Light Beer for Breakfast to Stay
Hydrated Through the Day

PART II: ON THE TEE

Chapter 4..........................How to Get More Distance off the Shank
Chapter 5........................When to Suggest Major Swing Corrections
to Your Opponent
Chapter 6............................Using Your Wood to Dig Deeper Divots

PART III: IN THE ROUGH

Chapter 7...........................How to Hit a Nike from the Rough When
You Hit a Titleist from the Tee
Chapter 8...........................How to Find the Ball That Everyone Else
Saw Go in the Water
Chapter 9...Bushwhacking with a 1-Iron
Chapter 10....How to Let a Foursome Play Through Your Twosome

PART IV: ON THE GREEN

Chapter 11......................Using Your Shadow to Maximize Earnings
Chapter 12.......God and the Meaning of the Birdie-to-Bogey 3-Putt
Chapter 13.....................How to Properly Line Up Your Fourth Putt
Chapter 14....Using Aerodynamics to Make Your Putter Fly Farther

PART V: AT HOME

Chapter 15............................How to Explain an Eight-Hour Round
Chapter 16...Why Your Wife Doesn't Care that You Birdied the 8th

---

KEEP YOUR SHIRT ON

Like oil and water, golf and nudity just don't mix.

SMILE, YOU'RE ON CANDID CAMERA

In July 2000, David Calhoun, manager of the Beaver Creek Golf Links in Oakland, Michigan, took out a full-page ad in the local newspaper...but not to advertise the links. He was apologizing for the TV footage of naked women prancing around his golf course. Acting on a tip about a "special event" at Beaver Creek, a local TV station secretly filmed it. Their footage of topless—and some bottomless—women mingling with golfers made it to their news program, where it was "aired and re-aired" for two weeks. Calhoun said that perhaps he shouldn't have let Mannequins, a Detroit topless bar, rent the course, but insisted that the 20 female employees had broken their promise to keep their bikinis on. "Maybe my judgment wasn't the best in the world," Calhoun told readers.

HOOKED IT!

In June 2002, police raided the Hidden Valley Golf Club in Norco, California, detaining 90 golfers, several staff members...and 17 prostitutes. According to police, the club was hosting a golf tournament where "sex acts were offered to participants for a fee." Manager Jason Wood, assistant Darren Bollinger, and event organizer Sandy Juarez had set up tents around the course where the women could provide their services—even putting up signs to advertise. The three were sentenced to 125 days of house arrest and three years' probation. Police noted that some of the "golfers" didn't even bother to bring golf clubs.

AND THE BOOBY PRIZE GOES TO...

Golfer Jim Furyk won the 2003 U.S. Open with a tie for the lowest score in the event's history. He was especially commended for keeping his composure on the 14th green, when a young woman with long blond braids and no shirt ducked under the ropes, walked up to Furyk, and offered him a rose. "It was a total shock," he said later. "I turned around and just went, 'Whoa!'" The topless woman was led off the course by security and charged with disorderly conduct. Furyk kept his cool and sank his putt.

Dale Douglass was once forced to tee off with a putter...because his caddie got lost.

RECORD BOOK

The longest, strongest, fastest, and smartest (through the 2004 season).

MOST PGA WINS

Sam Snead, 82
Jack Nicklaus, 73
Ben Hogan, 64
Arnold Palmer, 62
Byron Nelson, 52
Billy Casper, 51
Walter Hagen, 44
Tiger Woods, 42
Cary Middlecoff, 40

MOST MAJOR WINS

Jack Nicklaus, 18
Walter Hagen, 11
Ben Hogan, 9
Gary Player, 9
Tom Watson, 8
Tiger Woods, 8

MOST TOUR WINS IN A YEAR

Byron Nelson, 18
(1945)
Ben Hogan, 13
(1946)
Sam Snead, 11
(1950)
Ben Hogan, 10
(1948)
Paul Runyan, 9
(1933)
Vijay Singh, 9
(2004)
Tiger Woods, 9
(2000)

BEST SEASON SCORING AVERAGE

Tiger Woods
68.17 (2000)
Byron Nelson
68.34 (1945)
Tiger Woods
68.87 (2001)
Tiger Woods
69.00 (2002)
Davis Love III
69.03 (2001)
Vijay Singh
69.11 (2003)

MOST STROKES UNDER PAR IN A TOURNAMENT

Ernie Els, 31
(2003 Mercedes Championship)
Joe Durant, 29
(2001 Bob Hope Chrysler Classic)
Tim Herron, 29
(2003 Bob Hope Chrysler Classic)
John Huston, 28
(1998 United Airlines Hawaiian Open)
M. Calcavecchia, 28
(2001 Phoenix Open)
Stuart Appleby, 28
(2003 Las Vegas Invitational)

YOUNGEST WINNERS OF A MAJOR

Tom Morris, Jr., 17
(1868 British Open)
John McDermott, 19
(1911 U.S. Open)
Francis Ouimet, 20
(1913 U.S. Open)
Gene Sarazen, 20
(1922 U.S. Open)
Gene Sarazen, 20
(1922 PGA Championship)

LOWEST SCORE, 72 HOLES

Tom Armour III, 254
(2003 Texas Open)
Mark Calcavecchia, 256
(2001 Phoenix Open)
Mike Souchak, 257
(1955 Texas Open)
(3 tied at 258)

MOST CAREER CUTS MADE

Tom Kite, 587
Raymond Floyd, 583
Jay Haas, 575
Gene Littler, 566
Doug Ford, 561
Arnold Palmer, 543

The Superstick adjustable club claims to be "17 clubs in one."

HOW TO BECOME A GOLF PRO

You've got game…so how do you get a "Tour Card"?

GETTING CARDED
The most coveted item for a wannabe professional golfer: an official PGA Tour Card. Tiger has one, Ernie has one, Vijay has one, and it allows them to be one of the 150 to 180 golfers who get to compete in the big tournaments on TV. So if you're a very good golfer and think you can play with the big boys, how do you get your first card? There are several ways:

- **Special exemptions**—an invitation; a free pass
- **Open qualifying**
- **The "Nationwide Tour"**—the PGA's minor leagues
- **PGA Tour Qualifying School**—the dreaded "Q School"

Here are some of the details:

SPECIAL EXEMPTIONS

There are 34 different "exemption" categories for playing on the PGA Tour. Most of them apply to established pros. For example, if you finish in the top 125 on the money list, you're automatically "exempt" for all the PGA Tour events the following year—you get to keep your card. But some, such as the sponsor exemptions, make it possible for nonmembers to play with the pros. Here are two "special" categories:

Sponsor Exemptions. Sponsors of PGA Tour events (Buick at the Buick Open, Bell South at the Bell South Classic, etc.) are allowed to hand out four spots to whomever they choose. Just write them a letter and ask for one. The only requirement: you must have a registered USGA handicap index of zero (not just *any* hack can play with the pros). You're allowed to play in up to seven tournaments per season this way, and if in those seven tournaments you win enough prize money to end up in the top 125 on the year's money list, you're officially a member of the Tour for the following year. That's a tough challenge, considering that you

---

Arnold Palmer owned over 1,500 putters.

have to do it in seven tournaments while the average pro is playing in 25. But there's another way to do it: if you happen to win just one of those seven events, you're exempt for the rest of that year and get a PGA Tour card for the next two years. Some people who did it this way:

• Tiger Woods and Phil Mickelson both got their first cards by playing on sponsor exemptions and winning a tournament.

• Up-and-coming stars Matt Kuchar, Charles Howell III, and Hank Kuehne all got their first Tour Cards by playing sponsor exemptions and making the top 125 on the money list.

• The most amazing example: 24-year-old Jim Benepe from Sheridan, Wyoming, got a last-minute sponsor exemption at the 1988 Western Open. He had never played in a PGA tournament before…but he won. The virtual unknown was exempt for the full PGA Tour for the next two years. (It's still the only time anybody has won a PGA event on the first attempt.)

Foreign Exemptions. There are also foreign exemptions for tournaments. The PGA commissioner selects two international golfers per tournament to receive them. But even if you're good enough to get the exemption, that just gets you into the tournaments—you have to do the rest. In 2002 Argentinean Angel Cabrera, already a member of the European PGA, used both foreign and sponsor exemptions to play in as many U.S. tournaments as possible and to make as much money as possible to avoid having to go through Q School. In April he finished ninth at the Masters, bringing his season earnings up to $468,394. That was more than the player at number 125 on the money list in the previous year—another of the 34 exemption categories—and that got him his Tour Card for 2003. He was in.

QUALIFYING
Major Open Qualifying. Two of golf's four major tournaments are restricted—the PGA Championship is for pros only and the Masters is by invitation. The other two majors are not restricted. The "Open" in "U.S. Open" and "British Open" means exactly that: anybody, pro or amateur, with a USGA handicap not higher than 1.4 can attempt to qualify. Not *all* the spots are open, however, since many pros automatically qualify, but there are quite a few.

At the 2004 U.S. Open, 76 pros were automatically in, which left 80 spots open to anybody else. More than 7,000 golfers from around the world—including a 13-year-old and an 81-year-old—tried to qualify for those spots. You want in? Show proof of your handicap, pony up the $125 entry fee...and then play some really good golf.

But if you do get in and you play well, you could be set for a long time. The top-ten finishers in the U.S. Open automatically get a full Tour Card for the following year. And if you *win* either the U.S or British Open, you not only get the prize money, you're also fully exempt on the PGA Tour for the next five years.

Some major Open qualifiers who did pretty well:

• Ken Venturi won the U.S. Open as a qualifier in 1964.

• Orville Moody did the same in 1969. At the time, winning a major meant a lifetime Tour Card. (Not anymore—today it's good for a five-year exemption.)

• The last qualifier to win the U.S. Open: Steve Jones in 1996.

Monday Qualifying. Many PGA Tour events have an 18-hole qualifying round played the Monday before the event. A maximum of about 150 nonmember golfers are accepted; the top four get in. This used to be a fairly common way to fill out a field—tournaments accepted a lot more than four in the old days—and there was even a name for golfers who did it regularly: "rabbits" (because they jumped from event to event all over the country, usually living in their cars along the way). But the game, the money, and the number of stars grew, and today there are only four open spots per tournament (and not even for *every* tournament).

To use Monday qualifying to get a Tour Card, you must prove your handicap, pay a $400 entry fee, qualify for enough tournaments—and then do well. As with sponsor or foreign exemptions, you have to win enough money to make the top 125. Or you can enter just one tournament and win it, which gets you a two-year exemption. How often does a rabbit get on the Tour? Almost never:

• In 1986, Kenny Knox made it to the Honda Classic as one of the four Monday qualifiers...and won. Diehard rabbit Knox, who had $2,200 left in his bank account at the time, earned $90,000 for the win and got a Tour Card for the next two years.

No clue-ba: Kent Kluba is the only golfer ever to get lost during a tournament.

• That same year, Fred Wadsworth qualified for the Southern Open and won—the last time a rabbit won a PGA Tour event.

THE "NATIONWIDE TOUR"

In 1990 the PGA started a new tour, a "minor league" for players who weren't quite good enough to make the PGA Tour. They called it the Ben Hogan Tour. By 1993 it had gotten big enough for sponsors to notice and Nike bought in, renaming it the Nike Tour. In 1999 it became the BUY.COM Tour, then in 2003 it became the Nationwide Tour. Regardless of the changing names, the tour has proven to be a huge financial success and has helped a lot of players get ready for the big leagues.

Could the Nationwide Tour be a possible route for you? If you are one of the top 20 money winners on the Nationwide Tour, or if you win three events in a single year, you automatically get on the PGA Tour for the next year. Some golfers who have used the Nationwide Tour to get into the PGA: Ernie Els, John Daly, David Toms, Jim Furyk, and David Duval.

Q SCHOOL

Since its inception in 1964, the PGA Tour Qualifying Tournament is the most common way to get on the PGA Tour. Every year 30 new players get their Tour Cards this way. And "new" doesn't always mean rookies, since lots of former pros who lost their cards go to Q School to try to get them back. So, how do you get into Q School?

1) Pay a $4,500 fee for the first stage in October and finish in the top fourth of a 72-hole tournament. If you make the cut, you'll be one of more than 1,300 people trying to get one of those 30 spots.

2) Finish in the top fourth of a second 72-hole tournament. Now the field narrows to 325.

3) The final stage takes place in December. It's one 18-hole competition every day for six days in a row—a total of 108 holes of golf. Finish in the top 30 and you're on the PGA Tour for the coming year. Those who have gone through the process call it the most pressure-packed golf they have ever played, harder than any PGA Tour event because there's so little room for error.

Some golfers who made it to the PGA Tour through Q School:

The winning score in pro tourneys is improving at the rate of about one stroke every 25 years.

Curtis Strange (failed in 1976, then made it in 1977), Rich Beem, Luke Donald, Kirk Triplett, Jason Allred, Ty Tyron (at age 17), and Todd Hamilton, who won his first Tour Card through Q School in 2004 at the age of 39...and won the British Open that year.

Consolation Prize: If you don't make one of the top 30 spots at Q School, take heart. The next 50 automatically qualify for the upcoming Nationwide Tour, where you can try once again to do well enough to make it to the PGA.

Q SCHOOL HEARTBREAKERS

• In 2001 Roland Thatcher was on the final hole of the final stage of Q School and needed only a routine par to get his first PGA Tour card. But inexplicably, he sailed his ball over the green, where it bounced off a cart path and landed on top of the clubhouse. He ended up with a triple-bogey...and no Tour Card.

• In 2000 Jaxon Brigman shot a 65 on the last day to win his card by a single shot. But his partner accidentally wrote down "66". Brigman didn't notice the goof and signed the scorecard. Result: the 66 stood. So even though he had golfed well enough, Brigman missed getting on the Tour. "It was almost like a death in the family," he said later. "For five minutes, I had my PGA Tour card."

That's how to get on the Tour. The next thing you need to know is how to stay on the Tour, so hack on over to page 200.

*   *   *

RANDOM FACTS

• When he played on the Stanford golf team, Tiger Woods picked up a new nickname: "Urkel," after the nerd on TV's *Family Matters*.

• In 1996 a company in California introduced "Peace Missile" golf clubs, made from melted-down Soviet nuclear missiles.

• Golfers buy more than 500 million new golf balls every year.

• Results of a 2002 poll: 75% of professional golfers—whether religious or not—admitted to praying on the golf course.

THE GOLFER'S WIT

Golf, by its nature, is a very frustrating sport. The best way to deal with the agony is to have a sense of humor about it.

"I'll shoot my age if I have to live to be 105."
—**Bob Hope**

"But you don't have to go up in the stands and play your foul balls. I do."
—**Sam Snead arguing with Ted Williams about which is harder, golf or baseball**

"One of the advantages bowling has over golf is that you seldom lose a bowling ball."
—**Don Carter**

"My swing is so bad I look like a caveman killing his lunch."
—**Lee Trevino**

"Baseball players quit playing and they take up golf. Basketball players quit, take up golf. Football players quit, take up golf. What are we supposed to take up when we quit?"
—**George Archer**

"If profanity had an influence on the flight of the ball, the game of golf would be played far better than it is."
—**Horace G. Hutchinson**

"Golf is a game in which the ball lies poorly and the players well."
—**Art Rosenbaum**

"Art said he wanted to get more distance. I told him to hit it and run backward."
—**Ken Venturi, on Art Rosenbaum**

"If you drink, don't drive. Don't even putt."
—**Dean Martin**

"Give me the fresh air, a beautiful partner, and a nice round of golf, and you can keep the fresh air and the round of golf."
—**Jack Benny**

"You can make a lot of money in this game. Just ask my ex-wives. Both of them are so rich that neither of their husbands work."
—**Lee Trevino**

"Actually, the only time I ever took out a one-iron was to kill a tarantula. And it took a seven to do that."
—**Jim Murray**

The Pros and Cons Invitational is played by touring pros and prison inmates.

BAGS, SHOES, AND CARTS

The origins of three golfing accessories.

THE GOLF BAG

For the first few centuries of golf's history, there was no such thing as a golf bag: caddies simply carried the clubs of their "gentleman golfers" under their arms. That worked fine for the gentlemen golfers who could afford the luxury of a caddie, but by the late 19th century, a lot more common folks were playing the game. It was extremely tedious for a golfer to carry his clubs to the tee, put them down on the ground, pick one up, hit the ball, then pick the rest of his clubs back up and do it all again.

Sometime in the 1870s, a sail maker (and golfer) from North Devon, England, solved this problem by sewing together some pieces of canvas and creating the first golf bag. Other golfers quickly followed suit and made their own bags, but the first golf bag patent wasn't issued until 1890. A few years later, the first bags with retractable tripod legs appeared, allowing the bag to stand on its own. In the mid-1900s, the first patent was issued for a pull cart made for golf bags. In the 1970s, the first ultralight bags were made from high-tech fabrics, and in the 1980s, manufacturers added legs that extended automatically when the bag was set down. Today's bags come in hundreds (maybe thousands) of shapes and sizes, with multiple compartments for clubs, and pockets for tees, balls, gloves, bottles, cans, holy books, or whatever else you might need on the course. Golf bags are now a $300 million industry.

SPIKED SHOES

The first mention of cleated golf shoes comes from Scotland's *Golfer's Manual* (1857): "Let the novice invest in a pair of stout shoes (boots constrain the ankles too much), roughed with small nails or sprigs, and he will march comfortably and safely over the most slippery ground that can be turned out by the meridian sun in the dog days." And nails remained the spikes of choice for decades until screw-in spikes were invented.

Metal-spiked shoes were the norm for much of the 20th century, but they tore up the greens, leaving many country clubs no choice but to ban them. That problem was alleviated in the 1990s with the invention of "soft-spikes" made of plastic or rubber.

But spikes or no spikes, many golfers have asked the question: Do I really need spiked golf shoes to play better? According to Brent Kelley, author of *Your Guide to Golf*, not necessarily. "If you can't afford or just don't want to buy golf shoes yet, wear the pair of shoes with the most 'gripping' soles you can find—rubber with lots of ridges, bumps, etc."

THE GOLF CART

The father of the golf cart was R. J. "Dick" Jackson, a car salesman from Houston, Texas. One day in the late 1940s, he saw a teenager named Preston Moore toting his golf clubs around on a scooter at River Oaks Country Club. Jackson suffered from arthritis and had a difficult time lugging his clubs around all day long, so he recognized it as a great idea. He immediately went out and bought a small three-wheeled, gas-powered utility vehicle (used to carry airplane parts), and added a bench to the front and a compartment for his golf bags to the back. Jackson called this first golf cart the "Arthritis Special" and patented it in 1948. He only made a dozen or so of the carts, but one caught the eye of John T. Watson, owner of Watson Distributing in Houston, who bought the patent and started mass-producing them.

These early carts had one major drawback: noise. Many of the higher-end golf resorts banned the loud, smoke-sputtering contraptions that required a kick start to get going. Golf was a game of elegance, and gas-powered golf carts were anything but. That changed in 1962 when an inventor named Merlin L. Halvorson designed the first battery-powered golf cart. Its smooth, quiet ride was welcomed at courses all over the world.

Golf carts, now a $200 million industry, have since transcended the game and become a part of society. Retirement communities use them—so do airports, shopping malls, security companies, and universities. Even NASA's highly publicized Mars Rover has been called an "$820 million golf cart."

ASK THE EXPERTS

We admit it: we're writers, not golf experts. So we scoured hundreds of books (okay, not hundreds—four) by real experts to find the answers to a few of golf's most pressing questions.

LIKE A ROCK

Q: *Is it true that warm balls will go farther than cold balls?*

A: Yes, it's true. The colder the ball gets, the less resilient the plastics inside, and the harder the ball becomes. Your driving distance could go down by as much as 30 percent. It's akin to the difference between hitting a superball and a rock. When you hit a solid object, you lose a lot of energy on impact. Springy rubber, on the other hand, temporarily absorbs the impact, keeping the ball in contact with the club longer. The ball flattens a bit and then springs back to a round shape, launching itself like a shot from the clubhead.

TEASE FOR THE TEES

Q: *How come whenever a new "miracle" club or ball comes to market, the USGA bans it?*

A: The United States Golf Association does their best to thwart any big changes in the game that might come through technological advances. After all, if everybody could drive long, straight, and true, it wouldn't be much of a game, would it? So a good rule of thumb is that if something has dramatically improved your game, it is probably not legal in a tournament. Example: the ball that has a built-in radio transmitter to make it easier to find in the rough? Not legal.

UNWANTED VISITORS

Q: *I want to move into one of two houses available in a golfing community. Both are pretty much the same, but they're on opposite sides of a long, straight fairway. Does it matter which one I buy?*

A: Of course it does. Remember the three rules of real estate— location, location, location—and buy the one on the left side of the fairway. Since 1) most golfers are right-handed, and 2) more

---

It took four years of apprenticeship to become a featherie ball maker.

golfers tend to slice the ball rather than hook it, the house to the left of the fairway will attract far fewer errant balls than the one on the right.

GOLF = INTELLIGENCE?

Q: *What's the average golf score for all golfers—good, bad, and abysmal?*

A: Coincidentally, it's about the same as the average IQ for all humans: 100. For men, the average golf score is 97; for women, 114.

DUCK AND COVER

Q: *If someone yells "Fore!" and I have no idea where the ball may be coming from, what do I do?*

A: According to Kevin Dukes, an orthopedic surgeon with the Tulsa (Oklahoma) Bone & Joint Association, "Forty-two percent of all golf injuries are to the head and face, and 28 percent are caused by getting struck with a ball. So protect your head first. Take shelter or cover up with your forearms. Crouching down also makes you a smaller target."

YARDWORK

Q: *How much would it cost to build a professional golf course in my spacious backyard?*

A: Built to golf-course specs? The rule of thumb among designers is about $200,000 to $400,000 per hole. That's for digging, water hazards, landscaping, etc. If you want it designed by a top-end pro, add another $7 million for 18 holes, which adds another $390,000 per hole. Croquet, anyone?

*   *   *

STRANGE GOLF FACTS

Some odd prizes won by pro golfers:

• Abe Lemons won a bottle of Geritol at the Golf and Country Club tournament in Frederick, OK.

• Ian Baker-Finch won a cow in the 1988 Bridgestone/Aso (Japan) Open. He sold the cow back for $5000.

GOLF 101:
THE HANDICAP

*Someone once asked Chris Codiroli what his
handicap was. "My handicap? Woods and irons."*

W**HAT'S YOUR HANDICAP?**
It's one of those golfing terms that most golfers think
every other golfer understands...except them. But
what, exactly, does it mean? Basically, a USGA Handicap Index—
or just "handicap"—is a number that indicates how well (or poorly) you play. The lower the number, the better you are.

But golf handicapping wasn't introduced simply as a shorthand
rating system. The system was developed in Great Britain in the
1800s. Its original purpose: for gambling. If you regularly shoot 89
strokes on an 18-hole course, how can you compete (or successfully wager) against someone who regularly shoots a 74? You
can't—you'll lose just about every time. So the British invented
an organized method of determining how many strokes the better
player has to spot the other player in order to make a fair—and
fun—game.

In the early 1900s, the USGA standardized the system so that
clubs in the United States could issue handicaps, too. It was (and
still is) certainly used for gambling purposes, but was also a good
way to determine whether golfers were qualified to enter the growing number of organized tournaments.

Today, there are official and unofficial handicaps. Many golfers
just figure out their own, but if you want to play in a USGA tournament, you must have an official handicap. To do that, first you
have to be a member of a USGA-registered golf club. Then the
club takes your best 10 scores from a minimum of 12 rounds of
golf and comes up with the average score, from which your handicap is derived.

HERE'S HOW YOU FIGURE OUT A HANDICAP:
• Let's say that on 12 rounds of golf you take an average of 89
strokes to complete 18 holes.

- Now say par for those 18 holes is 72 strokes.
- Subtract 72 from 89.
- Your handicap is…17.

HOW TO SCORE IT

• **Stroke Play.** How a handicap is applied depends on whether you're playing *stroke play* or *match play* scoring systems. Stroke play is the system that you usually see the pros playing on TV—all the strokes for an entire round are counted.

To apply a handicap in this system, simply subtract your handicap from your total number of strokes, your "gross score," to determine your "net score." You're a 15 handicapper and you shot 90? Your net score is 75. If you were playing somebody with a 2 handicap and they shot a 78, you would have beaten them, because their net score would be 76.

If you're playing in a group, it's a little different. Everyone plays off the best player, which means they subtract his handicap from theirs. Example: In a group of three, if one golfer is a 5 handicapper, one's a 10, and the other's a 20, then the best player (the 5 handicapper) gets no strokes, the 10 gets 5, and the 20 gets 15. That's how it's done.

• **Match Play.** In match play you don't count the total strokes for a round, you just count them on each hole. If you complete a hole in four strokes and your opponent completes it in five, you win that hole and get one point.

To adapt the USGA Handicap Index to this system, every USGA course rates the difficulty of its holes from 1 to 18 (or from 1 to 9 on a nine-hole course), with 1 being the most difficult. If you've got a 6 handicap, you get to subtract a stroke on holes rated 1 through 6. A 10 handicapper gets to take one stroke on all holes rated 1 through 10. If you're a 25 handicapper, you take a stroke on all 18 holes, and an additional stroke on the holes rated 1 through 7 (because 25 – 18 = 7). Got it? Good, because there's another twist.

Say a 6 handicapper is playing a 10 handicapper. Many people play the logical way: the 6 takes a stroke on holes rated 1 to 6, and the 10 takes a stroke on holes 1 through 10. But that's the wrong way to do it. The correct way is to subtract the lower handicap from the higher: 10 – 6 = 4, and *that* becomes the 10 handicapper's number. He now gets to take a stroke on holes rated 1 through 4—and the better player gets no strokes. Why is it done this way? Because the other way, the 6 handicapper—the better player—would be getting 1 stroke on holes rated 1 through 6—the same as his not-as-good opponent, who would only be getting an advantage on holes rated 7 through 10. That's not fair. The lesser player needs those strokes on those harder holes. By giving the better golfer no strokes, the lesser golfer at least has a chance of winning those tough holes.

MORE HANDICAP FACTS

• The handicap system has some built-in protection: Equitable Stroke Control (ESC). If there's a hole at a course on which you *always* do terribly (like hitting into the water five times in a row), your handicap could balloon without really reflecting how good you are. The ESC helps you by putting a maximum amount of strokes you have to write down for any given hole, depending on your Course Handicap.

• A lot of recreational golfers don't have registered handicaps because they don't want to be a member of a registered golf club or there isn't one close enough to make it practical. So USGA rules allow any group of at least 10 golfers who play together on a regular basis to become an official "golf club" and register official handicaps. Just contact the USGA (www.usga.org) to find out how.

• In the early 1980s the USGA changed the system to also take into account the fact that every golf course is different. Today you combine your USGA Handicap Index with the USGA Course Rating for the specific course you're playing to determine your Course Handicap—which you use to adjust your score on that course. It sounds complicated, but it's actually easy. Each course will have its rating listed and a table for how to convert your Handicap Index into a Course USGA Handicap.

• And, of course, as you keep submitting scores to your home club, your handicap will go down as you improve…or up if your play gets worse. Good luck!

WARTIME RULES

During World War II, professional golf pretty much came to a standstill in Europe. But the Brits still found ways to play.

D-DAY
June 6, 2004 was the 60th anniversary of D-Day, the day the Allies began their invasion of Europe and their attack on Nazi Germany—the beginning of the end of World War II. In commemoration of that day, golf clubs around Great Britain issued copies of the special rules of golf from 1940's *The Golfer's Handbook*. The rules remain a testament to the importance of golf in Great Britain, as well as to the British sense of humor at its very driest.

Temporary Provisions

1. Players are asked to collect bomb and shell splinters to save causing damage to the mowing machines.

2. In competition, during gunfire or while bombs are falling, players may take cover without penalty for ceasing play.

3. The position of known delayed-action bombs are marked by red and white flags placed at a reasonably, but not guaranteed, safe distance.

4. A ball lying in a crater may be lifted and dropped not nearer the hole without penalty.

5. A ball moved by enemy action may be replaced as near as possible to where it lay, or if lost or destroyed a ball may be dropped not nearer the hole without penalty.

6. A player whose stroke is affected by the simultaneous explosion of a bomb or shell, or by machine gun fire, may play another ball from the same place.
Penalty: one stroke.

Duffer means "dull, stupid person" in Scottish.

THE HAWK

*He overcame adversity with steely-eyed determination
to become one of the best golfers ever.*

CHAMPION: Ben Hogan

BACKGROUND: Born William Benjamin Hogan on August 13, 1912, in Dublin, Texas.

HIS STORY: Hogan had a grim childhood. His father committed suicide when Ben was just nine years old, and some accounts say the young boy even witnessed the event. When he was 12, Hogan started caddying for 65 cents a round at the Fort Worth Country Club (with his childhood friend, Byron Nelson), and discovered he had a gift for the game—except for a very bad hook.

Still, he turned pro in 1929 at the age of 17, playing pro events in Texas for three years, then joined the PGA Tour in 1932. He didn't do well because of the hook, but the very determined Hogan spent years working on his game until he overcame his hook, finally getting his first win in 1940. He won the next two events he played and led the PGA Tour in prize money in 1940, 1941, and 1942. He then missed a few years, serving as a lieutenant in the Army Air Corps during World War II, but when he got back to the tour in late 1945 he not only continued his dominance, he expanded it. From late 1945 until 1949, Hogan won an amazing 37 times.

But the most remarkable part of Hogan's story is that he was a golfer at all after 1949. In February of that year, Hogan's car was hit head-on by a Greyhound bus in Texas. His wife, Valerie, received only minor injuries, possibly because he dove over her to protect her, but Hogan suffered a broken pelvis, collarbone, and ankle. Blood clots brought him close to death several times over the next few months, and his doctors said he'd probably never golf again. They were wrong. Eleven months after the accident Hogan was back on the golf course, and in 1950, in just his seventh tournament back, he won the U.S. Open (with his legs still wrapped in bandages).

Hogan was famous for his steely demeanor, and some of the other pros found him downright rude. He rarely spoke while he

---

Golf balls have a shelf life...they begin to lose their resilience after about a year.

played, concentrating on the game with an intense glare that earned him the nickname "the Hawk." The Scots called him the "Wee Ice Mon" (he was 5'9"). Fellow golfer Jimmy Demaret once joked about him, "When I play with him, he talks to me on every green. He turns to me and says, 'You're away.'" Demaret added, "Nobody gets close to Ben Hogan."

CAREER HIGHLIGHTS

- In 1946 Hogan won 13 times. In 1948 he won 10 times.

- Between 1946 and 1953 he played in 16 majors—and won nine of them.

- In 1953 he played in only six tournaments—and won five of them. Three were the Masters, the U.S. Open, and the British Open. (He didn't win the PGA championship that year because he didn't play it—it started too soon after the British Open.)

- He won one British Open (1953), two Masters (1951, 1953), two PGA Championships (1946, 1948), and four U.S. Opens (1948, 1950, 1951, 1953).

- He won the Vardon Trophy in 1940, 1941, and 1948.

- Hogan was PGA Player of the Year in 1948, 1950, 1951, and 1953.

- He was a member of two U.S. Ryder Cup teams and captain of the team in 1947, 1949, and 1967.

- Hogan finished in the top ten of 90 percent of the tournaments in which he played (241 out of 269).

- He had 64 PGA victories, third all-time behind Sam Snead (82) and Jack Nicklaus (73). He is also third in most majors won.

- Hogan was inducted into the World Golf Hall of Fame in 1974.

*   *   *

"I guess there is nothing that will get your mind off everything like golf. I have never been depressed enough to take up the game, but they say you get so sore at yourself you forget to hate your enemies."

—Will Rogers

The British term "dragon's teeth" refers to uncut grass in a bunker.

ANIMAL MAGNETISM

*Golf is a great way to get back to nature. It's also
a great way for nature to get back at golfers.*

• **Many geese** have discovered that migrating is for wimps. Entire
flocks will now "migrate" just a few miles, settling in on golf courses
for the winter. Surrounded by water and greenery, they don't worry
about hazards beyond the occasional bad slice. Golf course managers have tried numerous solutions, from sheepdogs to scarecrows
to noisemakers, without much effect.

• **Australian golfers** report that crows and currawongs (an indigenous black bird) swoop down and steal their balls. When one
bird's nest was blasted with a water cannon, nearly 50 golf balls
came raining down.

• **The second oldest course** outside the British Isles is the Royal
Calcutta Golf Club in Kolkata, India, built by British colonists in
1829. The story has it that monkeys enjoyed annoying the golfers
by stealing their balls and running off with them. The golf course
tried solution after solution, from fences to sharpshooters to giving
the monkeys their own supply of balls, until they finally gave in to
reality and posted a new rule: "Play the ball where the monkey
drops it."

• **In 1994 a farmer** in Germany sued a golf course, complaining
that errant golfers had been hooking balls into his field for years.
After the mysterious death of one cow, a veterinarian discovered a
golf ball lodged in its throat. Further investigation revealed that
30 of the farmer's cows had developed the habit of swallowing golf
balls, and that they collectively held a total of 2,000 balls lodged
in their stomachs.

• **An elderly man** reportedly trained an otter to retrieve golf balls
from a water hazard on a golf course near Florida's Homestead Air
Force Base. For every ball the otter brought up from the bottom,
the man gave him a small fish from a bucket.

• **Under the headline, "Fore! Wild Pigs on Worldwide Attack,"**
The Guardian reports that pigs are terrorizing golfers in Malaysia.
According to the London newspaper, they're worse than poisonous
snakes and are now invading courses in Sweden and France. "It's

King Edward VII owned a golf bag made from a male elephant's genitals.

like Hitchcock's *The Birds*," says the article, "only smellier."

• **While playing** a tournament in South America, Sam Snead was once attacked by an ostrich. The birdie bit him on the hand, putting him out of commission for two weeks.

• **A stampeding herd** of about 50 cows invaded the 18th hole of the 1984 St. Andrews Trophy, menacing several golfers in their path. A "cattle-clysm" was avoided when officials and golfers diverted the beasts by shouting and waving their clubs.

• **On a golf course** in Natal, South Africa, Molly Whitaker was all set to chip her ball out of a bunker when a monkey leaped from a tree and wrapped its arms around her neck. Her caddie chased it away, and the game continued.

• **An Icelandic course** carved out of the lava oceanfront has run into trouble from Arctic terns, who nest there. During the nesting season in late summer, protective tern parents land on golfers trying to play, and peck them without mercy.

• **In 1984** the Smith & Wesson Company opened a driving range for its employees in Springfield, Massachusetts. They were forced to close it a week later after flocks of seagulls began a continuous raid on its ball supply, bombarding buildings, cars, and people with hundreds of golf balls.

• **In 1981, on a par-3 hole** at Mountain View Golf Course in California, amateur Ted Barnhouse hit a wayward ball over a fence into a cow pasture. The ball bounced off a grazing cow's head and ricocheted off a lawn mower onto the green…where it bounced off the flag and into the hole.

*   *   *

ACTUAL WARNING FROM THE
FLORIDA DEPARTMENT OF FISH AND WILDLIFE

"Due to the extended drought, golfers should beware of alligators searching for water holes. For protection, wear little bells to alert the gators to your presence and carry pepper spray in case they get too close. Also, know the difference between the droppings of young and mature gators. The young gator droppings are small and round and usually contain fish bones. The mature gator droppings are larger and usually contain little bells and smell like pepper spray."

Poll results: 7 out of 10 golfers say they've had their clubs stolen, or know someone who has.

LEGENDARY LINKS

*Golf's leading experts and players regularly vote these
courses among the best in the entire world.*

C OURSE: The Old Course
LOCATION: St. Andrews, Scotland
STORY: The self-proclaimed "oldest golf course in the
world" is also probably the most famous. Records show that golf
was being played in the area as early as the 1400s. The Royal and
Ancient Golf Club of St. Andrews was founded around the Old
Course in 1754. According to club history, the course has evolved
over time and wasn't designed by one architect. Some of the peo-
ple who played a major role in shaping it: Daw Anderson (1850s),
Old Tom Morris (1860s–1900), and Dr. Alister Mackenzie (1930s).

Some famous features: the 14th hole's "Hell Bunker," a huge
sand bunker more than 10 feet deep (in all, there are 112 bunkers
waiting among the 18 holes) and the famous double greens—huge
greens shared by two holes…which means you can have a putt as
long as 100 yards.

Want to golf there? You can. Unlike many of the world's best-
known courses, St. Andrews is open to the public. Just remember,
golf's most famous course is difficult, which is why it's loved—and
hated—by golfers. The first time he played there, Bobby Jones
picked up his ball midway through the round and left. But over
time, he came to love the course. Shortly before his death, Jones
said, "If I had to select one course on which to play the match of
my life, I would choose the Old Course."

NOTE: There are four other 18-hole links courses built on the
dunes of St. Andrews Bay: the New Course (1895), the Jubilee
(1897), the Eden (1914), and the Strathtyrum Course (1993).
There's also a nine-hole course for children and beginners.

COURSE: Carnoustie Golf Links
LOCATION: Carnoustie, Angus, Scotland
STORY: This is another of the world's oldest golfing sites, with
records that show golf was played there in 1527. Like St. Andrews,
the club's history is filled with some of golf's most legendary

---

Despite precision manufacturing, no golf shaft is perfectly round throughout its length.

names. The first course was built in 1842 by Allan Robertson, extended to 18 holes in 1867 by Old Tom Morris, and reworked by legendary English course architect James Braid in 1926.

One of the signature holes is the 6th, a 585-yard par-5. If you use a driver off the tee, you have to hit an impossibly narrow strip of land between an out-of-bounds fence on the right and bunkers on the left. That's why no one had ever bothered trying it—until Ben Hogan came along. During the 1953 British Open, Hogan dared that gap on four consecutive days—and hit it every time, netting him four consecutive birdies on the hole. He went on to win, and the 6th fairway has been known as "Hogan's Alley" ever since. And like St. Andrews, Carnoustie is open to the public, so any golfer can try that shot, too.

COURSE: Pine Valley Golf Club
LOCATION: Clementon, New Jersey
STORY: Pine Valley is continually voted by golfers and golfing experts as the best golf course in the world because, they say, it has more world-class holes than any other course. That's pretty amazing, considering that it was once called "Crump's Folly." George Crump was a retired Philadelphia hotel owner who, with no knowledge of how to do it, decided he wanted to build a great golf course. He bought 184 acres of swampy forestland in 1912—and then proceeded to have 22,000 stumps removed. But he was smart enough to have some of the greatest course architects in the world contribute to the design. The result: a challenging course carved into a scrubby, piney landscape that one expert described as "the best 'most difficult' in the world." Unfortunately, Crump died in 1918, when only 14 holes were finished, and never got to see his masterpiece completed.

Chances are good that you'll never get to play Pine Valley—it's very exclusive. It's so exclusive, in fact, that two men once paid $10,000 each to friends who were members for a chance to play there. (They got caught; the members got suspended.)

COURSE: Cypress Point
LOCATION: Pebble Beach, California
STORY: This is one of the courses used for the famed Pebble Beach Pro-Am, founded by Bing Crosby. It was designed by Scot-

tish architect Alister Mackenzie in 1928. (Another of his famous courses: Augusta National.) Located in what many people consider one of the most beautiful locations on Earth, Cypress Point is built on the rocky cliffs of the Pacific Ocean on the Monterey Peninsula.

The signature hole is the 16th, a par-3 that requires a golfer to hit over 222 yards of ocean in what is usually an erratic, swirling wind. Only three holes in one have ever been made at the hole (one was by Crosby). Mackenzie wrote of his creation: "For years I have been contending that, in our generation, no other golf course could possibly compete with the strategic problems, the thrills, excitement, variety and lasting and increasing interest of the Old Course, but the completion of Cypress Point has made me change my mind."

MORE WORLD-CLASS COURSES

Shinnecock Hills (Long Island, NY): One of the first American clubs (built in 1891), it was the first to have its own clubhouse (built by architect Stanford White in 1892) and the first to allow women members. It was the site of the second U.S. Open in 1896 and has hosted the event four times since then. The name comes from the local Shinnecock Indians, who worked as laborers when the course was first built.

Teeth of the Dog (Dominican Republic): Frequently ranked in the top 40 courses worldwide, this course is at the Casa de Campo resort on the Caribbean island's tropical southeast coast. The signature hole is the 16th, a 185-yard par-3 on a rocky cove shaped like a set of jaws.

Royal Adelaide (Adelaide, Australia): Another Alister Mackenzie design, this was built on the sandy dunes of the south-central coast. It is the frequent home of the Australian Open and Amateur Championships, and is known as a very tough course. "The course is brutal," said Aussie pro Stuart Appleby. "If we had to play on this all year, I'm sure we'd give it away."

Cabo del Sol (Los Cabos, Mexico): By all accounts, a stunningly beautiful course overlooking the Sea of Cortez. Jack Nicklaus said the last three holes of this desert course, complete with large cacti, are the most beautiful he ever saw. (Then again, he designed the course.) Golfer's advantage: the area gets 300 sunny days a year.

Prairie Dunes (Hutchinson, Kansas): In 1937 Emerson Carey, founder of Carey Salt Company and an avid golfer, hired golf architect Perry Maxwell to build a links-style course like the ones he'd played in Scotland—in Kansas. Maxwell is reported to have said while walking the ragged site before construction, "There are 118 golf holes here…and all I have to do is eliminate 100." The course consistently ranks among the top 100 courses worldwide.

Ballybunion, Old Course (County Kerry, Ireland): When the first 12 holes were built on massive dunes in 1897, the *Irish Times* called it "a rabbit warren below the village, where a golfer requires limitless patience and an inexhaustible supply of golf balls." Tom Watson helped redesign and update it in 1995, and said of the course: "Ballybunion is a great links golf course with some of the best approaches of any course I have ever played. I love it, and I think it is the greatest golf course that God ever put on this earth, and make no mistake, God put it there."

* * *

IN THE NEWS: A CASE OF GOLF RAGE

Golfers: Todd Livingstone, 33, a correctional officer in Ontario, Canada; and Denny Mior, 41, a retail store owner.

Incident: In 1999, Livingstone was part of a large party of golfers who were on the links to celebrate his brother's upcoming wedding. Mior was part of a foursome golfing right behind them. After Livingstone finished his round, his brother told him that Mior's group had been hitting balls into their group since the 10th hole.

Teed Off: Livingstone confronted a member of Mior's group. When Mior intervened, Livingstone grabbed him around the throat with both hands and started choking him. Mior hit Livingstone several times on the torso with his sand wedge, which only made Livingstone angrier. He punched Mior several times and when it was over, Mior had cracked ribs, a dislocated knee, and a damaged ear. Livingstone, a much larger man, was relatively unscathed. He was later charged in the attack.

Aftermath: Livingstone was found guilty, ordered to pay $464 in restitution, and sentenced to three months of house arrest. (He still gets to work at the jail, but he doesn't have to live there.)

THE U.S. OPEN

*On page 28 we told you how golf in America
got organized with the founding of the USGA.
One of the main reasons they were needed: to
determine the golfing champions. And to
do that, they needed a tournament.*

WHO'S THE BEST?
The U.S. Open Championship is the second-oldest
American golf championship...by a day. It is held at a
different (and always very difficult) course every year, and is considered by many golfers to be the world's most prestigious major tournament. Today it attracts the sport's biggest stars and offers some of
the largest prizes in the game—but that's not how it started.

The first U.S. Open was held at the Newport Golf Club in
Rhode Island on October 4, 1895, one day after the real reason
the golfers were there—the first U.S. Amateur Championship.
The U.S. Open was almost an afterthought to the amateur match.
Professionals were still largely looked down upon in the golf world
and had no organization of their own—the USGA, which spon-
sored the event, was (and still is) primarily an amateur association. But since the pros—mostly Brits trying to make a living in
the United States—were ineligible to play in the U.S. Amateur,
the USGA decided to hold another tournament, open to pros and
amateurs alike. That's how the U.S. Open was born.

MAJOR CHANGES

For the premiere event, ten professionals and one amateur competed in the 36-hole stroke play tournament. Horace Rawlins, a 21-
year-old Englishman, won it with a score of 173. He received $150
of the $335 purse and a gold medal, and he got to keep the Open
Championship Cup for a year. With organized golf still so new in
the United States, British golfers dominated the "American Open"
for many years...but the Americans eventually caught up.

In 1911 a professional golfer named John J. McDermott became
the first native-born American to win the U.S. Open. At 19 years
old, he is still the youngest ever to win. But it was in 1913 that
the U.S. Open got its biggest boost when the world-famous British

---

Ted Hoz of Louisiana has the largest golf ball collection in the world—with 69,384 balls.

pros Harry Vardon and Ted Ray came to play the event at the Country Club in Brookline, Massachusetts. In front of the largest U.S. Open crowd to date, the two seasoned pros were beaten in an 18-hole playoff by 20-year-old American amateur Francis Ouimet. It was considered the biggest sports upset of its day and made headlines on both sides of the Atlantic. Ouimet, who had grown up in a working-class family in Brookline and had been a caddie at the club, became an instant American hero. The U.S. Open was on its way to becoming one of golf's four major championships.

U.S. OPEN STANDOUTS

Scotsman Willie Anderson won for the third time in a row in 1905, a feat that has never been matched. It was also his fourth win overall. Only he, Bobby Jones, Ben Hogan, and Jack Nicklaus have won that many U.S. Opens.

Bobby Jones gave golf one of its most famous tales of sportsmanship during the 1925 U.S. Open when he accidentally moved his ball while preparing to swing. No one else saw it, but Jones called a penalty stroke on himself—and went on to lose by one stroke.

Billy Burke and George Von Elm were tied at 292 after 72 holes of regulation play in the 1931 U.S. Open. After 36 playoff holes, they were tied at 149. After 36 more playoff holes, Burke won… by one stroke. It's still the longest playoff in U.S. Open history.

John Goodman won in 1933. He is the fifth—and the last—amateur to ever win the event.

Tiger Woods destroyed the U.S. Open record books in 2000 by winning with a score of 12-under—15 strokes ahead of his closest competitor. (He won again in 2002.)

*　　*　　*

SUCCESS STORY

"If Horatio Alger were alive today, he would love the rags to golf riches tale of Jose Coceres, from Argentina. The 38-year-old 140-pounder just won his second PGA Tour event, raising his 2001 take to $1.49 million. Not bad for a poor kid who learned to swing with a tree limb and subsequently helped raise 10 impoverished siblings."

—*Dallas Morning News*

It's in the bag: Raymond Floyd is the only pro golfer to have hit a drive into his own golf bag.

GATOR GRIPS AND HOSELS

The not-so-pro's guide to talking like a golfer, G–I.

Gallery: The spectators at a golf tournament.

Gator grip (also called the claw or psycho grip): An unusual grip for the putter, where the bottom hand grips the shaft from around the top, rather than from the bottom.

GHIN: The Golf Handicap Information Network, the USGA computer system used by most American golf courses to calculate handicaps.

Go to school: To study someone else's putt to see how yours is going to roll on the green.

Gorse: A dense, spiny shrub used in roughs, more common in Europe.

Grain: Direction of growth of the blades of grass, particularly on putting greens. The grain influences the direction and speed of the ball as it rolls.

Grand Slam: Winning all four major tournaments (the Masters, U.S. Open, British Open, and PGA Championship) in one calendar year.

Green: The very closely and smoothly mown area of the golf course specifically prepared for putting and on which the hole is placed.

Green in regulation: Getting the ball onto the green in the prescribed number of strokes (equal to par for the hole minus two strokes).

Greens fee: Fee charged to play a golf course.

Ground under repair: A marked area of a golf course from which a player may move a ball without penalty before playing his next shot. Common reasons: new constructions, damaged water lines, etc.

Hack(er): Slang term for a player of lesser ability.

Hammer hands: Players with "hammer hands" consistently overshoot their putts.

Hanging lie: A ball resting on an uphill slope.

Hardpan: An area of hard ground on which no grass will grow. It's difficult to get the club under the ball on hardpan, making hardpan shots among the toughest in golf.

Hazard: Any bunker or body

Among amateur golfers, lower back injuries are the most common ailment.

of water (sea, lake, pond, etc.) on or near the area of play.

Hole high: *See* "pin high."

Hole in one: A score of one on a hole; holing the tee shot. (Usually on a par-3 hole, less often on a par-4.)

Home green: The last-played green, usually the 18th.

Hook: A shot that curves dramatically to the left of the target (for a right-hander) due to spin.

Honor: The player with the lowest score on the previous hole gets the honor of teeing off first on the next.

Horizontal bulge: An integral part of club design—the curve of the face of a wood, from toe to heel, which aids shot accuracy.

Hosel (or neck): The part of the clubhead into which the shaft is inserted.

In: The last nine holes of an 18-hole course.

In play: Once the tee shot has come to rest, a ball is in play until it is holed or goes out of bounds.

Inside: 1. To the left of the target (right-handed). **2.** The closest to the hole.

Inside the leather: Closer to the hole than the length of the putter (to where the leather grip begins). Once used to determine if a putt was a "gimme."

Interlocking grip: A common golf grip where the little finger of the bottom hand interlocks with the index finger of the top hand.

*   *   *

WORD ORIGINS

Bunker. Comes from the Scottish *bunker*, *bunkart* or *bonkar*, meaning a storage hole dug into the side of a hill. Or it may have come from *bunke*, which is an old Swedish word referring to a protected part of a ship.

Chip. In old Scotland, chipping (instead of "chopping," as in England) was the word used for cutting wood with an ax.

Round. Why is a game of golf called a "round?" Because courses are traditionally laid out in a loose circular pattern, bringing players at the last hole back to where they started.

GOLF TIPS FROM...

Want to play like the best? Then listen to the best.

BEN HOGAN: "The average golfer's problem is not so much the lack of ability as it is the lack of knowledge about what he should be doing."

STEVE ELKINGTON: "Best tip I ever got was that on the backswing you have to turn your shoulder until it's under your chin, and on your follow-through, go all the way until the shaft touches your neck."

BABE DIDRIKSON ZAHARIAS: "When I start my swing, my paramount thought is to not quit hitting the ball."

DAVIS LOVE, JR.: "When it's breezy, hit it easy."

ARNOLD PALMER: "I guess the best tip I could give to older golfers would be to understand that physically they are not what they used to be and try to play within themselves, perhaps taking one or two more clubs than they used to on a lot of shots." (Taking "more club" means using a lower numbered, less lofted club—say, a 5-iron instead of a 7-iron.)

BEN HOGAN: "Good golf begins with a good grip."

JACK NICKLAUS: "I went to the movies—visualized the type of shot, the swing needed for that shot, and the perfect result—before stepping up to the ball."

PAM BARNETT: "To help your concentration, don't take too much time."

PHIL MICKELSON: "The best tip I could give is that growing up, it's most important to enjoy playing the game of golf. I would never practice if I didn't feel like practicing. Some days I'd practice 10, 12 hours, and other days I'd turn around and go home. I think it's so important that you have fun while you're playing so that your interest is always up when you're at the golf course."

QASS SINGH (ten-year-old son of Vijay Singh, in a note pinned to his father's bag during the 2000 Masters): "Papa, trust your swing." (Singh won.)

Over 2,500 putter models have been registered with the U.S. Patent Office.

THE FIRST RULES

*Isn't it comforting knowing that some
things remain pretty much the same?*

CODIFIED
In 1744 the Edinburgh Town Council presented the Gentlemen Golfers at Edinburgh with the Silver Club—a trophy for what is now known to be the world's first official, annual golf competition. It was a watershed moment for golf, not just because it meant the game was growing in popularity, but because in order for them to have an official tournament, they needed basic standards; they needed rules.

The 13 rules for this tournament would be the first codified set. Other clubs, such as St. Andrews, soon adopted them, but with their own variations. So, although the Gentlemen's 13 Articles didn't make the game uniform, they did lay out the basic foundation for what would become the modern game of golf.

Here are the Gentlemen Golfers' 13 rules of golf:
(Note on Article 1: the green of each hole was considered the tee of the next hole, and players were expected to start within a club's length of the hole they just played.)

ARTICLES & LAWS IN PLAYING AT GOLF

1. You must tee your ball within a club's length of the hole.

2. Your tee must be upon the ground.

3. You are not to change the ball which you strike off the tee.

4. You are not to remove stones, bones or any break club, for the sake of playing your ball, except upon the fair green and that only within a club's length of your ball.

5. If your ball comes among watter, or any wattery filth, you are at liberty to take out your ball & bringing it behind the hazard and teeing it, you may play it with any club and allow your adversary a stroke for so getting out your ball.

To golf in the Netherlands, you must pass a test and receive an official "Golf Ability Card."

6. If your balls be found any where touching one another, you are to lift the first ball, till you play the last.

7. At holeing, you are to play your ball honestly for the hole, and not to play upon your adversary's ball, not lying in your way to the hole.

8. If you should lose your ball, by its being taken up, or any other way, you are to go back to the spot, where you struck last, & drop another ball, and allow your adversary a stroke for the misfortune.

9. No man at holeing his ball, is to be allowed, to mark his way to the hole with his club, or anything else.

10. If a ball be stopped by any person, horse, dog or anything else, the ball so stop'd must be play'd where it lyes.

11. If you draw your club in order to strike, & proceed so far in the stroke as to be bringing down your club; if then, your club shall break, in any way, it is to be accounted a stroke.

12. He whose ball lyes farthest from the hole is obliged to play first.

13. Neither trench, ditch or dyke, made for the preservation of the links, nor the scholar's holes, or the soldier's lines, shall be accounted a hazard; but the ball is to be taken out, teed, and play'd with any iron club.

*   *   *

LEAP OF FAITH

In old match play rules, if another ball landed in front of yours and was six or more inches away, you couldn't move it. The "stymie" rule said that you had to hit around the other ball. This was especially tricky on the green, as American Olin Dutra found out during a 1933 Ryder Cup match when an opponent's ball blocked his path. Dutra tried to jump his ball over the other ball—but hit it, instead…and knocked the other guy's ball right into the cup.

Babe Ruth golfed in the high 70s and routinely made 300-yard drives.

WIE? OUI!

*Meet Michelle Wie, the teenage sensation
who is tearing up the LPGA before she's
even old enough to drive (a car).*

"I'm happy out of my mind. I like beating a lot of people."
—**After winning the 2003 U.S. Women's Amateur championship**

"If you expect a bad lie even for one second, the gods will know it and *give* you a bad lie, because you deserve it for thinking that way."

"I'm not really interested in sports psychology. It makes me feel like a crazy person."

"Men on tour should be allowed to wear shorts when the temperature is in the 90s. Gosh, long pants are a health hazard when it's that hot. If I were one of those guys, I'd pass out. Or pretend like I was passing out, so they'd let me wear shorts."

"My favorite young golfer is Annika Sorenstam, but my favorite old golfer is JoAnne Carner. I wouldn't mind getting older if I could be like her."

"I don't mind it when I hit a ball into the woods. I think of it as an adventure."

"You mean the PGA Tour media guide lists a player's weight and the LPGA guide doesn't? That's awesome—I think I'm overweight."

"There is no such thing as jet lag for me. I can sleep anywhere. Don't be offended, but I could fall asleep right now."

"My autograph is ugly, but I like it. It'll be very hard to forge."

"Getting angry is bad for your karma. In a tournament once I chunked a chip in front of a lot of people. After I finished the hole I stomped toward the next tee. There was a gallery rope there, and I tripped on it and cut my leg. I still have the scar. It was the golf gods getting even with me."

"Modern comedies aren't as good as the ones they used to make. I'm old school. I love *Dumb and Dumber*."

"By the time I'm old, golfers will be shooting 54s. You probably won't live to see it, but I'm sure I will."

Thanks, Mom: Patty Berg began playing golf because her mother forbid her to play football.

MORE GREAT ONES

Their statistics may be dwarfed by the superhuman feats of a Jack Nicklaus, Tiger Woods, or Sam Snead, but there are plenty of great golfers out there—lesser known…but true champions.

JOHNNY MILLER

He is now known as an outspoken TV broadcaster, but in his playing days Miller was an exceptional golfer. During his 25-year career (1969 to 1994), he won 25 tournaments. In 1973 he won his first major, the U.S. Open at Oakmont, and shot what many call the best round of golf ever played: a 63 in the final round, the lowest score ever by a U.S. Open winner. According to the World Golf Hall of Fame: "In golf's modern era, it's commonly understood that no player has ever achieved the brief but memorable brilliance of Johnny Miller…in 1974–75 Miller hit the ball consistently closer to the flag than any player in history." In 1974 alone he won eight tournaments, the money title, and the Player of the Year award. (The only year between 1971 and 1980 that the title wasn't won by either Jack Nicklaus or Tom Watson.) He won his last tournament, the 1994 Pebble Beach Pro-Am, at the age of 47.

RAYMOND FLOYD

Floyd entered the PGA in 1963 at the age of 20. When he won a tournament in his first year, it made him the fourth youngest ever to win a PGA event. He went on to win 22 tournaments, four of them majors: the 1969 and 1982 PGA Championships, the 1976 Masters, and the 1986 U.S. Open, which he won at the age of 43, making him the oldest winner to date. He's won 14 events on the Champions Tour and is one of two players (the other is Sam Snead) to win PGA events in four different decades. Floyd was also a U.S. Ryder Cup player eight times, and the team captain in 1989.

DOW FINSTERWALD

The man with the odd name may well have become the next great champion after Ben Hogan…if Arnold Palmer hadn't come

---

Tallest golfer in Masters history: Gordon Sherry (6' 8").

along. His numbers are still impressive: between 1955 and 1963 he won 11 tournaments, one of them the 1958 PGA Championship, and was among the top three money winners from 1954 to 1960. He played on four U.S. Ryder Cup teams, and in 1977 he was captain, leading the team to a win in England.

CURTIS STRANGE

Strange turned pro in 1976 and became one of the best golfers of the 1980s, topping the money list in 1985, 1987, and 1988. He was also voted Player of the Year in 1988. He won 17 tournaments over his career, including two U.S. Opens in a row (1988 and 1989). In 1989 he became the first golfer to earn more than $1 million in a single season.

ROBERTO DE VICENZO

When you see his stats, they may not look that impressive at first: de Vincenzo won 5 PGA events, one of them a major, the 1967 British Open, which he won at the age of 44. But the PGA isn't the only place the Argentinean played. He won national opens in 16 countries—including the Argentina Open, which he won nine times, the last one in 1985 at the age of 62—and in total won more than 230 tournaments around the world. After helping to kick off the Senior Tour in 1980, he went on to win three more events on that tour. De Vicenzo was inducted into the World Golf Hall of Fame in 1989.

CARY MIDDLECOFF

Middlecoff had a degree in dental surgery and served in the U.S. Army Dental Corps during World War II. But when he beat Gene Sarazen and Ben Hogan to win the 1945 North and South Open, he decided to play pro golf instead of being a dentist. He became one of the great golfers of the 1940s and '50s, winning 40 PGA Tour events, including two U.S. Opens (1949 and 1956), and the 1955 Masters. He also led the tour in wins in three different seasons, played on three U.S. Ryder Cup teams, and in 1956 won the Vardon Trophy. Bobby Jones once said of Middlecoff: "I'd give the world to have a swing like that."

Q: What color are the flags that mark water hazards? A: Yellow.

NICK PRICE

Born in South Africa and raised in Rhodesia (now Zimbabwe), Price started golfing when he was eight. He became a pro in 1977 on the South African Tour and European PGA Tour. In 1983 he joined the PGA Tour and by the 1990s had become one of the best golfers in the world. In 1992 he won the PGA Championship and in 1993 he won four PGA events, including the Players Championship, and was named Player of the Year. But there was more to come. In 1994 he won six times, including the British Open and his second PGA Championship, and was again named Player of the Year. He has won 18 PGA Tour events in the United States and has 24 more wins internationally. He was inducted into the World Golf Hall of Fame in 2003.

*   *   *

NINE LAWS OF GOLF...

that aren't in the rule book (but you can find them on the Internet).

1. Your best round of golf will be followed almost immediately by your worst round ever. The probability of the latter increases with the number of people you tell about the former.

2. Brand-new golf balls are water-magnetic. Though this cannot be proven in a lab, it is a known fact that the more expensive the golf ball, the greater its attraction to water.

3. The higher a golfer's handicap, the more qualified he deems himself as an instructor.

4. Every par-3 hole in the world has a secret desire to humiliate golfers. The shorter the hole, the greater its desire.

5. Trees eat golf balls.

6. Sand is alive. If it isn't, how do you explain the way it works against you?

7. Golf carts always run out of juice at the farthest point from the clubhouse.

8. The person you would most hate to lose to will always be the one who beats you.

9. The last three holes of a round will automatically adjust your score to what it really should be.

Average 18-hole course size: 150 acres.

HELLHOLES

*Golf game got you down? Let these horrifying tales of some of the
worst holes ever played help put things into proper perspective.*

ROW, ROW, ROW YOUR BOAT

During the 1913 Shawnee Invitational for Ladies, M. H.
Meehan hit a shot into a small tributary of the Delaware
River. Rather than take a penalty, Meehan and her husband commandeered a rowboat. As he piloted the craft, she kneeled in the
boat and frantically swatted at the drifting ball with her five-iron.
Forty swats later, the ball finally found land in the middle of a
dense forest about 200 yards from the green. Meehan bushwhacked
for a while until the hole was in sight, then drove the ball toward
it…where it wedged firmly between two rocks. She banged away
for a dozen or so more strokes before getting it to the green. Meehan sunk the putt on stroke number 161.

BETWEEN A ROCK AND A HARD PLACE

Willie Chisholm holds the record for worst-played hole in a U.S.
Open. At the 1919 event, his ball got lodged under a boulder.
Refusing to move the ball and take a penalty stroke, Chisholm
tried to play it. It took him 13 strokes to pry the ball loose and 18
total shots to hole out.

BARNES STORMING

At the 1968 French Open, Brian Barnes had to sink a three-foot
putt. It should have been an easy play for a man regarded as one of
the game's top putters. It wasn't. He gave the ball an easy tap—it
hit the lip of the cup and rolled out. Barnes missed again, lost his
cool, then tried raking the ball into the hole, batting it back and
forth like a hockey puck, swatting at it like a broom, even hitting it
croquet-style. After the ball was finally holed, the perplexed scorekeeper admitted that he'd lost count during Barnes's tirade. "When
you catch your *ss in a buzz saw," the scorekeeper said, "it's not too
easy to tell how many teeth bit you. What score did you make?"

"Twelve!" Barnes bellowed back. He then stormed off the
course and dropped out of the tournament. (He actually made 15.)

Arnold Palmer was the first pro to earn over $100,000 in a single year (1963).

TWENTY-THREE FOR THE RECORD BOOKS

Tommy Armour (read more about him on page 278) was an excellent golfer despite being blind in one eye. Only a week after winning the 1927 U.S. Open, Armour teed up for the Shawnee Open in Pennsylvania—and wished he hadn't. On the 17th tee, Armour hooked 10 balls out of bounds. He set a still-standing PGA Tour record: 23 strokes on one hole.

AUGUSTA'S EASIEST HOLE?

Tommy Nakajima made his Masters debut in 1978 at only 23 years old. After shooting an 80 in the first round, he was in danger of not making the cut, but a front-nine 36 on Friday put him back in the running...until the par-5 13th (known as one of Augusta's easiest). Attempting to eagle the hole, Nakajima tried to cut the corner of the 485-yard dogleg. The ball landed in a creek. He took a penalty drop and hit his third shot farther up the fairway. The fourth shot landed in a creek, right in front of the green. Nakajima tried to hit it out of the water, but the ball went straight up and came down on his shoe. Two-stroke penalty. The frustrated rookie asked his caddie to clean his club, who mishandled the handoff and dropped the handle in the water, or as the rule book calls it, "grounding a club in a hazard." Another two-stroke penalty. Nakajima's next shot flew all the way over the green. He had to chip it back to the green and still needed two putts to finally sink the ball. His final tally on the hole was 13 (an Augusta record), and after his front-nine 36, he ended the round with another 80. Nakajima would get his revenge on the 13th eight years later, when he eagled the hole at the 1986 Masters.

MORE HELLHOLES

• In the final round of the 1998 Bay Hill Invitational, John Daly hit a three-wood into the water six times on the par-5 6th. He ended the hole with an 18.

• England's Chris Gane hit into the rough on the 18th at Gleneagles in the 2003 Diageo Championship in Scotland. After several futile hacks, he holed out with a 17.

• Philippe Porquier took 20 shots to finish a hole at the 1978 French Open at La Baule.

A spectator picked Les Madison's pocket as he walked the fairway at the 1936 U.S. Open.

URBAN LEGENDS

*At one time or another, everyone's heard about a poodle
that exploded when its owner tried to dry it in a microwave,
the shrink-to-fit jeans that crushed a woman to death, or
some other story so unbelievable…that people believe it.
It turns out there are a few of these too-good-
to-be-true stories just for golfers.*

STORY: In the early days of golf, the sport was restricted to men. In fact, that's how it got such a funny-sounding name: "golf" is an acronym for "Gentlemen Only, Ladies Forbidden."
TRUTH: This has been presented as fact in countless trivia books (the BRI even gets letters attesting to its truth). But golf is an odd word. Linguists say it may come from the Dutch word *kolf*, for a stick or mallet, or the Scottish word *gowf*, a verb that means "to strike." And while it's true the sport was traditionally dominated by men, women have been playing golf for hundreds of years.

STORY: At an 1858 meeting of the Royal and Ancient Golf Club of St. Andrews, one member informed the rest of the club that it took him 18 shots to finish a fifth of Scotch. By allowing himself one shot per hole, the golfer decided that when the Scotch was finished, the round was, too. And that's why there are 18 holes in a round of golf.
TRUTH: The number of holes on early golf courses varied wildly, anywhere from five to 24 holes. St. Andrews had ten holes, but eight were routinely played twice. In 1764, when the Royal and Ancient Golf Club of St. Andrews formulated the rules of golf, they went with 18 holes because that's how *they* played. Scotch had nothing to do with it (but it might make a round of golf far more interesting).

STORY: In 1996 *Sports Illustrated for Kids* magazine printed a page of "trading cards" of young athletes on the rise, including PGA rookie Tiger Woods. When Woods won the career Grand Slam (the "Tiger Slam") five years later, interest in Woods memorabilia skyrocketed and one collector paid a whopping $125,000 for that old magazine page.

According to most court decisions, home owners are responsible for…

TRUTH: This one's true. Sports memorabilia firms verify that the $125,000 sale took place. But the only reason the buyer was willing to pay that much (variations on the legend put the figure as low as $22,000) was because it's probably the only card in existence and it was in perfect condition. That's because it was in a magazine with a relatively low circulation, most copies of which had long been thrown away, deteriorated, or become crumpled, creased, or torn. The lesson: save your golf magazines. (Fun fact: $125,000 is more money than Ben Hogan made in his entire career.)

STORY: Early one morning in 1998 at Palm Beach's Breakers Golf Course, an impatient member of a foursome went ahead of his group to play through. When the group couldn't locate their friend, they assumed he had already finished and was waiting in the clubhouse. He never turned up. Three days later, an occasional course visitor appeared: a crocodile called Ole Mose. Course and city officials quickly put two and two together and decided to kill and dissect Ole Mose…and there they found the missing golfer.

TRUTH: The story is a fake—it made the rounds via e-mail, complete with a picture. But the picture was taken in Borneo in 1997, not in Florida. And someone made up a fake story to go with it. No one was eaten by a crocodile at the Breakers Golf Course. Nevertheless, the story has circulated on the Internet for years, complete with the bogus photo of the dissected, man-filled croc.

STORY: A man was playing a couple rounds of golf. He'd always had a nervous habit of chewing tees while he played, but on this day he kept getting sicker and sicker, and he died a few days later. An autopsy showed he had been poisoned by pesticide from grass that had gotten on the tee.

TRUTH: It actually happened. In 1982 Navy Lieutenant George M. Prior complained of headache, fever, and nausea after a routine day of golf at the Army-Navy Country Club in Arlington, Virginia. Four days later, he had a temperature of 104.5 degrees and his body was covered in blisters. He died shortly thereafter, having ingested a lethal dose of Daconil, a fungicide sprayed on the golf course twice weekly, from chewing his tee.

KNOW YOUR GOLF

A few things you should know...

WHAT ARE "LINKS?"

Golf courses are often called "links" or "the links," but a links course actually refers to a particular kind of golf course that requires a particular style of play. Links courses are the original golf courses, founded in Scotland centuries ago. They were built on the sandy dunes of Scotland's east coast and got the name "links" because this was the land that "linked" the sea to the more fertile land used as farmland further inland. Perhaps the fact that it was not being used for farmland was why it was chosen for golf.

What makes a course a links course? The hilly terrain, sandy soil, lack of trees, proximity to the sea, and the near-constant and often very strong winds. And the strong winds make for another requirement—deep bunkers, so the sand won't be blown away. Those features demand a different kind of game from the one played on courses more common to the United States. Experts refer to it as a "ground game," because the shots are lower to avoid the wind and the fairways are built to accommodate those lower shots and let the ball roll.

And because they're built on narrow strips of land, links courses are usually laid out with the first nine holes going straight out from the clubhouse and the last nine coming straight back in alongside them. Today they're built all over the world. The most famous links course in the United States: Shinnecock Hills Golf Links on Long Island in New York.

WHAT'S THE "STABLEFORD SYSTEM?"

Like match play and stroke play, this is a way to score a round of golf. It was invented in 1931 by Dr. Frank Stableford, a member of the Wallasey Golf Club in Wales. The story goes that Dr. Stableford had seen his handicap soar ever since he joined the club on the windy Welsh coast (his 1 handicap had ballooned to an 8). As he was playing one day, he came to the treacherous 2nd hole, a long par-4 made all the more treacherous by strong, blustery winds

---

Studies show: balls that are colored "optic orange" have a 25% better chance of being spotted.

coming off the Irish Sea. He knew he would get a high number on the hole, and he thought it was unfair that he should have an entire round ruined because of one bad hole. So he invented a new system, assigning a score to the number of strokes on a hole, with the worst score being zero, no matter how badly one did:

• For two strokes (a double bogey) or more over par, you get zero points. (This way you aren't unduly punished, even if you take 20 strokes on one hole.)

• For a bogey, you get one point.

• For par, you get two points.

• For a birdie, you get three points.

• For an eagle, you get four points.

• For a double eagle, you get five points.

At the end of the round, you total your points, not your strokes, for all 18 holes. (And unlike stroke play, with Stableford play, you want the highest score possible.)

The first Stableford Rules tournament was played at Wallasey on May 16, 1932. Golfers took to it right away. Anybody could play it; it gave lesser golfers a better chance against better ones, and like match play, it made the game faster because you never had to wait for someone to finish their quadruple bogey. It's still used all over the world today. One PGA event in the United States, the International, held at Castle Pines Golf Club in Colorado, uses the system—sort of. They use the Modified Stableford Scoring System, which pays a higher reward for birdies and eagles and actually punishes for bogeys:

• For a double bogey or worse, you subtract two points.

• For a bogey, you subtract one point.

• For a par, you get zero points.

• For a birdie, you get two points.

• For an eagle, you five points.

• For a double eagle, you get eight points.

WHAT'S AN INVITATIONAL?

An invitational is just what it sounds like—an invitation-only golf tournament, such as the Buick Invitational. This is in opposition to an open, such as the British Open, where anyone can attempt

Amateur Henry Poli once made a 150-yard ace using a putter.

to qualify for one of the spots. How do you get invited? On the PGA Tour, most players are automatically invited because of their standing on the money list, having won the particular event in the past, or exempt status—others are just invited. To get invited, a golfer has to fill out the proper forms, mail them to the tournament…and wait. If you're someone like Tiger Woods or Vijay Singh, consider yourself in. (If you're Uncle John, you should probably plan something else for the weekend, just in case.) The most famous invitational in the world: the Masters.

WHAT'S A "REDAN HOLE?"

A redan hole is a type of golf hole design. It's usually a par-3, has a wide, shallow green situated diagonally to the tee box (the left end being farther away as you stand on the tee). The green slopes down from right to left, and is guarded at the front by deep bunkers. It got the name from the Crimean War, when the British captured a fort, or *redan* in the local language, from the Russians. This particular fort had deep pits dug around it for protection. British officer John White-Melville is credited with naming the 15th hole at North Berwick Golf Links (the West Links) in Scotland the original Redan Hole.

WHO PLAYS AND WHEN

PGA Tour events begin with a very wide field. The 2004 U.S. Open, for example, started with 156 players. To speed the proceedings along, the PGA Tour assigns tee times through a ranking system that places golfers into categories based on number of victories, money ranking, and tour status.

Category 1

• PGA Tour members who have won an event that season.

• The PGA Tour's "Life Members," who have been on the tour for at least 15 years and have won at least 20 times.

• The top 25 of the PGA's career money list through the end of the previous season.

• There's also the subcategory 1A, for tour veterans who have no recent wins but are past career Grand Slam winners.

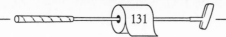

Category 2

• Players ranked in the PGA Tour's top 125.

• Those who have played 50 or more tournaments in their career or in five PGA events the previous year.

• Players in the top 50 of the official World Golf Rankings.

Category 3

• Everybody who doesn't fall into the first two categories, such as rookies and new open qualifiers.

Pairings are made by matching golfers from the same categories into groups of two or three. Generally, the higher the category, the better the tee time: late mornings or early afternoons for Category 1 players in round one of a tournament; early morning for Category 3 rookies. The 2003 PGA Championship kicked off at 7:30 a.m. for Joe Durant, Anders Hansen, and John Guyton. Fred Couples and David Duval didn't start until 1:25 p.m.

For the last two days of a tournament, the standings determine pairings and tee times. Like the category system, better golfers get better times. For example, in the 2003 U.S. Open, Ryan Dillon was 13 over par and J. P. Hayes was five over par after three rounds. They were first up for the Fourth round at 9:30 a.m. Leaders Stephen Leaney and Jim Furyk were 13 under and 16 under, respectively, and started at 3 p.m.

TV is also a big factor. Networks do not air every minute of a tournament, usually just a few hours of it. The 2004 Masters spanned four entire days, but was on television for just 12 hours. And though players might begin teeing off at 7 a.m., CBS or NBC doesn't start broadcasting until midafternoon. Vijay Singh and Phil Mickelson end up with later tee times, which not-so-accidentally coincides with the TV broadcast schedule.

HOW DO PRO TOURNAMENTS DIVVY UP THE PURSE?

• The PGA Tour has an elaborate system for figuring out who gets exactly how much money in an event. The system covers all the many possible scenarios, but here are the basics: first prize for winning a tournament is 18 percent of the total purse; last place, or 70th, gets 0.2 percent. So, if the total purse is $5 million, the winner gets $900,000 and 70th place gets $10,000.

• What happens if a PGA tournament finishes in a tie? It can't.

Ties are always decided with a playoff, either sudden death or a designated number of holes. So what happens when one player wins outright, say with a score of five under par, and many players tie for second at four under par? Do they all get second-place money? No. That would throw the purse off.

Say three people are tied for second place. Although technically they all finished in second, in terms of the money they finished in second, third, and fourth place. So add up the winnings for second, third, and fourth place and divide that amount equally between the three players.

• Amateurs often play in professional tournaments, and they're not allowed to win any money. So what happens to their prize money? They just kick it down to the golfer below. If an amateur wins a tournament, the guy in second place gets the first-place money. Second-place money goes to the third-place finisher, and so on, all the way down the line.

• What if people are disqualified after the cut? If there was designated prize money for 70 golfers and five of them are disqualified after the cut, then the last five places' prize money is simply subtracted from the purse and the first 65 players are paid.

• Think making the cut means you're guaranteed some money? Think again. The PGA usually cuts the field to 70 golfers after two days, but sometimes they cut it to more. So a handful of golfers can golf all four days, finish in 71st place or worse, and not make a dime.

*   *   *

NAYSAYERS

"Golf appeals to the idiot in us and the child. Just how childlike golf players become is proven by their frequent inability to count past five."

—John Updike

"They call it golf because all of the other four-letter words were taken."

—Raymond Floyd

"Golf is typical capitalist lunacy."

—George Bernard Shaw

Polls show that of the top ten sports Americans hate, golf is rated fifth.

LINKS QUIZ

*Test your knowledge of golf. These questions range from easy
to difficult, and some of the answers can be found in other
articles in this book. (Answers at the end of the quiz.)*

WHO AND WHERE

1. Who won the first Open
Championship in 1860?
a. Old Tom Morris
b. Young Tom Morris
c. Willie Park
d. John Ball

2. Tiger Woods won the 2000
U.S. Open by 15 strokes, a
record for a major. What
course was it played on?
a. Pinehurst Number 2
b. Pebble Beach
c. Valhalla
d. Augusta National

3. At the 1977 Danny Thomas
Memphis Classic, who became
the first player to shoot 59 in a
PGA Tour event?
a. Hale Irwin
b. Johnny Miller
c. Lee Trevino
d. Al Geiberger

4. Who is the only golfer to
lose three U.S. Open playoffs?
a. Arnold Palmer
b. Greg Norman
c. Lee Trevino
d. Sam Snead

5. Which one of the following
does *not* golf left-handed?
a. Phil Mickelson
b. Mike Weir
c. Ben Hogan
d. Curtis Strange

6. In what state is Doral's
Blue Monster course located?
a. Texas
b. California
c. New Mexico
d. Florida

7. Who's the better golfer—
Jack Nicklaus or Tiger Woods?

BY THE BOOK

8. How many rules are there
in the USGA rule book?
a. 34
b. 78
c. 122
d. 211

9. How many minutes do pros
have to find their ball before
it's deemed lost?
a. 3
b. 5
c. 7
d. 10

The Llanymynech Golf Club has 15 holes in Wales, 2 holes in England, and 1 on the border.

10. True or false: A player can replace his ball when he reaches the putting green.

11. The diameter, in inches, of a regulation hole is:
a. 4
b. 4 ¼
c. 4 ½
d. 5

12. Which of the following is *not* a part of a golf club?
a. hosel
b. heel
c. toe
d. indent

13. The yardage for a regulation par-4 ranges from:
a. 250–400
b. 251–470
c. 275–500
d. 300–475

14. A marker should be placed:
a. behind the ball
b. in front of the ball
c. beside the ball
d. any of these is fine

TALKING GOLF

15. Nick Faldo said: "My Sunday best is a Wednesday afternoon compared to him." Who?
a. Tiger Woods
b. John Daly
c. Davis Love III
d. Vijay Singh

16. Who said: "If you drink, don't drive. Don't even putt."?
a. Bob Hope
b. Chi Chi Rodriguez
c. Lee Trevino
d. Dean Martin

17. Bobby Jones said of this golf great: "He played a game with which I am not familiar." Who was he describing?
a. Gary Player
b. Tom Watson
c. Jack Nicklaus
d. Arnold Palmer

ANSWERS

1. c; **2.** b; **3.** d; **4.** a; **5.** d (Ben Hogan was left-handed, but golfed right-handed); **6.** d; **7.** Jack Woods, no wait, Tiger Nicklaus…what was the question? **8.** a (Although there are many subsets for different situations, there are technically only 34 rules in the game of golf.); **9.** b; **10.** False (Rule 15-1. A player must hole out with the ball played from the teeing ground, unless that ball has been declared unfit for play.); **11.** b; **12.** d; **13.** b; **14.** d (There is no restriction except that the surface surrounding the ball may not be altered.); **15.** b; **16.** d; **17.** c

In one of his first tournaments, Gary Player got knocked out by his own ball.

TREE'S COMPANY

Some shots don't win tournaments, they just make memories.

THINKING OUTSIDE THE BOX

Players: Lon Hinkle and Chi Chi Rodriguez

Event: The 1979 U.S. Open at the Inverness Club in Toledo, Ohio

First Shot: Hinkle and Rodriguez were paired together in the first round. When they got to the 8th tee, a 528-yard par-5 with a considerable dogleg (bend) in the fairway, Rodriguez noticed something: a gap in the tree line that allowed him to see over to the 17th fairway, which ran right alongside the 8th. If a player could put a shot over there, he reasoned, he would be shooting straight at the 8th green, instead of having to follow the dogleg. It wasn't exactly proper…but it wasn't exactly against the rules, either. They both shot through the gap. Rodriguez ended up parring the hole, but Hinkle got a birdie from the shortcut, putting him in a tie for the lead. The press loved the story and ran with it, but USGA officials weren't amused—someone had discovered a flaw on their course.

Second Shot: When Rodriguez and Hinkle got to the 8th tee the next day, there was a surprise waiting for them: officials had planted a 20-foot spruce tree right in the middle of the gap. The golfers thought it was funny. So did the hundreds of spectators who showed up to see what the pair would do. "I sharpened up a pencil and put my ball on the top of the pencil," Rodriguez said later, "and hit it over that tree." Hinkle did too—and he made another birdie. The USGA huffed and puffed, but they couldn't stop the two old pros from having a little fun. Neither of them won the tournament, but the incident became part of PGA history.

Parting Shot: When Hinkle returned to the course on the Champions Tour in 2003, reporters were all over him about the infamous tree. "The only good thing about the whole deal," he told them, "is that Inverness, which is a beautiful old golf course, has pictures of all the great players on the wall, Gene Sarazen, Ben Hogan, and Byron Nelson. And right alongside them there's a picture of Lon Hinkle. Not only that, everybody still calls that tree the "Hinkle Tree."

Q: What is the "scoring zone"? A: 10 feet or closer to the hole.

PGA WEEK

When you watch golf on TV, you only get to see a few hours of it over a few days. But there's much more to a tournament than that. Here's the "PGA Week" schedule for the 2005 John Deere Classic in East Moline, Illinois.

THE 2005 JOHN DEERE CLASSIC
TOURNAMENT SCHEDULE

Monday, July 4 (free admission)
- 11:00 AM   John Deere Golf & Turf One Source Pro-Am

Tuesday, July 5 (free admission)
- All day   Professional Practice Rounds
- 9:00 AM   Classic Pro-Am "Final Tune-Up" golf day
- 3:00 PM   Free Alcoa Youth Clinic (Deere Run driving range)
- 7:00 PM   Wednesday Pro-Am Pairings Party (Outing Club)

The tournaments always set aside time for the pros to practice on the course that the tournament will be played on. If there's not enough time on that course, they'll find another course or driving range close by. All the events also have youth clinics, where pros and sometimes celebrity amateur guests give the children of ticket buyers a golf lesson.

The Pro-Am Pairings Party is where the amateurs and pros mingle and have dinner together, and then the amateurs get to pick the pro they're going to play with (for the Wednesday Pro-Am). After attending his first pairings party, pro Scott McCarron said, "I had flashbacks of waiting to get picked for the kickball team in elementary school."

Wednesday, July 6
- Noon   Classic Pro-Am (AM and PM tee times)
- After play   Free live music behind the clubhouse
(The Fry Daddies)

Every tournament on the PGA Tour (except the four majors, the Players Championship, and the four World Golf Championships) has at least one pro-am event. They feature two to four local big-

---

First PGA golfer to appear on the cover of *Time* magazine: Arnold Palmer.

local bigwigs who pay big bucks to play a round with a PGA Tour pro. The pros are "strongly encouraged" to play—they can be penalized for not complying. Why? Because pro-ams are a major source of revenue for the PGA Tour.

After play, the party begins. Many of the tournaments have live music in the evenings for at least a couple of the event's six days. In this case, it's a Jimmy Buffet-style band from Iowa.

Thursday, July 7

- 7:00 AM   First round of the John Deere Classic
- After play Free live music behind the clubhouse (The Fry Daddies)

Friday, July 8

- 7:00 AM   Second round of the John Deere Classic
- After play Free live music behind the clubhouse (The Funktastics)

Saturday, July 9

- 7:00 AM   Third round of the John Deere Classic
- 3:30 PM   David Ogram world record attempt (most golf balls hit in half an hour)
- After play Free live music behind the clubhouse (The Funktastics)

Sunday, July 10

- 7:00 AM   Final round of the John Deere Classic
- After play Free live music behind the clubhouse (The Fry Daddies)

On Thursday morning, the tournament begins with the first tee times at 7 a.m. sharp. From Thursday until Sunday, there is golf all day long and—golf being the wild and crazy sport that it is—live music every night behind the clubhouse. And then, of course, there's the awards ceremony, which takes place whenever the tournament ends on Sunday.

THEN... After Sunday's work and fun are wrapped up, all the pros hit the road and get ready to do it all again (unless they're taking the next tournament off) in another town, at another golf club, in another tournament on the PGA Tour.

A nude woman once chased Jose Maria Olazabal down the fairway.

Golf in the Year 2000

If someone living 100 years ago wrote a book predicting what golf would be like today, how well would they do? Read on and find out.

LOOKING FORWARD

In 1892 a Scottish professional golfer named J. McCullough wrote a book titled *Golf in the Year 2000, or, What We Are Coming To*. It's a Rip Van Winkle–like story about a golfer named Alexander J. Gibson who falls asleep in 1892 and wakes up in the year 2000. He makes friends with a man named Adams, and they go golfing together.

The book is popular with collectors because some of the things McCullough predicted in 1892—digital watches, television, subways, and bullet trains, for example—did come to fruition. He had more misses than hits with his golf predictions, but that's what makes the book fun to read. Some of his predictions:

Handicapping golf clubs: "I took out what I supposed was a driver. It was a very powerful weapon with a remarkably thin shaft, which, on closer inspection, turned out to be made of steel—the head, too, was made of that metal. The shaft terminated in a little white disc, under glass, with figures on it and a hand like the face of a small watch. There was another small disc on the sole of the club. This one was, however, quite plain. 'It seems a wonderful weapon,' I replied; 'but what are those dials for?'

"'That one,' he said, pointing to the one at the top of the shaft, 'registers every stroke you take with the club. It is on every club, and as the strokes you have taken with each club are registered, the total of the set is your score for the round. At the end of the round your clubs are handed in to the secretary, who with his clerks counts the scores....We have got handicapping as near perfection as possible, for you see we have a record of every round a man plays, and by taking his average from day to day, and from week to week, we soon arrive at his right figure.'"

Robot caddies: "Two players had just driven off and were leaving the teeing ground, and sure enough behind each followed what I supposed was the caddies Mr. Adams spoke of; a perpendicular rod

---

A 1995 poll found that 37% of Americans thought the Ryder Cup was a horse race.

about four feet long, supported on three wheels, the whole rather resembling a tricycle with a small mast where the saddle should have been. This rod was weighted at the foot and hung on the wheels, so that it was always perpendicular, however steep the gradient it was going up or down.

"They followed wherever we went, at a distance of twelve feet or so, and regulated themselves to our pace, stopped when we stopped, and so on. Their wheels shot out spikes when necessary, so that they might not slip going up steep bits or through bunkers. My friend explained that we had a sort of magnet behind our jackets which attracted them, but did not allow them to come nearer than the twelve feet before mentioned. Of course you could go up to them when they had stopped; but when you moved on they remained stationary until you were the twelve feet away, and not till then did they follow."

Jackets that yell "Fore!": "'Another new invention for you—the sound comes from under your arms when you swing. It acts like a concertina: draws the air in when you take the club back, and when you bring the club down out comes the voice.'

"'Well,' I said, 'you have certainly brought golf to a nice pass. The clubs keep their own score; your jacket shouts "Fore," your caddie keeps his mouth shut—everything seems to be turned topsy-turvy. You ought to have an invention for swinging the club, and all you would have to do would be to walk round smoking your pipe and superintending operations.'"

Mechanical niblicks (nine-irons): "The niblick was the funniest of the lot. It had a double head, and when you swung it, it revolved like the paddle-wheel of a steamboat, only very much faster. You addressed the ball with the one head, while the other came up behind the shaft, it being of course quite stationary. As soon as you swung the club the two heads began to revolve—the opposite way from a paddle-wheel, of course—and threw the ball out of the bunker, with no end of sand. You had to look out for your eyes if there was any wind."

Hammer clubs: "And the clubs—a queerer collection I never saw. As I said before, they were all made in one piece, and were of steel. The faces all protruded about half an inch beyond the place

The word *divot* means, appropriately, "piece of turf" in Scottish.

where the shaft and head met. The heads were very small, which gave the clubs the appearance of hammers, and some looked as if you could reverse them and play left-handed. Of course, though the clubs were entirely of steel, they were painted so that they did not look so very unlike the old tools."

Programmable putters: "The head was an oblong block, with the shaft coming up from the neck as usual. The grip was all right, but below it was a spring, which joined it to the shaft. The slightest motion of your hands on the grip made the club oscillate backwards and forwards, like a pendulum, the grip, however, remaining steady in your hands.

"On the back of the grip were a row of figures, 1, 2, 3, 4, 5, 6, 8, 10, 12, 15, 20, 25, 30, 40, 50, with a hand which you could push along to indicate any of them. The way in which you played the shot may be described thus: you put the hand at the figure corresponding to the distance you were from the hole, held the club over the ball, and with a slight motion of your hands set it in motion. When you had got the right line to the hole, you just put it down behind the ball, and thereupon it would send it the prescribed number of feet. Success was then a simple matter of judging the right line; if you were on that, you would hole out, or at the very least lie dead. Such was the latest thing in putters."

Compressed-air golf balls: "To all appearance, as I have said, the balls were the same as we used in 1892; but though innocent enough to look at, they had more work in them than even the heads of the clubs. In the centre of the ball was a small chamber of compressed air; outside that was a rim of some hard substance like gutta-percha [rubber], about a quarter of an inch thick; then came the shell of the ball, which was made up of oblong little blocks, of a hard, white substance.

"These blocks were each separate, and fixed to the inside layer by strong springs—four springs to every single square—crossing each other. When they were all fixed on the ball quite resembled one of the old-fashioned gutties. Even handling them you did not detect the difference, and the flying power was extraordinary."

Part II of "Golf in the Year 2000" is on page 231.

At many exclusive clubs in Japan, caddies are female.

THE WALKER CUP

*Like many presidents, George H. W. Bush and George
W. Bush are both avid golfers. But golf runs a little deeper
in their family: the "W" is for George Herbert Walker,
founder of the Walker Cup amateur tournament.*

A CUP IS BORN

In 1920 the Royal and Ancient Golf Club of St. Andrews
invited top officials from the USGA to St. Andrews for a
conference. The reason: the rule book. The R&A set the standard
for Europe, while the USGA interpreted the rules for the United
States. Golf had now become popular enough in the United States
that the difference between the two rule books was becoming a
problem. They wanted to standardize the rules.

Among the Americans who attended the meetings was wealthy
businessman and USGA president George Herbert Walker. The
meetings were so cordial and productive that both sides expressed
interest in an international amateur golf tournament. Walker took it
on as his pet project. His plan: countries would send a team of golfers
to square off in match play. He even offered to pay for the trophy.

SLOW START

The following year the USGA invited numerous nations in which
golf was popular (Canada, France, Spain, and Great Britain) to
send teams to the competition in Scotland. Not a single one
accepted. Undeterred, Walker persuaded William Fownes, the
1910 U.S. Amateur champion, to put a team together. Fownes
rounded up a group and took them to Scotland. Then he had to
round up a team of British golfers (they were there anyway, to play
in the British Amateur Championship) to play what amounted to
the first—but unofficial—Walker Cup. The Americans defeated
the Brits.

In 1922 Walker invited the British to play again, and this time
the R&A accepted. The match would be played at the National
Golf Links of America in Southampton, New York, not coincidentally the home club of George H. Walker. Fownes again captained
the American team, which included U.S. Amateur champion Jesse

Guilford. This provided credibility and celebrity to the new tournament. Robert Harris captained the British team, but fell ill and was replaced by Bernard Darwin, a *Times* of London reporter who had accompanied the team to cover the event. (Darwin actually beat Fownes in their singles match.) The first winner: the U.S. team by a score of 8 to 4. Walker was finally able to present the large silver trophy he had donated, which the press had dubbed the "Walker Cup." The tournament has been called by that name ever since.

THE TRADITION CONTINUES

The Walker Cup was played again in 1923 and 1924, but it proved too much of a financial strain to send teams on annual transatlantic trips. St. Andrews and the USGA also feared interest would drop if the matches were too frequent. The solution: the tournament would occur every other year, with the location alternating between the United States and Britain. The tournament continued to be played in even-numbered years until 1938, when it was suspended due to World War II, and was resumed in odd-numbered years in 1947. As of 2003, the U.S. has a distinct Walker Cup advantage, winning 31 events to Britain and Ireland's five, with one match tied. But the British are coming... the 2003 victory was their third win in a row.

THE GOLFING BUSHES

In 1921 Walker's daughter Dorothy married Wall Street banker Prescott Bush. Long before going into politics and becoming a U.S. senator from Connecticut, Bush worked at the USGA as secretary, vice president, and then president from 1928 to 1935. The Bush family still says Prescott Bush was the best golfer of the clan; he had a handicap no higher than 3 and often as low as scratch. On his home course in Kennebunkport, Maine, he won the Cape Arundel Golf Club championship eight times, and once held the course record of 66.

Bush's son is former U.S. president George Herbert Walker Bush. He didn't begin golfing until his teens because he was so intimidated by his father's prowess. He's a frequent golfer, but is known to be impatient, which may explain why his putting game isn't the greatest. Bush even installed a nine-hole practice green on

---

There is approximately one golf hole for every 139 people in the United States.

the South Lawn of the White House, but according to reporters, it didn't help. It's also been reported that George H. W. Bush has a "no laughing rule" for his playing partners and favors "speed golf": he gets to the ball, hits it, and moves on as quickly as possible.

George W. Bush golfs only on vacation, both at his Crawford, Texas, ranch and the family retreat in Maine. He usually shoots in the mid to high 80s and friends describe him as an aggressive golfer who always goes for long drives and aims for the green with every shot.

But neither George H. W. Bush nor George W. Bush ever cheats (probably because their family worked for so many years at the USGA to promote the rules and traditions of golf). Professional golfer and family friend Ben Crenshaw says the closest they come to doing so is an occasional mulligan, and only on the first tee.

*   *   *

HAPPY MEALS

On the Tuesday before the Masters, previous champions assemble for the annual Masters Club meeting, also called the "Champions Dinner." Ben Hogan suggested the idea and hosted the first dinner in 1952. The previous year's winner gets to pick the menu (and foot the bill). Some savory selections from the last 20 years:

1986: Bernard Langer—weiner schnitzel

1989: Sandy Lyle—haggis, mashed potatoes, turnips

1993: Fred Couples—chicken cacciatore

1994: Bernard Langer—turkey, dressing, black forest torte

1995: Jose Maria Olazabal—paella and whitefish

1996: Ben Crenshaw—Texas-style barbecue

1997: Nick Faldo—fish and chips, tomato soup

1998: Tiger Woods—cheeseburgers, chicken sandwiches, French fries, milkshakes

1999: Mark O'Meara—chicken or steak fajitas, sushi, tuna sashimi

2004: Mike Weir—Elk, wild boar, char (a fish), Canadian beer

2005: Phil Mickelson—lobster ravioli in tomato cream sauce, Caesar salad, garlic bread

President George H. W. Bush once accidentally beaned Dan Quayle with a golf ball.

THE GOLFER'S WIT

Golf, by its nature, is a very frustrating sport. The best way to deal with the agony is to have a sense of humor about it.

"I enjoy the *oohs* and *ahhs* from the gallery when I hit my drives, but I'm getting pretty tired of the *awws* and *uhhs* when I miss the putt."
—John Daly

"Samuel Ryder, the original patron of the Ryder Cup, was buried with his five-iron, the only sensible thing to do with any golf club, really."
—Bernie Lincicome

Ralph Kramden: How do you know so much about golf?
Ed Norton: I've been working in the sewer for ten years. If that doesn't qualify me as an expert on holes, I give up.
—*The Honeymooners*

"Have you ever noticed what golf spells backwards?"
—Al Boliska

"My game is so bad I gotta hire three caddies—one to walk the left rough, one for the right, and one for the middle. And the one in the middle doesn't have much to do."
—Dave Hill

"I play in the low 80s. If it's any hotter than that, I won't play."
—Joe E. Lewis

"The rest of the field."
**—Roger Maltbie,
on what he had to shoot
to win a tournament**

"My favorite shots are the practice swing and the conceded putt. The rest can never be mastered."
—Lord Robertson

"I'll always remember the day I broke 90. I had a few beers in the clubhouse and was so excited I forgot to play the back nine."
—Bruce Lansky

"Why am I using a new putter? Because the last one didn't float too well."
—Craig Stadler

"His nerves, his memory, and I can't remember the third thing."
**—Lee Trevino,
on the three things to
go on an aging golfer**

GOLF LIBRARY

There are other golfs book out there. Here
are some of Uncle John's favorites.

WHO'S YOUR CADDY? by Rick Reilly
Review: A *Sports Illustrated* writer's account of caddying for golf
superstars (Jack Nicklaus, David Duval) and celebrities (Donald
Trump, Bob Newhart) on the pro-am circuit. "Reilly takes the time
to delve into personalities here, but the discussion always humor-
ously—and lovingly—comes back to golf. A terrific book for both
casual and serious fans." *(Book Page)*

DUEL IN THE SUN by Michael Corcoran
Review: "Corcoran highlights the stirring battle waged between
Tom Watson and Jack Nicklaus for the 1977 British Open championship. He tells how Arnold Palmer's 1960 quest for the title rekin-
dled the interest of America's top pros in the event that most golfers
consider the world's most important. Even for those who recall the
event in detail, this book will prove entertaining and enlightening,
with riveting hole-by-hole accounts." *(Library Journal)*

THE GOLF OMNIBUS by P. G. Wodehouse
Review: "Wodehouse's status as golf's Shakespeare, its master
comedian and tragedian, is borne out by this collection of short
stories in which golf and love are the two constants. 'I doubt if
golfers should fall in love,' says one character. 'I have known it to
cost men 10 shots per medal round.'" *(Sports Illustrated)*

THE GRAND SLAM: BOBBY JONES, AMERICA, AND THE STORY OF GOLF by Mark Frost
Review: "Before Arnold, Jack and Tiger, there was Bobby. After
winning golf's Grand Slam in 1930, Jones stood like a colossus
over the American sporting scene. Frost has written a swift, sure-
footed account of Jones's remarkable life and career, from Jones's
precocious early days on the Atlanta links to his sudden retreat
from the media spotlight. As bedside reading for the literate duffer,
this is a hole in one." *(Publisher's Weekly)*

1954 U.S. Open winner Ed Furgol's left arm was six inches shorter than his right.

A GOOD WALK SPOILED: DAYS AND NIGHTS ON THE PGA TOUR by John Feinstein

Review: "Chronicles the struggles of the game's top golfers, as well as those trying to get onto the PGA Tour. These are gifted players who've devoted their lives to the game, and on any given day they could just flat out stink. Completely engaging from first page to last, a wonderfully observed and masterfully told story of pain and profit in the world's most frustrating sport." (*Amazon.com*)

BEN HOGAN'S FIVE LESSONS by Ben Hogan and Herbert Warren Wind

Review: "Originally serialized in 1957, Hogan's lessons proved to be an enduring hit. Tremendously detailed, down to how to waggle the club properly, this is the definitive primer on the sport from its hardest-working perfectionist." (*Sports Illustrated*)

THE GREATEST GAME EVER PLAYED: HARRY VARDON, FRANCIS OUIMET, AND THE BIRTH OF MODERN GOLF by Mark Frost

Review: "Vardon was a top professional earning fame and fortune on both sides of the Atlantic, while Ouimet was the self-effacing, up-and-coming amateur. When the two battled it out at the 1913 U.S. Open, they changed the game of golf forever. The author's enthusiasm is infectious as he writes about each day's drama at the U.S. Open, including the thrilling 18-hole playoff." (*Book Page*)

THE ETERNAL SUMMER: PALMER, NICKLAUS, AND HOGAN IN 1960, GOLF'S GOLDEN YEAR by Curt Sampson

Review: "Sampson examines a pivotal year in the history of golf, when Arnie was in his prime, the great Ben Hogan was struggling for one last bit of glory, and a 19-year-old chubby kid named Jack Nicklaus was starting to get noticed." (*About.com*)

DEAD SOLID PERFECT by Dan Jenkins

Review: "Follows the exploits of one Kenny Lee Puckett on the PGA Tour. No one has captured the essential lunacy of the twentieth-century sports (and TV) scene as accurately and hilariously as this." (*Los Angeles Times*)

PGA pro Frank Nobilo's ancestors were Italian pirates.

GOLF "FASHION"

*Why does down keep a duck up? Why are there five windows
at the bank, but only two tellers? Why do golfers wear
such strange clothes? To some questions, there are no
answers. (Except for the one about golf clothes.)*

THE FORMAL ERA

1400s: Golf is beginning to be played in Scotland. Golf
clothes are ordinary Scottish clothes—elaborate and colorful kilts, scarlet waistcoats, and tams—woolen caps with wide
circular crowns and a pom-pom in the center. The loose-fitting
garments (especially those breezy kilts) allow for free movement.

1500s: Golf becomes a sport of royalty, with James IV of England
being the first known royal golf addict. Golf wear becomes the
very formal wear of "lord" and "lady" golfers.

1700s: The first private golf clubs are founded by gentlemen
golfers in eastern Scotland. The Royal Burgess Golfing Society of
Edinburgh, one of the earliest, has a strict dress code for members:
red jacket, white shirt, trousers, and club-issue tie, all to be worn
while golfing.

1800s: European women golfers wear bustles and large hats, either
tied on or pinned. Their play is restricted mostly to putting, partly
due to their cumbersome clothing, but also because it is against
social decorum to swing a club above shoulder height. The middle
of the century sees the first golf professionals, who aren't upper
class but are rather from the lower class—mostly caddies and
craftsmen. Their attire is still formal, but in a much less expensive
way. (And they're not allowed to be members of golf clubs.)

1888: Scotsman John Reid opens one of the first American golf
clubs, New St. Andrews, in Yonkers, New York. With it comes the
strict European dress code, including the red jacket. Most British
and American clubs are now issuing jackets, and members can be
fined for wearing improper attire on the course.

1890s: Women golfers get a little breathing room—literally—as
they are now allowed to wear long skirts, buttoned-up boots,

billowy blouses, and straw hats. But showing ankle during play is forbidden.

1910s: At both private golf clubs and newly emerging public courses, standard dress for American men is a woven dress shirt with a stiff collar, slacks, a coat, and a tie. Women wear expanding pleats down the sides of their tweed jackets to prevent clothes from ripping mid-swing. The tweed golf sweater becomes the first casual golf garment and is worn off the course as well.

1920s: Professional golfers (the lower-class golfers) begin to take over from the gentlemen at the clubs—but they still have to play at the clubs. The flamboyant Walter Hagen sets new trends during the equally flamboyant Jazz Age. Hagen wears plus-fours—knee-length knickers that got their name from the extra four inches of fabric that billow around the knees—two-tone shoes, a sleeveless argyle sweater, and a loose-fitting blazer. One journalist comments that the sight of Hagen "was enough to make the flappers choke on their gum."

1940s: The postwar era sees the colors fade, as drab, though still elegant, comfort wear comes in. *Esquire* magazine calls it "the grey flannel world of golf." Ben Hogan rules the golf world in dark gray slacks, a light-colored shirt, a cashmere sweater, and his ever-present white cap.

1960s: Color TV is in—and color comes to golf as never before. Doug Sanders earns the nickname "Peacock of the Fairways" for his purple pants and turquoise sweaters and is named *Esquire* magazine's "Best Dressed Athlete." Tony Jacklin wears all purple (including a turtleneck) when he wins the British Open in 1969. Gary Player sticks out by not sticking out, dressing head to toe in solid black.

1970s: Former pro (and current broadcaster) David Feherty shares some painful memories:

> I can't help but think that the decades of the 1970s and '80s were the lowest point in golf fashion…High-waisted, beltless slacks infested our pro shops, making it impossible to retrieve a scorecard from the hip pocket, unless you went for it over your shoulder. The white patent belt was almost compulsory and shirt collars were so long and pointed they became extremely dangerous in high winds. They could put your eye out, for heaven's sake! The only solace I could find was in the fact that my teammates looked equally absurd.

Why did David Frost drop his pants at the 1994 Presidents Cup? A wasp crawled up his leg.

PGA player Johnny Miller defines the era with his countless pairs and varieties of plaid pants, tight at the waist and flared—almost belled—at the bottom.

1980s: Greg "the Shark" Norman defines golf's new (and cool) look with comfortably loose slacks and colorful polo shirts. And he always wears his trademark straw Panama hat. Polo shirts, also called "golf shirts," become immensely popular off the course. Payne Stewart straddles the traditional and modern, matching his polo shirts with retro wear—plus-fours, argyle socks pulled up to the knees, and a tam.

1990s to present: What's worn on the course become largely indistinguishable from the casual look worn in office buildings around the country. Today, golf wear has become almost a billion-dollar business with designers such as Tommy Hilfiger and Ralph Lauren bringing out entire lines of golf clothes. You can also get Arnold Palmer, Jack Nicklaus, and Greg Norman golf wear, as well as the biggest seller: Nike's Tiger Woods Collection, featuring Tiger's undeniable contribution to pro golf fashion, the baseball cap. (Swedish golfer Jesper Parnevik is one of the era's mavericks, appearing at PGA events in a rainbow of brightly colored, skintight pants.) Still, to keep golf wear from becoming *too* casual, many golf clubs enact strict dress codes, banning denim, sleeveless shirts, T-shirts, and sweatshirts.

*   *   *

A JACK ATTACK

"In 1994 actor Jack Nicholson allegedly jumped out of his car at an intersection and attacked motorist Robert Blank's Mercedes-Benz with a golf club when Blank cut him off in traffic. After smashing the car's windshield and denting its roof, Jack allegedly got back into his own Mercedes and drove away. Nicholson was later charged with misdemeanor assault and vandalism; Blank sued him, claiming assault and battery. But the civil suit was settled out of court, and the criminal case was dropped. Jack later said, in his defense, that a friend of his had just died, and that he (Jack) had been up all night playing a maniac in a movie."

—*Hollywood Scandals*

Before the 1920s, it was considered poor taste to unbutton your jacket on the course.

THE FINE ART OF THROWING YOUR CLUB

Oh, those stupid stupid STUPID GOLF CLUBS! They should know better than to make us play so badly.

THUNDER BOLT

Tommy Bolt won 15 PGA tournaments in his career, including one major, the 1958 U.S. Open. If that doesn't sound like a lot of wins, consider that Bolt is 55th on the all-time list, and that he didn't join the PGA until he was 32 years old. All those wins came in one 11-year period, from 1951 to 1961. He went on to win 12 more times on the Champions Tour and was inducted into the World Golf hall of Fame in 2002.

But Bolt was better known for something else: he was one of the most competitive and explosive men to ever play the game. His various nicknames—Thunder Bolt, Terrible Tommy, Tempestuous, and Vesuvius—were all well earned. "You could sense the lava rising, the ash spewing, the top about to come off," *Los Angeles Times* columnist Jim Murray wrote. "Mt. Bolt was about to erupt."

THROWING THE GAME

When Thunder Bolt's game went awry, his fellow players, his caddie, and the gallery all knew to watch out…a club (or clubs) would be flying. There's a famous photo of Bolt taken at the 1960 U.S. Open at Cherry Hills, just after he'd hit two consecutive shots into the water. It shows him in a full, two-handed backswing, about to launch his driver into the lake. There were numerous other incidents. Many of his fellow pros thought Bolt's inability to control his emotions cost him tournaments. "If we could've just screwed another head on his shoulders," said his friend Ben Hogan, "Tommy Bolt could have been the greatest who ever played."

Bolt's club-chucking antics were so notorious that he earned a dubious honor from the PGA. Because of him, a new rule was instated: any player who throws a club at any time during play receives a two-stroke penalty. The rule was affectionately known as the "Tommy Bolt Rule." (The day after the rule took effect,

---

Bill Clinton once caddied for Tommy Bolt.

Bolt became the first golfer to break it; not because he was mad, he just didn't want some other player to be the first to break "his" rule.)

Bolt's other rule: "If you are going to throw a club," he advised, "it is important to throw it ahead of you, down the fairway, so you don't have to waste energy going back to pick it up."

INCOMING!

Tommy Bolt may be the most famous tosser of shafts, but he certainly wasn't the only one.

Bobby Cruickshank. During the 1934 U.S. Open, he hit a shot on the 11th hole that went straight into the creek in front of the green—and it bounced off a rock and ended up 10 feet from the hole. In celebration, Cruickshank—who was leading at the time—threw his club high into the air...only to have it come back down and land on his head. After he regained consciousness a few minutes later, a dazed Cruickshank resumed playing, but never regained his composure. He lost the lead and finished third.

John Daly. Going into the third round of the 1997 PGA Championship at Winged Foot, Daly was one under par and just three strokes off the lead. Then he tanked. At the 12th hole, his drive sailed onto the fairway—the 17th fairway—and he snapped. He turned around and launched his club over the gallery and into the woods. Two marshals had to jump the chain-link fence to retrieve it.

Tiger Woods. He won the Bay Hill Invitational four years in a row, from 2000 to 2003. One more and he'd have the PGA record for most consecutive wins at one tournament. But it must have been too much pressure. In the final round, he found himself in 46th place. On the 6th hole, he sent a shot into the water. Then, according to witnesses (he wasn't on camera), he threw his club after it—but accidentally hit his caddie, Steve Williams, instead. "Steve was just as hot as I was," Tiger said later, "so it doesn't really matter." (Williams probably disagreed.)

*   *   *

"The ardent golfer would play Mount Everest if somebody would put a flagstick on top."

—Pete Dye

The Druid Hills Country Club in Atlanta staged a club-tossing competition in 1936.

RECORD BOOK: LPGA

And now, a little something for the ladies.

MOST MAJOR WINS

Patty Berg, 15
Mickey Wright, 13
Louise Suggs, 11
Babe Zaharias, 10
Betsy Rawls, 8
Annika Sorenstam, 7
Juli Inkster, 7

LOWEST SCORE IN A ROUND

Annika Sorenstam, 59
(2001 Standard Register PING)
Meg Mallon, 60
(2003 Welch's/Fry's Championship)
Jung Yeon Lee, 60
(2004 Welch's/Fry's Championship)
A. Acker-Macosko, 60
(2004 Longs Drug Challenge)

LOWEST SCORE, 72 HOLES

Karen Stupples, 258
(2004 Welch's/Fry's Championship)
Wendy Doolan, 259
(2003 Welch's/Fry's Championship)
Se Ri Pak, 261
(1998 Jamie Farr Kroger Classic)

MOST HOLES IN ONE, CAREER

Kathy Whitworth, 11
Vicki Fergon, 8
Meg Mallon, 8
Jan Stephenson, 8
Mickey Wright, 8
Betsy King, 7
Sandra Palmer, 7

MOST BIRDIES IN A ROUND

Annika Sorenstam, 13
(2001 Standard Register PING)
(Seven tied at 11)

MOST LPGA TOUR WINS

Kathy Whitworth, 88
Mickey Wright, 82
Patty Berg, 60
Louise Suggs, 58
Betsy Rawls, 55
Annika Sorenstam, 56
Nancy Lopez, 48

BIGGEST COME-FROM-BEHIND VICTORIES

Mickey Wright
10 strokes (1964 Tall City Open)
Annika Sorenstam
10 strokes (2001 The Office Depot)

BEST SEASON SCORING AVERAGE

Annika Sorenstam
68.70 (2002)
Annika Sorenstam
69.42 (2001)
Karrie Webb
69.43 (1999)
Grace Park
69.99 (2004)
Annika Sorenstam
69.99 (1998)

LARGEST MARGIN OF VICTORY

Cindy Mackey, 14
1986 MasterCard International Pro-Am
(72 holes)
Jan Stephenson, 11
1981 Mayflower Classic (54 holes)
Annika Sorenstam, 11
2002 Kellogg-Keebler Classic (54 holes)

CAREER GRAND SLAM WINNERS

Pat Bradley
Juli Inkster
Annika Sorenstam
Louise Suggs
Karrie Webb
Mickey Wright

LPGA winner Kim Williams signed a deal with Bullet...shortly after having been shot.

JIGGERS AND LOOPERS

How to talk like a golfer. (Whisper.) J–M.

Jail: A golfer is "in jail" when his ball cannot be swung at or advanced at all, such as when it lands in a clump of bushes.

Jigger: An old term for a four-iron.

Jumper (also flier or shooter): A shot that goes much farther than intended.

Jungle: Slang for thick rough.

Kickpoint (or flex point): The point where a golf club's shaft bends the most when the head is pulled down. A lower kickpoint is believed to produce a higher trajectory.

Kikuyu grass: Tough, creeping grass species used for rough in warm, dry regions.

Kitty litter: Slang for a sand bunker.

Knee knocker: A short, nerve-racking putt.

Knife: Slang for a one-iron.

Knock-down (or punch) shot: A shot intentionally played low, in windy conditions.

Lag (or lag putt): A long putt intended to stop close to the hole, but not necessarily to go in.

Lateral water hazard: A water hazard that runs parallel to the fairway.

Lead tape: Thin, adhesive strips of lead used to add weight to a clubhead.

Leading edge (or blade): The lowest and forwardmost edge of a clubhead.

Level (or level par): A British term for par.

Lie: The position of the ball at rest. ("I had a bad lie.")

Lift, clean, and place: Type of play that, usually because of wet or poor course conditions, allows the ball to be picked up, cleaned off, and replaced (within a specified area) in another position.

Line of putt: Intended path of a ball struck on a green.

Lip: The edge of the hole.

Lip out: When a ball rolls over the lip of a hole but doesn't go in.

Lob shot: A high, short, softly hit shot, usually to the green.

Lob wedge: A high-lofted iron —usually around 60 degrees— designed for playing lob shots.

Local rules: Recognized rules that individual courses may

With a wedge? Swedish golfer Jesper Parnevik eats volcanic sand "to improve his game."

have in addition to official rules.

Loft: The amount, in degrees, a club's face is angled, which determines a struck ball's trajectory. (A one-iron has very little loft; a nine-iron has a lot.)

Long iron: The longer, less-angled irons, generally 1 through 3, that are used for long shots.

Looper: A caddie.

Loose impediments: Natural objects, such as stones and leaves that may be moved without penalty as long as the ball doesn't move (not allowed in a hazard).

Lost ball: A ball that cannot be located within five minutes is officially lost.

Mallet: A type of putter with a head shaped like that of a mallet.

Marker: 1. A small object used to mark a ball on the green (usually a coin). **2.** The person who records a player's score (usually another player).

Marshals: Low-level officials at tournaments who control crowds and regulate golfers' pace of play.

Mashie: Old term for a five-iron.

Mashie iron: A four-iron.

Mashie niblick: A seven-iron.

Medal play: Another name for stroke play.

Member's bounce: A lucky bounce.

Mid-irons: Five-, six-, and seven-irons.

Mid-mashie: A three-iron.

Movable obstructions: Large objects in the line of play that may be moved without penalty. However, they must be able to be moved without "unreasonable effort," great delay of play, or damage to the course. Example: a chair or camera truck.

Mulligan: A "do-over" after a badly hit shot in recreational play—forbidden in the official rules of golf.

*   *   *

GOLF'S OTHER MAJOR

The University of Birmingham in England now has an accredited program offering a degree in golf. According to Sandy Jones, British Professional Golfers Association chief executive: "The university is about providing knowledge to anybody that requires it, and we now live in a world where leisure time is a great deal more important than it used to be."

THE KING

Golf's everyman.

CHAMPION: Arnold Palmer
BACKGROUND: Born on September 10, 1929, in Latrobe, Pennsylvania.

HIS STORY: Palmer's father, Deacon, was a greenskeeper at the local golf club, so Arnie was introduced to golf at an early age. He won five West Penn Amateur Championships while still a teenager and three Atlantic Coast Conference championships while attending Wake Forest University. He might have won another there, but his best friend and golfing teammate, Bud Worsham, was killed in a car accident during their senior year. Palmer was unable to cope with the loss and quit school, joining the Coast Guard for a three-year stint. After ignoring golf briefly, he started playing again while stationed in Cleveland, Ohio, and won a few small tournaments.

Palmer got back into the game full time when he got out of the Coast Guard in 1954, immediately winning the U.S. Amateur. That year he turned pro and continued to win. By 1957 Palmer led the PGA Tour in victories.

With his rugged, regular-guy good looks, his natural charisma, and his aggressive go-for-broke style of play, he attracted enormous galleries of fans that became known as "Arnie's Army." Because he was a risk-taker, he often found himself trailing near the end of a tournament, but that just set him up for some of the best come-from-behind victories in golf history. Fellow legend Bobby Jones once said, "If I ever had to have one putt to win a title for me, I'd rather have Arnold Palmer hit it for me than anybody I ever saw." Palmer's immense popularity made him a major force behind golf's huge following as it entered the TV age, and that popularity remains to this day.

CAREER HIGHLIGHTS

• Palmer won his first major, the Masters, in 1958. He would go on to win three more (1960, 1962, 1964).

• In 1960 he won the U.S. Open with one of the greatest comebacks in the history of the game (see page 213). That year he received *Sports Illustrated*'s "Sportsman of the Year" award.

• In 1961 he won the British Open at a time when most Americans didn't bother making the trip. When he won again in 1962, he helped turn golf's oldest championship back into the must-win tournament it once was.

• In 1960 and 1962 he led the PGA Tour with eight victories for the season.

• From 1960 to 1963 alone, he won 29 tournaments.

• In 1964 he became golf's all-time money leader with more than $500,000. In 1968 he became the first golfer to earn $1 million in his career.

• He won the Vardon Trophy for lowest scoring average four times in the 1960s and was named the Associated Press Athlete of the Decade.

• He played on six winning Ryder Cup teams and was the winning team captain twice.

• Palmer won 62 events on the PGA Tour, fourth on the all-time victories list. He won 10 more times on the Champions Tour, which he helped become a successful tour of its own.

• He is tied with Jack Nicklaus for the most consecutive years with at least one victory (17, from 1955 to 1971).

• Palmer was elected to the World Golf Hall of Fame in 1974.

• The Palmer Course Design Company has designed over 200 golf courses around the world.

• In 1995 he helped to raise the necessary $80 million to cofound the Golf Channel.

• In 2004 Palmer competed in his 50th—and last—Masters Tournament.

*   *   *

"Golf satisfies the soul and frustrates the intellect. It is at the same time rewarding and maddening—and it is without a doubt the greatest game mankind has ever invented."

—**Arnold Palmer**

GOLF TREK

Space: the final back nine. These are the voyages of astronaut Alan Shepard. His primary mission: to seek out new lies, new par-3s—to boldly golf where no man has golfed before!

S TARDATE: FEBRUARY 6, 1971
The *Apollo 14* crew has been on the Moon for nearly 36 hours. At the end of the second extravehicular activity assignment, 47-year-old astronaut Alan B. Shepard, Jr. revealed that he'd smuggled on some extra equipment for the mission: the detachable head of his six-iron and two golf balls. The following transcript comes directly from official NASA records:

> **Shepard:** Houston, while you're looking that up, you might recognize what I have in my hand as the handle for the contingency sample return. It just so happens to have a genuine six-iron on the bottom of it. In my left hand, I have a little white pellet that's familiar to millions of Americans. I'll drop it down. Unfortunately, the suit is so stiff, I can't do this with two hands, but I'm going to try a little sand-trap shot here. [His first swing misses.]

> **Ed Mitchell:** You got more dirt than ball that time.

> **Shepard:** Got more dirt than ball. Here we go again. [His second swing pushes the ball about three feet.]

> **Mission Control:** That looked like a slice to me, Al.

> **Shepard:** Here we go. Straight as a die. One more. [His third swing finally connects and sends the ball off-camera.]

> **Shepard:** Miles and miles and miles…

> **Mission Control:** Very good, Al.

EPILOGUE

So in addition to being the first American in space (he made his first flight in 1961), Alan Shepard was, and still is, the only human to play golf on the Moon. Actual estimates of how far his ball went—and remember this is a golfer talking—were about 300 yards. Shepard brought the club back to Earth, where it is now on display at the USGA Hall of Fame in New Jersey. The golf ball, as far as we know, is still on the Moon.

Golf lingo: a "Captain Kirk" is a shot that goes "where no man has gone before."

SCANDAL!

*Baseball has its Black Sox, boxing its fixed matches,
football its wardrobe malfunction. Golf, sadly,
has had its share of scandal, as well.*

EVENT: The 1985 Indonesian Open
GOLFER: Vijay Singh
THE STORY: Singh, a native of Fiji, joined the Asian Tour in 1982 and won his first victory at the 1984 Malaysian PGA Championship when he was 21 years old. Things were looking good for Singh…until the Indonesian Open. At the end of the second round, tournament officials disqualified Singh for cheating. He doctored his scorecard, they said, making it read one stroke better than it actually was. That one stroke would have allowed him to make the cut and continue playing through the weekend, but he was suspended from the Asian Tour for two years instead.

Singh has vigorously denied that he cheated. He admits that his scorecard was incorrect, but claims the son of an "Indonesian VIP" that he was partnered with was the one who changed it. "To save some embarrassment," he said, "they chose to get me." But don't cry for Singh: he went on to become the number-one golfer in the world, joining the PGA Tour in 1993 and eventually winning more than 20 events—nine of them in 2004 alone.

EVENT: The 1997 Lancome Trophy, Versailles, France
GOLFER: Mark O'Meara
THE STORY: After the tournament, Sweden's Jarmo Sandelin accused the winner, O'Meara, of cheating. He said that when O'Meara replaced his ball on the 15th green during the final round, he put it closer to the hole than his marker indicated. O'Meara denied the claim. Unfortunately for him they had video. It shows him putting the ball a little closer than it should have been. O'Meara insisted that it was an honest mistake, saying that it was "maybe a quarter-inch, half-inch" closer. "To expect someone to replace their ball in exactly the same spot where they mark it is impossible," he said. Officials watched the video and took no action, so O'Meara kept the trophy. He had won the tournament

---

"The 19th hole…the only one where golfers don't complain about the shots they take." —Anon.

by one stroke…over Sandelin. (See next entry.)

EVENT: The 1998 Lancome Trophy Championship, Versailles, France

GOLFER: Jarmo Sandelin

THE STORY: After the third round of play, Europe's number-one player, Ireland's Lee Westwood, refused to sign Sandelin's card, accusing him of cheating. He claimed Sandelin had hit a moving ball with his putter and hadn't penalized himself. (According to the rules, if you don't penalize yourself, you're disqualified.) Sandelin denied the charge and officials backed him up, but it didn't matter—he went on to lose the tournament by two strokes, anyway. "I don't appreciate it when one player doesn't trust another," he said later. (See previous entry.)

EVENT: The 1958 Masters

GOLFERS: Ken Venturi and Arnold Palmer

STORY: During the final round, Palmer and Venturi were paired together. At the par-3 12th hole, Palmer hit his tee shot over the green. The ball landed with such force that it became embedded in the ground. Palmer thought he was entitled to "relief," meaning he thought the rules allowed him to pick the ball up, clean it, and drop it and play it from where it stopped. But the official on hand disagreed. So Palmer played the ball and got a double bogey 5 for the hole. Then he dropped *another* ball and played *it*. He got a 3 with that one. Which ball counted? A few holes later the top officials ruled that the 3 was the proper score. Palmer went on to win his first Masters—by one stroke. Venturi finished two strokes back. But Venturi wasn't satisfied with the ruling and accused Palmer of signing an incorrect scorecard. He said that Palmer should have announced his intention to play two balls before he hit the first one. Palmer countered that he *did* announce it, and that Venturi just hadn't heard him.

The story—and the controversy—traveled around the golf world for decades and was almost forgotten…until Venturi, a CBS golf analyst for 35 years, brought it back up again in his 2004 book, *Getting Up & Down: My 60 Years in Golf*. He stood by his contention that Palmer should have announced he was going to play two balls. "Nobody, not even Palmer, is bigger than the game," he wrote. The only problem: most experts say he's wrong.

Shortly after the book came out, Tom Meeks, senior director of rules and competition for the U.S. Golf Association, said that even if Palmer *hadn't* announced that he was playing a second ball, the rules still stood with him. Rule 11-5 of the 1958 rule book says:

> Should the competitor fail to announce in advance his procedure or selection, the score with the second ball shall be his score for the hole if played in accordance with the Rules.

And that means Palmer's 3 stands.

Oddly enough, Venturi *still* says that Palmer deserved a 5 for the hole and won the 1958 Masters improperly. He strongly insists that he never accused Palmer of cheating, but simply of not knowing the rules. Venturi had good timing, though: his book came out a month before Palmer was to play his 50th (and final) Masters. Result: the accusation—and the book—got a lot of press.

EVENT: The 2002 British Open
GOLFERS: 47 golfers from the Nigerian PGA
STORY: Before the tournament, 47 golfers from Nigeria paid the $160 entry fee to get into the qualifying rounds of the competition. Apparently, officials at the Royal and Ancient Golf Club of St. Andrews didn't find that strange and took the golfers' money. But only four of the "golfers" actually showed up. It turned out that the others had used the event as a scheme to illegally obtain visas to get into the country. Officials with the Nigerian PGA promised to investigate the incident and to make sure it never happens again.

*   *   *

WORD ORIGIN

Word: Tee

Origin: "The first *tees* were just handfuls of sand or dirt off which golf balls were hit. The Scottish word was first recorded in 1673 as *teaz*, but people seemed to think this was the plural of tee, so over the years 'tee' became the singular form." (From *Grand Slams, Hat Tricks & Alley-oops*, by Robert Hendrickson)

A *Golf Digest* study found that the driving distance for the average golfer is 205 yards.

THE PHYSICS OF GOLF

Get out your calculator—we're going golfing!

SWINGIN'

Golf is a game of calculations and angles. The best golfers in the world have learned not just to pick the right club for the right shot, but how to take into account such factors as wind, temperature, air density, and the unique lie of any given fairway or green. Some have even studied the effects of plaid pants and striped shirts on their bunker play. (Their findings: it only affects *other* people's bunker play.) The mind of a pro golfer acts like a computer, running complicated programs to determine the optimum trajectory for each shot.

There are many different types of golf clubs (see page 255). Here's what happens when you actually swing one. High school science teaches that force equals mass times acceleration. In golf, this means that the force applied to the ball is equal to the mass of the clubhead multiplied by the speed it is traveling when it hits the ball. In other words, the faster the swing, the longer the drive.

But a really fast swing must also be efficient. The ideal swing is one that moves the clubhead in a perfect circular arc. Energy spent trying to get the club into the proper position to hit the ball is wasted and will slow the clubhead down, decreasing the distance of the shot.

And the shaft of the club affects energy, too. If you've ever seen a slow-motion shot of a golfer's swing, then you've seen how much the shaft bends. That's stored energy. If your timing is right, that stored energy is released in a whip motion as it hits the ball. That's why there are flex ratings on shafts. A golfer with a very fast swing wants a stiff shaft—it stores the energy of the swing better than a very flexible one would. Beginners will have more success with clubs with flexible shafts.

MAKING CONTACT

Now you've got your speeding clubhead—but that's only part of the program. That speeding head has to hit the ball correctly if the ball is going to go where you want it to go. This brings out the essential difference between striking the ball with a wood (especially the driver) and an iron.

Think of the golf swing as drawing a U-shape with the clubhead. When you swing a driver correctly, the bottom of the U comes *before* the ball. That means the clubhead makes contact with the ball just after it's reached its lowest point and is on the rise. When you swing an iron correctly, the bottom of the U comes *after* the ball, meaning the clubhead makes contact with the ball before it hits its lowest point and is still descending. That's why when you see a good golfer swing an iron, you see him take a divot—this is the ground in front of the ball. With a driver, there is no divot taken because the ball is generally sitting on a tee. These two different types of contact affect the most important part of what happens next: the spin of the ball.

AERODYNAMICS

The spin of a flying golf ball affects how straight and far it will go. This was first discovered in 1887 by British scientist P. G. Tait. He was taught in his youth that "all spin is detrimental," so he worked very hard at developing a golf swing that would produce very little spin on the ball. Then he started experimenting with golf balls, attaching string to them and having different people hit them. He discovered that a ball spinning quickly on a horizontal axis—with the top of the ball spinning toward the golfer—actually stays in the air longer than a ball with little or no spin. (As for his golf game, he said: "I understand it now, too late by 35 years at least.")

Here's how it works. A spinning golf ball creates the aerodynamic force called *lift*—the same as an airplane. This is because of a law of physics known as the Bernouilli Principle (named after Daniel Bernouilli, who discovered it in 1738), which says that when the speed of a fluid, liquid, or gas increases, its pressure decreases. Simply put: a golf ball with backspin is inducing the air it meets to pass more quickly over its top than its bottom—meaning there will be less air pressure above it and more below it. Result: lift.

Spin also affects the ball when it lands. Getting back to the difference between the driver and the iron: an iron's glancing contact produces more spin than a driver's square contact. In driving, you don't want the backspin—you want the ball to roll on contact. With irons, especially highly lofted ones, you want a lot of spin to create lift and to keep the ball from rolling when it lands.

HOOKS AND SLICES

Now that we know backspin is good, here's the bad news: if the axis of the spin isn't perfectly (or close to) horizontal, then the spin will not only not help the shot—it can make it worse. That off-horizontal spin is caused by not making square contact with the ball. For right-handers, if your swing comes from too close to your body and across the ball from left to right as it hits it—known as an inside-to-out swing—it will give the ball a counter-clockwise spin. By the Bernoulli Principle, this will create lift on the right side of the ball (lift doesn't neccessarily have to be "up"), causing it to curve to the left. That's what causes a hook. If your swing comes from too far from your body, back across the ball from right to left—an outside-to-in swing—it'll make the ball spin clockwise and the lift will curve it to the right. That's a slice.

DIMPLES

On page 243 we told you about the history of the golf ball and how golfers realized that scarred balls flew better than smooth ones, and how that led to golf balls with dimples. But we didn't tell you *how* the dimples help. Simple explanation: dimpled balls, by their effect on airflow around the ball, create less drag than smooth balls.

A rough, dimpled surface creates a more turbulent airflow around a ball than a smooth one—that's easily understood, even by nonphysicists. That flow is called a *turbulent boundary layer*. A smooth ball creates a more streamlined flow, called a *laminar boundary layer*. You'd think the smooth flow would create less drag, and it does when it's on the ball, but the flow is also prone to "separation," meaning that it breaks from the surface of the ball quickly. This creates a large and turbulent wake—and *that* creates a lot of drag.

The turbulent flow causes more drag on the ball initially, but it also tends to "hug" the ball as it flies, not separating from the surface until much later than a smooth ball. That creates a much narrower wake and much less drag, so your turbulently flying dimpled golf ball flies a lot farther—as much as twice the distance of a smooth ball.

A fully loaded deluxe Deusenberg Estate Golf Cart costs about $28,000.

GOT A WEATHER IRON?

Weather has some obvious effects on the golf ball, too. Raindrops act as resistance on the ball and sap its momentum; hitting a ball into a headwind is more difficult than hitting with a tailwind. But what about less obvious factors like air density or the elevation of a particular golf course?

Dense air offers more resistance to the traveling ball than thinner air would. It slows the ball down, decreasing distance. Air density is determined by pressure and temperature. Higher elevations have less air pressure, which means less air density. Result: golf balls travel farther in the mountains than they do at sea level.

Similarly, warm air is less dense than cold air. With the pressure the same, the ball will go farther on a hot day than on a cold one. Contrary to popular belief, humidity has little effect on driving distances. Humid air is slightly less dense than dry air, but not enough to make much difference.

So now, with the right club for the shot—adjusted according to weather conditions and air density—and with the ideal swing at the proper speed to generate enough force and applying the correct amount of backspin so as to gain lift appropriate to how the wind happens to be blowing at any given moment...all you'll need to work on is your chip shots and putting game.

*   *   *

GREAT GOLF GIFTS

• **Poor Putter's Pacifier.** "For the crybaby golfer," a golf ball with a pacifier attached.

• **THE EXPLODER!** This ball explodes into a cloud of talc when struck.

• **Wacky Flat Top Tees.** "Carry these tees for a mooching friend. The angled, flat top makes is impossible to tee up a ball."

• *Everything I Know About Golf*, by <u>Your Friend's Name Here</u>. Give him this hardcover, leatherbound book, with gold-pressed lettering on the cover...and 228 blank pages inside.

• **Camouflaged Golf Ball.** "The ULTIMATE Hard-to-Find Gift!"

PASTURE GOLF

*Ah, golf. Crowded courses, long waits, exorbitant greens fees,
irritating dress codes. Has your "nice walk spoiled" gotten more
spoiled in recent years? If so, pasture golf may be the perfect antidote.*

COMMON SCENTS

David Jones is a sheep rancher in Lillooet, British Columbia. In the mid-1980s, he was losing too many of his sheep
to the coyotes, mountain lions, and bears that lived in the surrounding wilderness. He had to do something to protect his business. So he thought about the different ways he might keep
predators off his land...until he came up with a good one: intro-
duce the scent of *their* predators—humans—into the area. But
how could he do that?

Jones also happened to be an avid golfer, which was tough in
Lillooet because there were no courses nearby. He figured that
there had to be other aspiring golfers in the area, so he got some
flags, dug a few holes...and soon he had a "golf course" right in the
middle of his 50-acre sheep pasture. For a couple of bucks, locals
were welcome to come out to the pasture and play a round of golf
in and around the sheep. With any luck, Jones figured, the golfers
would stink the place up enough to keep the predators away.

SWEET SMELL OF SUCCESS

In 1985 Jones estimated that there were maybe 100 golfers living in
the area; today the Sheep Pasture Golf Course attracts more than
15,000 golfers a year, each of whom pays $9 for a round of nine
holes (or $15 for 18 holes). And their scent has driven predators off
the land, just as Jones had hoped. In the nearly 20 years that the
course has been in business, he hasn't lost a single sheep to predators—or to golfers. It's pretty easy to play around the flock, and even
when a sheep does get hit by a stray shot from time to time, there's
no harm done. "Sheep are pretty well padded," Jones says.

If you think about it, golf at the Sheep Pasture Golf Course
probably has a lot in common with what golf was like hundreds of
years ago. The Scots didn't play on overwatered, overgroomed
fairways designed by landscape architects, they played on pastures

Lloyd Mangrum was once assessed a penalty for blowing a bug off of his ball.

where natural grasses were kept low by sheep, cows, and other ani-
mals. Nor did they have to deal with crowds, inconvenient tee
times, or any of the other frustrations associated with the modern
golf experience. If a Scotsman had a ball, a stick, and a place to
swing it, he had everything he needed to enjoy a round of golf.

BACK TO BASICS

Jones probably didn't realize it at the time—he was just trying to
protect his sheep—but he was part of a growing movement to take
golf out of overpriced, overcrowded golf courses and return it to its
simpler roots. Another pioneer in the pasture golf movement is an
Oregon golfer named Bruce Manclark. In 2001 he played a round
of golf at a neglected course in Alaska called Fishhook Glen. "It
was totally raw, totally unmanicured," he says, "but at the same
time amazingly beautiful and really fun." The experience prompted
Manclark and his wife to launch a Web site to help promote odd,
unconventional, and affordable "courses."

The Manclarks started out by listing the courses they knew of
and invited visitors to the site to post their own listings. At last
count, the site lists more than 60 courses in 23 states and six countries around the world, and the number is growing. Some courses
have only nine holes; others have 18. In most places listed, a round
of golf will set you back $10 or less.

PASTURE GOLF AROUND THE WORLD

Annie Lake Golf Course, Whitehorse, Yukon Territory
Description: The course has sand for greens instead of grass. $2
for 18 holes. Par 66.
Comments: "Greens must be swept after play. You can play as late
as you want in the summer months, but don't forget the mosquito
repellent."

Downs Golf Club, Downs, Kansas
Description: A small, no-frills nine-hole community golf course.
$3.00 for nine holes. Par 35.
Comments: "Outside toilets on hole 1 and hole 3. Shake the door
before entering to chase out the bull snakes."

Frozen Lake Golf, in the Matanuska Valley near Palmer, Alaska

Description: A frozen lake. Free. Par varies each winter depending on how the new course is laid out.

Comments: "Rules of lake golf vary depending on course conditions, size of lake, and lake usage (watch out for the ice fishermen). Interestingly, lake golf is best played wearing ice skates."

Bert Lee Park Golf Course, Flagstaff, Arizona

Description: The course is in a privately owned meadow. Free with permission of owner. Nine holes. Par 35.

Comments: "There are no greens on this course so don't worry about bringing your putter. We just have PVC pipes for pins. We had to give up on flags, because the elk kept chewing them off."

PASTURE GOLF TOURNAMENTS

Cowpatty Golf Classic, Lytton Springs, Texas

Description: Held each spring in a cow pasture outside of Lytton Springs, Texas. "Entry fee is $15, a 12-pack of beer or soft drinks, one Miller Lite per player, and two bags of ice per team."

Comments: "No tees allowed—must use cowpatties, horse doo, or fire ant mounds."

Cow Pie International Golf Tournament, held each Fourth of July at the Greens at Yanik Manor, Lebanon, Oregon

Description: A three-hole course in a horse and cow pasture. Holes are played three times for a total of nine holes. Par 36.

Comments: Tournament rules: "Watch for livestock. One added stroke for hitting a cow with a golf ball. No pushing your team members or other team members into pond (unless they deserve it). No playing naked until after dusk. Must have a beer in hand at all times. Cheating allowed if everyone on team agrees."

Cowboy Cow Pasture Golf Tournament, Nenzel, Nebraska

Description: Held in a cow pasture every June. The $30 entry fee includes dinner, a barn dance, and the use of a horse if you don't bring your own.

Comments: "Participants must ride horses between holes. On one hole golfers must tee off from a cow chip, on another, a praire dog village will be a hazard. The exact penalty for losing a ball in a prairie dog hole has not yet been decided."

Our favorite hole: the Cow Pasture Open includes a toilet seat hole.

GOLF IS...

More random thoughts on this perplexing game.

"...a game in which the ball lies poorly and the players well."
—**Art Rosenbaum**

"...a passion, an obsession, a romance, a nice acquaintance-ship with trees, sand, and water."
—**Bob Ryan**

"...not, on the whole, a game for realists. By its exactitudes of measurements it invites the attention of perfectionists."
—**Heywood Hale Broun**

"...like solitaire. When you cheat, you cheat only yourself."
—**Tony Lema**

"...20% mechanics and tech-nique. The other 80% is phi-losophy, humor, tragedy, romance, melodrama, com-panionship, camaraderie, cussedness, and conversation."
—**Grantland Rice**

"...the most overtaught and least learned human behavior. If they taught sex the way they taught golf, the race would have died out years ago."
—**Jim Murray**

"...a game invented by the same people who think music comes out of a bagpipe."
—**Anonymous**

"...essentially an exercise in masochism conducted out-of-doors."
—**Paul O'Neil**

"...in part, a game; but only in part. It is also in part a reli-gion, a fever, a vice, a mirage, a frenzy, a fear, a joy, a thrill, a disease, an uplift, a brooding, a melancholy, a dream of yester-day, and a hope for tomorrow."
—***New York Tribune*** **(1916)**

"...a day spent in a round of strenuous idleness."
—**William Wordsworth**

"...mystifying. It would seem that if a person has hit a golf ball correctly a thousand times, he should be able to duplicate the performance at will. But this is certainly not the case."
—**Bobby Jones**

"Golf is golf. You hit the ball, you go find it. Then you hit it again."
—**Lon Hinkle**

Clint Eastwood and Jack Lemmon are both members of the Golf Nuts Society of America.

SUPER SHOTS

There may be some doubters out there who think golfers are just wimpy guys in plaid pants. Obviously, they've never heard of these golfing supermen, athletes who scorned adversity, never gave up, and created some of the most memorable moments in sports history.

NOT BAD FOR AN OLD GUY

The Player: Hale Irwin

The Event: The 1990 U.S. Open at Medinah Golf Club, Illinois

The Shot: Hale Irwin had won the U.S. Open in 1974 and 1979, but by 1990, at age 45, he wasn't considered a real threat to win, especially in a major—he hadn't won *any* PGA tournaments in five years. Yet at the final hole he was just a birdie away from tying leader Mike Donald. He had birdied four out of the last six holes to get this close, but this one was a little harder—a 45-foot putt on the notoriously difficult greens of Medinah.

Irwin confidently stroked the putt. The ball went up over a crown in the green, swept right to left more than six feet, and 45 feet later, dropped into the cup. The gallery exploded and the normally contained Irwin exploded with them. He jumped into the air and then ran a lap around the green, high-fiving every fan he came near. The next day he won the playoff by birdieing the sudden-death 19th hole…and became the oldest U.S. Open champion in history.

THE GUM TREE INCIDENT

Player: Arnold Palmer

Event: The 1964 Australian Wills Masters in Melbourne

The Shot: In the second round of the tournament, Palmer bogeyed the 9th hole. What's so special about that? His third shot came from 20 feet in the air. He had hooked his second shot into a gum tree next to the fairway—and it stayed there, lodged in the fork of two branches. Most golfers would have probably just gotten a new ball and shot again, counting the first stroke and adding a penalty stroke…but Palmer wasn't most golfers.

He got some fans to boost him up to the first branch of the tree and then he climbed the 20 feet to his ball—with his one-iron in his hand. He turned the club backward and hammer-stroked the ball with the butt of the head. It popped out of the fork and shot 30 yards forward, straight toward the pin. He followed that with a chip to the green and a putt to finish with a bogey. He didn't win the tournament, but he'd made a shot that golf fans will never forget.

THE COMEBACK KID

Player: Gene Sarazen

Event: The 1935 Masters, Augusta, Georgia

The Shot: In the final round of the tournament, things weren't looking good for Sarazen. He was down by two strokes to leader Craig Wood with just four holes to play. As he was getting ready for his second shot at the 15th, a roar went up in the distance: Wood had birdied the 18th. Sarazen was now down by three.

The 15th was a par-5. If he could get on the green in two shots, he'd have a chance to complete the hole in three strokes for an eagle and be just one behind the leader. He was 230 yards from the pin, and his caddie didn't want him to risk it. "He was the minister in town," Sarazen said later. "He told me that the collection box [at church] was light, so I should play conservative." Sarazen didn't take the advice. He took out his four-wood.

Golf legend Bobby Jones was watching the shot from about 50 yards away. He later described the shot like this: "His swing into the ball was so perfect and so free, one knew immediately that it was a gorgeous shot. I saw the ball strike the tongue of the green, bound slightly to the left, directly towards the hole, and then the whole gallery began dancing and shouting." Sarazen holed the shot. He'd gotten a double eagle (three under par on a single hole—the rarest shot in golf), and he was now tied with Wood. The next day he won a 36-hole playoff to complete the dramatic comeback.

Sarazen's double eagle is still called the most famous shot in the history of golf. It helped launch the fledgling tournament (it was only the second Masters) into international prominence and is still known as the "Shot Heard 'Round the World."

Bonus: It was this shot that coined the term "double eagle"—it was made up on the spot by sportswriters.

TEE HEE HEE

Golfing necessities: A flashlight, a machete, a shotgun, and some good jokes to tell while looking for your ball (again).

Two dimwitted golfers are teeing off on a foggy par-3. They can see the flag, but not the green. The first golfer hits his ball into the fog and the second golfer does the same. Then they proceed to the green to find their balls.

One ball is about six feet from the cup while the other had found its way into the cup for a hole in one. Both are playing the same brand of balls, and they can't figure out whose ball was whose.

They decide to ask the golf pro to rule. After congratulating both golfers on their fine shots, the golf pro asks, "Which one of you used the orange ball?"

Golfer: "Caddiemaster, this boy isn't even eight years old!"
Caddiemaster: "Better for you, sir. He probably can't count past ten."

Q: Why do golfers always carry two pairs of pants with them?
A: Just in case they get a hole in one.

First golfer: "Your trouble is that you're not addressing the ball correctly."
Second golfer: "Yeah, well, I've been polite to the damn thing long enough."

Golfer: "I just got a new set of golf clubs for my wife."
Caddie: "Great trade, sir."

Q: How many golfers does it take to screw in a light bulb.
A: Fore!
Q: No, really. How many golfers does it take to screw in a light bulb?
A: Five. Okay, fine—it's seven!

Joel got home from his Sunday round of golf later than usual and very tired. "Bad day at the course?" his wife asked.

"Everything was going fine," he said. "Then Harry had a heart attack and died on the 10th tee."

"Oh, my," said his wife. "That's awful!"

"You're not kidding. For the whole back nine it was hit the ball, drag Harry, hit the ball, drag Harry…"

Hazards at the Stanley Golf Course in the Falkland Islands include minefields.

OLD TOM MORRIS

If you love golf, say "thank you" to this guy.

HOME IN THE HOME OF GOLF
It would be difficult to exaggerate Morris's contributions to golf. In the 50-year span during which the game evolved into an international professional sport, he influenced everything from how balls and clubs were made to how a course was laid out and—as one of the best golfers of his era—how the game should be played.

Morris was born in St. Andrews, Scotland, in 1821, where, he would often say, "We were all born with webbed feet and a golf club in our hand." He began his career in 1837 as an apprentice to featherie ball-maker Allan Robertson (called the "world's first golf professional"). Twelve years later, Morris opened his own ball- and club-making shop. In 1851 "Old Tom"—so called because his son, also a champion golfer, was also named Tom—became the first "Keeper of the Greens" at the Prestwick Club in west Scotland, and would be instrumental in hosting the world's first professional golf championship, the British Open. He won four of the first eight titles.

BACK TO ST. ANDREWS
In 1864 Morris went back home to become the first greenskeeper at the Royal and Ancient Golf Club of St. Andrews. He stayed at St. Andrews for nearly 40 years, where he became best known for his genius as a course architect. His design work can still be seen on parts of the Old Course, as well as on some of Scotland's most famous courses, including Muirfield, Carnoustie, and Royal County Down.

When Morris died in 1908 at age 86, his mourners flooded the streets of St. Andrews. Scottish golf historian James K. Robertson would write of him: "As St. Andrews became increasingly a mecca of golfers, so too did the sturdy patriarchal bearing of Old Tom come to symbolize all that was the finest in Scottish character and in the ancient Scottish game." The 18th hole of the Old Course is named in his honor, and Old Tom's portrait still hangs in the R&A's clubhouse.

Three German golfers once played three different continents in one day.

CURIOUS RULES

*Loony laws even make it into the world of golf.
Here are some official—but odd—rules of the game.*

• Other than glasses or contact lenses, you're not allowed to enhance your vision or estimate distance from the hole through the use of binoculars, a range finder, sextant, or global positioning system.

• The dress code of the PGA Tour dictates players wear long pants and collared shirts. In 1992 Mark Wiebe showed up at the Anheuser-Busch Classic in shorts—to deal with the 102-degree temperature—and was fined $500.

• If an opponent asks how many strokes you've taken on a hole, you must tell the truth.

• When you hit a ball out of play, you must take a "drop," by holding it out at arm's length, shoulder high, and letting it go. You must then play it from that spot. At one time, however, the rule was that you dropped the ball over your shoulder. Result: the ball would often bounce off the player's body and roll away, so the rule was changed.

• If a ball comes to rest near a bird's nest, the player may take a drop without penalty, provided that playing through would damage the nest.

• A free drop is also permitted for directly dangerous situations, such as if the ball lands near, on top of, or inside an alligator, rattlesnake, or bees' nest.

• Drops are not allowed in plant-related dangerous situations. If the ball falls into a patch of poison ivy or poison oak, for example, golfers must play it where it lies.

• The PGA assesses a two-stroke penalty for accidentally hitting your partner with a ball…but no penalty for hitting anybody else.

• If wind or an earthquake knocks your ball off the tee after you've addressed it, it counts as a stroke under an "acts of God" rule.

• In years past, golfers couldn't legally replace balls on the green

---

Rule at Yellowknife Golf Club, Canada: "No penalty assessed when ball carried off by raven."

with markers because maneuvering around other players' balls while putting was considered part of the game. The rules were changed in the 1950s after several pro tournaments were decided by players intentionally hitting their opponents' balls to move them farther from the hole.

• It's possible to become an amateur again after going pro, but you have to do it within five years of becoming a pro.

• In PGA tournaments, once a player gets to the ball, he is penalized a stroke for taking longer than 45 seconds to hit it.

• It's against the rules to ask for advice from anyone but your caddie or partner. You also can't give advice, solicited or not.

• Straddling the ball and putting it croquet-style was banned in 1968. The USGA banned the use of pool cues for putting in 1895.

• If a ball is hit off the course, onto the parking lot, and comes to rest underneath a parked car, the ball must remain in place. The car should immediately be moved and the ball played where it lies.

• Ant hills are considered "movable obstructions" and may be moved if they get in the way of playing a ball.

• A golfer may move another player's ball, but only under one of two conditions: 1) an opponent's ball may be lifted and replaced with a marker if it is physically in the way of one's shot; 2) an opponent's ball may be moved if the golfer feels the other person's ball is mentally interfering with his play.

*　　*　　*

WHATEVER IT TAKES TO WIN

Jack Nicklaus and Lee Trevino were tied for the lead at the end of the 1971 U.S. Open, forcing a playoff. Shortly before the first playoff hole, Trevino pulled a rubber snake out of his bag and tossed it to Nicklaus. Nicklaus had seen the snake earlier and had a pretty good idea that it was meant for him. He caught it and playfully threw it back to Trevino…but the tactic worked: Nicklaus hit his balls into bunkers on the second and third holes. Trevino won the tournament by three strokes, becoming the only player to ever beat Jack Nicklaus in a major playoff.

In 1968 the LPGA officially sanctioned miniskirts for tournament play.

THE GHOSTS OF GOLF

Blaming a lousy golf game on supernatural forces may not be so far-fetched after all.

THE GALLOPING GHOST

Location: Galloping Hill Golf Course, Kenilworth, NJ

Ghost Story: Several people have reported seeing a headless man riding a galloping horse across the golf course. Ghost hunter Dennis William Hauck, who investigated the hauntings, thinks it's the ghost of a Hessian soldier who fought for the British during the Revolutionary War—the same ghost that's been sighted in other New Jersey locations. According to Hauck, the fairway apparition could be the original inspiration for the "headless horseman" in Washington Irving's classic tale, "The Legend of Sleepy Hollow."

FAIRWAY TO HEAVEN

Location: The Victoria Golf Course, Victoria, British Columbia

Ghost Story: One of the main features of Victoria's annual Ghosts of Victoria Festival is the story of Doris Gravlin, who they say was strangled on the golf course by her husband, Victor, in 1936. According to one version of the story, he dragged her body across the 7th fairway to the beach, and then hid it under a pile of logs. Other accounts say he killed her on the 7th green and then buried her in a sand trap. Ever since then, she has repeatedly appeared on the course, described by festival organizers as a "gliding figure in white, twinkling lights, or a pulsating globe of light." She also spooks cars near the fairway by sometimes "passing right through their windshields."

THE WHITE WITCH OF ROSE HALL

Location: The Ritz-Carlton White Witch Golf Course, Montego Bay, Jamaica

Ghost Story: White Witch gets its name from Annie Palmer, a practitioner of voodoo and former owner of the 6,000-acre estate where the golf course now sits. In the 1800s, Palmer was the brutal mistress of the more than 2,000 slaves who worked her sugar plan-

---

18% of all money spent on sporting goods in the U.S. is used to buy golf equipment.

tation. After a slave rebellion in the 1830s, Annie Palmer, the White Witch, was found murdered in her bed. Since then, her ghost haunts the bedrooms and stairways of the Great House, known as Rose Hall.

BANKRUPT BERNIE

Location: Poolesville Golf Course, Maryland

Ghost Story: Even though it's only been there for about 40 years, this Maryland course is known as the most haunted in the United States. Visitors have reported seeing lights and TVs turn on and off by themselves, doors opening and closing, a figure standing in the clubhouse or walking down the stairs, and even someone touching them. People who know the place's history say the ghost is Bernie Siegel, the man who built the course and clubhouse, and then committed suicide when the failed project left him bankrupt in 1966. Why does he haunt the place? According to local legend, Bernie is so bitter that he refuses to leave the place that drove him to ruin.

STILL HANGING AROUND

Location: Fort MacLeod Golf Club, Alberta, Canada

Ghost Story: This course was built on the site of an old Royal Canadian Mounted Police fort. In the early 1900s, two smugglers were hanged near what is now the 2nd tee box and buried under the area of the 1st fairway. Sometimes, staff and players say, you can see two ghostly figures "hanging" above the 2nd tee.

UNREQUITED

Location: Upminster Golf Club, Essex, England

Ghost Story: This course's clubhouse was built as a monastery in the 1100s and became a manor house in 1653. The lord of the manor fell in love with a local woman who did not return his affections. Furious, he kidnapped and imprisoned her in a hidden room. She eventually died there, her body entombed within the manor walls. And to this day her ghost, a figure in a long white gown, is sometimes seen moving around the house. Club members have named her Mary, and some believe they'll find her bones one day…when they find the hidden room behind the walls of the clubhouse's bar.

BABE

The other Babe.

CHAMPION: Babe Zaharias
BACKGROUND: Born Mildred Ella Didrikson in Port Arthur, Texas, on June 26, 1914.

HER STORY: She was a true tomboy who, as a young girl, loved sports and quickly found out that she was very good—better than most of the boys. (The neighborhood boys nicknamed her the "Babe," for her Babe Ruth–esque batting.) In the 1932 Olympic Games, Zaharias won gold medals in the javelin toss and the 80-meter hurdles, and a silver medal in the high jump. She set new world records in almost every event. Then she discovered golf.

Many men give a polite nod to women golfers—but don't do it with this one. Bobby Jones said the Babe was one of the top ten golfers ever to play the game. He meant women *and* men. Her record as a golfer is possibly the best record of any athlete playing any game in the modern era of sports.

CAREER HIGHLIGHTS

• The Babe won 55 amateur and professional golf events in her career, including the U.S. Women's Amateur tournament in 1946.

• Over a 14-month stretch from 1946 to 1947, she won 14 consecutive tournaments and 17 overall. Later in 1947, she won another 12 straight tournaments. That run included the 1947 British Women's Amateur, making her the first American to win the event.

• After turning pro in 1948—at the age of 34—she won 41 tournaments, including ten majors.

• If all those achievements aren't impressive enough, add to the list the fact that her pro career lasted only seven years. Zaharias died from cancer at the age of 42.

• In 2000 *Golf Digest* made their own list of the 100 best golfers of all time: Babe was number 17...ahead of Nick Faldo, Larry Nelson, Ben Crenshaw, Hale Irwin, Johnny Miller, and Greg Norman.

DESPOT DUFFERS

*Think the foul-mouthed guy taking too long on the next
tee is a jerk? Try playing with one of these guys.*

KIM JONG IL. According to the North Korean government, dictator Kim is possibly the world's greatest golfer. Want proof? Kim claims to have shot an all-time world record of 34 (that's 38 under par) at Pyongyang Golf Club. That score includes five holes in one. Even more amazingly, it was *the first time Kim had ever played golf.* (Could this be true? Probably not…but who's going to argue with him?)

ADOLF HITLER. Hitler's plan to showcase "the master race" at the 1936 Berlin Olympics fizzled when American track star Jesse Owens won four gold medals. Undeterred, he organized the Hitler Cup, an international amateur golf competition in Baden-Baden. Although Germany had no golfing heritage, no well-known players, and only a few courses, the German team held a surprising five-stroke lead after two rounds. Excited by the possibility of a German win, Hitler went to Baden-Baden to present the prize (an amber-plated brass disk) personally, but quickly returned home when England and France surged ahead in the final rounds to best Germany.

FIDEL CASTRO. In 1959 Castro made plans to visit Washington, D.C., in hopes of meeting with President Eisenhower. Told the president enjoyed playing golf, Castro arranged for a tutoring session with fellow revolutionary (and one-time caddie) Che Guevara. Castro shot 150, and never got to meet Ike. After the Cuban revolution, Castro razed all but one of the country's dozen golf courses.

BENITO MUSSOLINI. Gene Sarazen was in Scotland for the 1927 British Open when he got a telegram from the American ambassador to Italy, asking if he'd go to Rome to play a round of golf with Mussolini. "Yeah," he replied, "but I don't think I'm going to get a great reception—I changed my name from Saraceni to Sarazen." He lunched with Il Duce, but never golfed with him. Mussolini, who apparently thought golf was a waste of time, looked over the golf course and said, "This should be a cornfield."

ANCIENT ORIGINS OF GOLF, PART III

Did golf come from paganica, colf, daiku, pukku-mikku,
gambuca, or some other game? Here are a few more
theories. (Part II of the story begins on page 83.)

CHOLE: THE FLEMISH THEORY

Some historians say golf's most direct recent ancestor was a game played by the Flemish peoples of northern France, parts of which are now Belgium. One theory, put forward by the prominent golf historian Robert Browning in his book *A History of Golf*, revolves around the Hundred Years' War, a long period of nearly constant warfare between England and France in the 14th and 15th centuries.

During the latter half of this bloody era, the embattled French leaders enlisted, and received, the help of another archenemy of the English—the Scots. Thousands of Scottish soldiers fought side-by-side with French soldiers well into the 1400s. There, says Browning, the Scots were introduced to a Flemish game called *chole*, which records show was already a popular sport in northern France as far back as the 1300s. The game: a rock or ball was hit by a curved stick toward a goal, such as a pole, a rock, or a gate, but could be miles away. According to Browning, the Scots took the game home, changed the goal to a hole, and—voilà—golf was born! (Chole is still played in Belguim and northern France today.)

JEU DE MAIL: THE FRENCH THEORY

Jeu de mail (game of mail) was played in France since at least the 1500s. In *The Story of Golf*, author George Per says of the game:

> Originally developed in Italy, it was a curious blend of billiards, croquet, and golf, played with long-handled mallets and large wooden balls within a well-defined area. The object was to hit the ball through one or more iron hoops, using the fewest possible strokes.

According to Anthoine Ravez, president of the French Croquet Federation, jeu de mail has an even farther-reaching influence. "Borrowed by the British around 1300," claims Ravez, "jeu de mail was modified over the centuries: the Scots made golf out of it, the Irish turned it into croquet. Louis XIV, suffering from being unable to play jeu de mail during the winter, miniaturized it on an indoor table and laid the basis of billiards."

What is known is that jeu de mail spread to England, where it was played as the game *pall-mall*. That game became so popular that the London street that runs between Buckingham Palace and Piccadilly Circus is still called Pall Mall.

CHUIWAN: THE CHINESE THEORY

Yes, you read correctly: golf was invented in China. At least that's what some experts, like Professor Ling Hongling in Lanxhou, China, say. Ling believes that games involving the hitting of a ball into a pit or hole were played in China as far back as 300 B.C. The earliest verified records date to A.D. 943, when *chuiwan*—literally, "whack ball"—is mentioned in Chinese literature.

Further proof: Ling claims that in the Palace Museum in Beijing is a Ming dynasty painting called "Xuanzong at Play." It is a painting of Emperor Xuanzong playing chuiwan. He says it shows the emperor with many different types of clubs to choose from, "caddies" (probably court eunuchs) waiting on him, and even sticks marking the holes with flags on them. Chuiwan was introduced to Europe by the Mongol armies of the khans in the 1300s. It found its way to Scotland, he says, where it was stolen and claimed as Scotland's invention.

TO SCOTLAND

Which theory is accurate? The answer is unknown. But whatever its ancient origin, few dispute that golf is Scotland's game. For that story, hook on over to page 233.

* * *

CADDIE-LAC

At the Talamore Golf Course in Southern Pines, North Carolina, golfers have the option of renting an old-fashioned golf cart for $20…or a llama caddie for about $100 (free llama T-shirt and hat included).

A fifth of the world's population earns $425 a year—the cost of a day's golf at Pebble Beach.

GOLF AND THE ENVIRONMENT

*For those who love the game, a well-manicured golf course
is one of the most beautiful sights in the world. But there are
also people who can look at the same course and see a poisoned
landscape built by snooty people for their own selfish pleasure.
Can these two groups ever see eye to eye?*

THE GRASS ISN'T ALWAYS GREENER

If you were out on the links on April 29, 1993, then you played golf on World No-Golf Day. The event was set up by an environmental group called the Global Anti-Golf Movement (GAG'M). Its charges were serious: golf courses contribute to water depletion, soil erosion, deforestation, and pesticide contamination. Building courses in fragile ecosystems also has a negative impact on endangered animal and plant species.

In addition to the environmental impact, GAG'M cites the social implications of the industry:

> Golf course and golf tourism development often creates skewed land use, displacing local communities…[and] aggressively promotes an elitist and exclusive resort lifestyle and notion of leisure.

In short, they say golf is a violation of human rights. The GAG'M manifesto calls for an "immediate moratorium on all golf course development."

TOMORROW'S GOLF COURSE TODAY

These claims have not fallen on deaf ears. While there will be no moratorium on building new courses, some of the biggest names in golf are looking for new ways to lessen its negative impact—both environmentally *and* socially. In 2000 Arnold Palmer became a partner in one of the game's boldest innovations ever: the Arbor-Links Home Course in Nebraska City, Nebraska.

The brainchild of the National Arbor Day Foundation, this 310-acre, 18-hole championship golf course is not only environmentally friendly, it's educational as well. Even more, it's an ongoing science project. Palmer's hope is that ArborLinks will be the prototype for the golf courses of the future. (He's so passionate about the course that he waived his usual designer fee.)

Some of the course's unique features:

• Each hole is named after a tree and has a placard explaining different aspects of golf's environmental impact.

• Instead of changing the topography of the land to adapt to the course, Palmer designed the course to work with the existing curves and hills in the area.

• Whenever possible, native grasses, shrubs, and trees were planted to more easily coexist with the ecosystem.

• The native planting reduces the need for pesticides, but when they are needed, organic pesticides are used.

• Different greens feature different species of grass and types of soil. Filters below the greens analyze the runoff to determine which combinations of soil and grass are the safest.

• Silt fencing protects trees and streams from erosion.

• Ponds and waterways are designed to catch the rest of the runoff, meaning the water needed for irrigation can be recycled.

• Areas not in play are off limits and act as wildlife sanctuaries.

SO FAR, SO GOOD

ArborLinks is still new, but preliminary results are promising. And not only have other new courses utilized some of these innovations, but environmental groups have begun working with existing courses to find inexpensive ways to improve them as well. "Close monitoring of ArborLinks," says Palmer, "will allow us the opportunity to educate our industry and the public by providing factual data, as well as provide a golf course that is fun, beautiful, and accessible to all golfers." In 2004 *Golf Digest* voted ArborLinks one of the ten best new courses in the United States.

*   *   *

THE ART OF GOLF

Art Lefelar, a 91-year-old golfer, has shot his age more than 1,600 times.

BING AND BOB

They made seven movies together and were two of Hollywood's biggest stars. But they weren't even in the PGA, so how'd they get into the World Golf Hall of Fame?

THE CROONER

Bing Crosby was inducted into the World Golf Hall of Fame in 1978. It wasn't for his abilities as a golfer—although he did play in the 1950 British Amateur Championship (score unknown), and even got his handicap down to 2 at one point. He received the honor because he may have done as much for the popularity and success of professional golf as Walter Hagen or Arnold Palmer did. It all started in 1937 when Crosby, already a huge star, decided to start a small golf tournament. The idea was that he and his Hollywood golfing buddies would get to play against the leading pros of the day. He probably wasn't aware of it then, but he had invented one of golf's most popular and lucrative formats—the "pro-am" (professional and amateur) tournament. He called it the Crosby Clambake and it was an immediate success.

After World War II, the tournament was moved to California's Monterey Peninsula, and is known today as the AT&T Pebble Beach National Pro-Am. The combination of the world's best golfers, the biggest Hollywood stars, the majestic Pebble Beach landscape, and the relaxed party atmosphere—guaranteed by the presence of such comic talent as Groucho Marx, Jack Lemmon, and Bill Murray—has made it one of the most popular tournaments on the PGA Tour. (In 2005 more than 135,000 people attended the event.) Crosby hosted the Clambake until 1977, the year he died (while playing golf—for that story, see page 221). Today two of Crosby's sons, Harry and Nathaniel, are on the board of directors of the Pebble Beach Pro-Am.

THE COMIC

Bob Hope was inducted into the World Golf Hall of Fame in 1983. He was a pretty good golfer and actually took lessons from Ben Hogan and got his handicap down to a 4. Like Crosby, Hope played in the 1951 British Amateur Championship. "I got beat in the first round by a man smoking a pipe," Hope said, "which of course

---

To qualify for the Bionic Invitational, you must have an artificial joint.

delighted Bing Crosby." (Crosby smoked a pipe.) But that's not how he got into the Hall of Fame. Along with Crosby, Hope is credited with helping golf become the hugely popular sport it is today.

Bob Hope became an international golf ambassador, traveling the world with his clubs, playing with American GIs, celebrities, and royalty. He played regular rounds with eight U.S. presidents, from Eisenhower to Clinton. He even teamed up with his long-time friend Arnold Palmer to win the pro-am at the 1962 Palm Springs Desert Classic. In 1965, he took over the Palm Springs event, making it the Bob Hope Chrysler Classic (Phyllis Diller would often caddie for him). It is still one of the PGA's most suc-cessful—and generous—events. As of 2004, it had generated more than $38 million for charities. Hope died in July 2003, a few months after his 100th birthday, leaving the world with—among many other things—some great observations on golf:

HOPE-FUL QUOTES

• "Golf is a game that needlessly prolongs the lives of some of our most useless citizens."

• "In the Bob Hope Golf Classic, the participation of President Gerald Ford was more than enough to remind you that the nuclear button was at one stage at the disposal of a man who might have either pressed it by mistake or else pressed it deliber-ately in order to obtain room service."

• "I went to play golf and tried to shoot my age, but I shot my weight instead."

• "Isn't it fun to go out on the course and lie in the sun?"

• "Titleist has offered me a big contract not to play its balls."

• *Upon receiving balls inscribed with "Happy Birthday, Bob"*: "Now, when I hit one in the water, the fish will know who to send it back to."

*   *   *

GOING...GOING...GONE

A Web site called *wowwhatawaytogo.com* once offered unique ways to dispose of departed loved ones' ashes: 1) mix them into clay and fire them into bone china plates; or 2) for a golfer, insert the ashes into golf balls, so he can keep playing...and playing...and playing...

Q: Which U.S. Open winner was on a 1988 postage stamp? A: Francis Ouimet (1913).

DUFFERS ANONYMOUS

It's been said that golf is the hardest sport to be good at. Here's proof.

HIGHEST SCORE WINS, RIGHT? What's the average winning score for a PGA Tour event? Around 270 for four rounds. In June 1985, amateur Angelo Spagnolo shot 257... in *one* round. *Golf Digest* named him "America's Worst Avid Golfer." (It was probably the 66 strokes on the 17th that sealed the deal.) Officials estimate he lost 60 balls that day—27 of them in the 17th hole's water hazard before officials let him skip to the green. His prize: a green plaid jacket, a parody of the Masters' green jacket.

THE COMMON TOUCH. Vice President Spiro Agnew played in the pro-am of the 1971 Bob Hope Desert Classic. He didn't last long. With his first two tee shots, he hit three spectators, then decided to pull out of the tournament "in the interest of public safety." When Agnew resigned the vice presidency in 1973, he was succeeded by another golfer known for hitting spectators with errant shots—Gerald Ford.

BUTTERFINGERS. Raymond Russell was heading to the 17th green at the 2001 Compass English Open with a virtual lock on a top-ten finish and the big prize money. The Scotsman wanted to clean his scuffed golf ball before attempting his putt, so he picked it up and tossed it to his caddie... who missed it. The ball rolled off the green, down a hill, and into a lake. They looked and looked, but couldn't find it. Result: A two-stroke penalty...and...no top-ten finish. Cost of the gaffe: $15,000.

INSERT YOUR OWN "BIRDIE" JOKE HERE. In 1987 the small African nation of Benin had no golf courses. This didn't stop Mathieu Boya from practicing his game. One day he was hitting golf balls in an open field adjacent to the Benin Air Base. He hit a high drive that struck a bird in flight. The stunned bird fell into the open cockpit of a fighter plane preparing for takeoff. The startled pilot lost control of the jet and crashed into four other planes parked on the runway. All five planes—the entire Benin Air Force—were destroyed.

GOLF MOVIE GUIDE

After reading several film reviews, we came up with this rating system:
EAGLE, *a must see;* BIRDIE, *very good;* PAR, *pretty good; and*
BOGEY, *not a great film, but hey…it features golf.*

TIN CUP (1996) *Romantic comedy*
Rating: EAGLE
Review: "From the opening song by the Texas Tornadoes
("A Little Bit Is Better than Nada") to the U.S. Open showdown
with Don Johnson, this Kevin Costner vehicle strikes the perfect
pitch. It helps that Costner can actually play. And it helps that
Cheech is around, too." (Brent Kelley, "Your Guide to Golf")
Stars: Kevin Costner, Rene Russo, Cheech Marin. *Director:* Ron
Shelton.

BANNING (1967) *Drama*
Rating: BOGEY
Review: "A golf pro has sporting and amorous adventures at a
country club. Tedious, complexly plotted melodrama of life among
the idle rich." (*Halliwell's Film and Video Guide*) *Stars:* Robert
Wagner, Anjanette Comer, Jill St. John. *Director:* Ron Winston.

THE LEGEND OF BAGGER VANCE (2000) *Drama*
Rating: PAR
Review: "This golfing fairy tale is classy, dignified, eminently big-
hearted. It's also simple-minded to the point of banality. Even so,
it's hard to resist falling in step with the onlookers who crowd the
links to follow a washed-up golfer as he tries to exorcise his
demons and reclaim the promise his life once held." (Associated
Press) *Stars:* Matt Damon, Will Smith. *Director:* Robert Redford.

BABE (1975) *Biography*
Rating: BIRDIE
Review: "Susan Clark won an Emmy for her performance as legendary athlete Babe Didrikson. Able to excel in practically any
sport, Babe becomes a pro golfer, tennis player, and billiard

---

Trivia quiz: In which film does James Bond play golf with the villain? A: *Goldfinger.*

champ. In 1940 she meets and marries ex-wrestler George Zaharias (Alex Karras), who becomes her mentor and manager and stays by her side during her three-year ordeal with terminal cancer." (Hal Erickson, *All Movie Guide*) *Director:* Buzz Kulik.

PAT AND MIKE (1952) *Comedy*
Rating: BIRDIE
Review: "Cameo appearances by a host of tennis and golf greats, including Babe Didrikson, stud this five-iron tale of athlete Katharine Hepburn and her promoter-manager Spencer Tracy at odds with each other on a barnstorming golf and tennis tour. As always, the Hepburn and Tracy chemistry assures good comedy." (*Video Movie Guide*) *Director:* George Cukor.

FOLLOW THE SUN (1951) *Biography*
Rating: BIRDIE
Review: "The biography of Ben Hogan, his ups and downs. Golf fans vote it great—others, the usual sports saga." (*Movies on TV*) *Stars:* Glenn Ford, Anne Baxter, Dennis O'Keefe. *Appearing as themselves:* Sam Snead, Jimmy Demaret. *Director:* Sidney Lanfield.

CADDYSHACK (1980) *Comedy*
Rating: BIRDIE
Review: Being golf fans, we at the BRI have a soft spot for this movie. Much to our dismay, though, it didn't get many good reviews. But we give it an Birdie because—however sophomoric the humor may be—*Caddyshack* somehow manages to portray what is both absurd and sublime about the game of golf. *Stars:* Chevy Chase, Rodney Dangerfield, Ted Knight, Michael O'Keefe, Bill Murray. *Director:* Harold Ramis.

HAPPY GILMORE (1996) *Comedy*
Rating: PAR
Review: "True Adam Sandler fans will love this movie, but non-Sandler fans also may enjoy it as *Happy Gilmore* is actually one of his tamer films. The jokes are simple yet effective, and while the plot is admittedly predictable, the movie still scores points with its comedic charm. It's no *Caddyshack*, but *Happy Gilmore* is still a great golf comedy." (Bullz-Eye.com) *Director:* Dennis Dugan.

ONCE YOU KISS A STRANGER (1969) *Psychological thriller*
Rating: BOGEY

Review: "Remake of Hitchcock's *Strangers on a Train*. A mentally unstable woman seduces a golf pro at a country club, then suggests that she murder his archrival and he kill the psychiatrist who wants to commit her to an asylum. Neither role is believable, and what suspense the story has comes through chase sequences or other such tried-and-true devices." (*TV Guide*) *Stars:* Paul Burke, Carol Lynley. *Director:* Robert Sparr.

THE CADDY (1953) *Comedy*
Rating: BIRDIE

Review: "Dean Martin and Jerry Lewis tee each other off on a PGA Tour. Introduced the Dean Martin classic "That's Amore" to the world of kitsch and features a bevy of real life golfers in cameo roles—including Sam Snead, Byron Nelson, and Julius Boros." (*The New York Times*) Director: Norman Taurog.

BOBBY JONES: STROKE OF GENIUS (2004) *Biography*
Rating: BOGEY

Review: "Any suspense that comes in watching Jim Caviezel sink a putt as golf legend Bobby Jones fades with constant repetition. What's left is the flat but not uninvolving story of a sickly Georgia boy with a fiery temper who went on to conquer golf. Jones deserved better than a biopic with a TV-movie heart." (*Rolling Stone*) *Director:* Rowdy Herrington.

THE MAN WITH THE PERFECT SWING (1995) *Comedy*
Rating: BIRDIE

Review: "Middle-aged, faded athlete Babe Lombardo barely survives on the rare profits from his line of dubiously conceived golf accessories. One day he discovers 'the key' to the perfect golf swing and gets a friend to help him produce a video. A funny, touching, and affectionate character piece." (*The Austin Chronicle*) *Stars:* James Black, Suzanne Savoy. *Director:* Michael Hovis.

Highest-grossing golf movies: *Tin Cup* ($53.9 million) and *Caddyshack* ($39.8 million).

NIBLICKS AND POT BUNKERS

Our guide to golfspeak continued. N–P

Nearest point of relief: If a ball is obstructed by an immovable object or abnormal ground condition, it may be dropped within one club length of the "nearest point of relief," the point closest to the ball at which it is no longer obstructed.

Niblick: Old-fashioned term for a nine-iron.

19th hole: The clubhouse bar.

O.B.: Out of bounds, usually marked with white stakes. If you hit the ball OB, it's a one-stroke penalty.

Offset: A clubhead whose face is set back from the shaft.

One-piece takeaway: A popular swing style in which one's shoulders, arms, and club begin the backswing in unison.

One-putt: When a golfer takes only one putt to get in the hole (once on the green).

Oscar Brown: Slang for out of bounds.

Outside: 1. To the right of the target (right-handed). **2.** The farthest from the hole, and therefore the first to hit (same as "away").

Overlapping grip: (Also called the "Vardon grip" after Harry Vardon.) The most common club grip, wherein the pinky finger of the lower hand rests on the index finger (or between the index and middle fingers) of the top hand.

Overseeding: Bermuda grass courses are often "overseeded" with rye grass because Bermuda grass goes dormant in winter.

Par: From the Latin word for "equal," the number of strokes a good golfer should take to complete a given hole (or course). It is the number of strokes needed to reach the green, plus two for putting. A good golfer should be able to play a par-5 in three strokes and then take two putts. Most courses have a total par of 72.

Past parallel: When a golfer's backswing brings the club to a position beyond parallel with the ground. Generally used as a negative.

Arnold Palmer once drove balls off the second tier of the Eiffel Tower. His longest: 403 yards.

Pin: The flagstick.

Penalty stroke: A stroke that must be added to a player's score for various reasons under the rules of golf.

Pin high: When a ball lands on the green, even with the hole but on one side or the other.

Pin position: Also "pin placement," the location of the hole (and flagstick) on a green, which, in a PGA Tour event, is changed every day.

Pitch: A short, high shot to the green with a very lofted club like a pitching wedge or sand wedge.

Pitch and run: A pitch that is intended to roll on the green rather than stop quickly. (Also called "bump and run.")

Pitch mark: The indentation a ball makes when it lands on the green. (Also called a "ball mark.")

Plane (or swing plane): The imaginary plane that a clubhead's arc travels through during a swing.

Play club: In the days of all-wooden clubs, the equivalent of today's driver.

Playing through: When a slower group of golfers allows the faster group behind them to play their hole, instead of making them wait. Result: the slower group ends up behind the faster one.

Plugged ball: A ball that gets embedded in the ground (shallowly or deeply) when it lands.

Plumb bob: A common technique whereby a golfer stands in front of the ball and allows the putter to hang loosely from his fingers in order to view a straight line from the ball to the hole.

Postage-stamp green: A very small green. One of the most famous: the 7th hole at Pebble Beach.

Pot bunker: A small but deep sand bunker.

Pro-am: A tournament featuring professionals and amateurs playing together.

Provisional ball: A second ball played from the same spot as the first, such as when a ball is lost or out of bounds.

Pull: A ball hit straight, but left (for right-handers) of the intended line. (As opposed to a "hook," where the ball goes left due to spin.)

Pull cart: A two-wheeled golf bag holder.

Push: When the ball goes to the right (for right-handers) of the intended line. (The opposite of "pull.")

AMATEURS

Usually it's an insult to call somebody
an amateur. Not this time.

THE U.S. AMATEUR

The U.S. Men's Amateur is America's oldest golf championship—it's one day older than the U.S. Open. It was first held by the newly formed United States Golfing Association (USGA) on October 3, 1895, at the Newport Golf Club in Rhode Island. (It's no coincidence that the USGA's first president, Theodore Havemeyer, owned the Newport Golf Club, or that the tournament's trophy is called the Havemeyer Trophy.) The 36-hole match play event was won by native Scot Charles B. MacDonald.

A month later the USGA held another tournament, the U.S. Women's Amateur Golf Championship, the third-oldest golf championship in the country (the U.S. Open was the second). It was held at the Meadow Brook Club in Hempstead, New York. The winner, as reported in the newspapers of the day: Mrs. Charles S. Brown, who beat 12 other women with a score of 132. For her win, Mrs. Brown took home the silver pitcher that had been donated for a trophy. The following year, the Cox Cup became the prize, and was held by the winner for one year, then passed on to the next champion.

PEAKS AND VALLEYS

Both amateur tournaments grew in popularity every year, the men's becoming one of the sport's four major tournaments along with the British Amateur, the U.S. Open, and the British Open. It saw its biggest heyday in the 1920s, when the nation's (and possibly the world's) most famous golfer, Bobby Jones, was winning his numerous amateur titles. In 1930 he won his fifth and final championship.

The popularity of the U.S. Amateur waned after Jones retired, as the best golfers became increasingly attracted to the growing purses and glamour of the professional game. But some chose to remain in the amateur ranks, hoping to earn no more than a trophy for their work. And even the biggest pros still revere the event: Arnold Palmer, Jack Nicklaus, and Tiger Woods all won

---

Dream trip: In 1997 amateur golfer Jeff Thorner played 50 courses in 50 states in 50 days.

U.S. Amateur championships, and they all consider them major titles. (Imagine how popular the event would be, or how different golf in general might be if any of those greats had decided to remain amateurs for their entire careers.)

AMATEUR STANDOUTS

Walter J. Travis, an Australian-born American, won in 1900 at the age of 39—and he had only started golfing when he was 35. He repeated the win in 1901 and again in 1903. As a golf course designer, a golf writer, publisher, and inventor, Travis is considered one of the great pioneers of the game in the United States. He was also the first non-Brit to win the British Amateur, in 1904.

Louis N. James won in 1902 at 19 years of age, becoming the first American-born golfer to win the Havemeyer Trophy.

Charles "Chick" Evans was the first golfer to win the U.S. Amateur and U.S. Open in the same year (1916). He would never become a pro but would compete in 56 consecutive U.S. Amateurs. (He won it again in 1920.)

Edith Cummings won the Women's Amateur in 1923. In 1924 she became the first golfer—and the first woman—to appear on the cover of *Time* magazine. (She was also the model for the character Jordan in F. Scott Fitzgerald's *The Great Gatsby*.)

Tiger Woods won the Men's Amateur in 1994 at the age of 18. He won again the following year, on the 100th anniversary of the championship. In 1996 Woods was already one of the most recognizable—and best—golfers in the game. The 20-year-old held off on going pro, though…until he won the 1996 U.S. Amateur. He's the only golfer to have won it three times in a row.

Ryan Moore of Puyallup, Washington, won the U.S. Amateur in 2004. He also won the U.S. Amateur Public Links Championship, another of the USGA's championships. He is only the fifth golfer to win both events in the same year. Not only that, the University of Nevada–Las Vegas senior won the NCAA Division I individual title *and* the Western Amateur, another prestigious amateur event. The four wins in one year rank as one the best amateur seasons in golf history.

Floyd Rood hit a golf ball across the continental United States. It took him 114,737 strokes.

THE TIGER TIMELINE

Since his "slump" in 2003 and 2004 (he won only six tournaments), some of the hype is gone, but don't be fooled: Tiger Woods's accomplishments are simply phenomenal.

TIGER was born Eldrick T. Woods on December 30, 1975, to Earl and Kutilda Woods. Earl was a retired U.S. Army Lieutenant Colonel and Kutilda a native of Thailand. Earl gave him the nickname "Tiger" in memory of his friend, Vuong Dang Phong, a Vietnamese soldier.

1976: Tiger started imitating his father's golf swing. He was six months old.

1978: Earl gave Tiger a cut-down club and he immediately showed an ability to swing and hit balls. That year, two-year-old Tiger appeared on *The Mike Douglas Show*, showing off his swing and engaging in a driving contest with Bob Hope.

1979: He shot a 48 over nine holes at the Navy Golf Club in Cypress, California.

1984: He won his first Optimist International Junior Championship. He was eight. (He won again at 9, 12, 13, 14, and 15.)

1991: At age 15, Tiger became the youngest U.S. Junior Amateur champion in history. That year he was voted *Golf Digest* Amateur Player of the Year.

1992: He won the U.S. Junior Amateur again, becoming the first to win the title more than once. (He won it in 1993, too.)

1994: At 18 years old, he became the youngest-ever winner of the U.S. Amateur Championship, and the only person to win both the Junior Amateur and the Amateur.

1995: He won the U.S. Amateur again. He was also the Pac-10 Player of the Year at Stanford.

1996: He became the first golfer in history to win three consecutive U.S. Amateur titles. He also tied the record for the lowest ever score for an amateur at the British Open with a 281. He turned pro that year, playing in just nine PGA tournaments, but won two of

---

Swing speed of the average male golfer: 93.75 miles per hour. Tiger Woods: 125 mph.

them and earned nearly $800,000. That was eclipsed by the endorsement deals he signed: $40 million with Nike and $20 million with Titleist. At the age of 20, and in his first year as a pro, he was voted the *Sports Illustrated* Sportsman of the Year.

1997: Woods won four PGA Tour events and was the tour's leading money winner with a record $2,066,833. He also won his first major, the Masters, lapping the field to win by a record-shattering 12 strokes. He was the youngest Masters winner ever. He also became the number one golfer in the world rankings, less than a year after turning pro.

1999: He broke the money record by earning $6,616,585. That was $2,974,679 more than David Duval's second-place earnings, and 52 percent of all he could have possibly won that year. In 21 tournaments, he made the cut in every one, finished in the top ten in 16, and won eight of them. He also won his second major at the PGA Championship.

2000: He did his 1999 season one better by winning nine events and earning $9,188,321. The nine wins were the most in a season since Sam Snead won 11 in 1950. He won his third major, the U.S. Open at Pebble Beach, again in obliterative fashion by a record 15 strokes. He also won his fourth major, the British Open, by eight strokes and with the lowest major tournament score in history (269). He also got his fifth major title and his third in a row when he won his second consecutive PGA Championship. He and Ben Hogan are the only players to win three majors in one season.

2001: He got the "Tiger Slam" when he won the Masters, making him the first player in history to win four consecutive major tournaments. (It's called the "Tiger Slam" because the wins weren't all in the same year. If they had been, it would've been a "Grand Slam.") He also won five other events.

2002: Woods won five of the 18 events he entered. He won his second consecutive Masters and the U.S. Open, giving him eight major wins, tying him with Tom Watson for fourth on the all-time list. At the age of 26, he has more majors than Harry Vardon, Bobby Jones, Gene Sarazen, Sam Snead, and Arnold Palmer had over their entire careers.

Billionaire Warren Buffett once paid $100,000 to caddie for Tiger Woods in a charity event.

2003: Once again he'd won five of the 18 events he entered. The wins included a three out of four run from February to late March. His win at the Western Open gave him a 29-2 record when going into the final round with at least a share of the lead.

2004: His worst year on the PGA Tour, Woods won only one PGA tournament. His number one world ranking, which he had held for a record 264 weeks, was lost to Vijay Singh. In the meantime, he became the first golfer to pass $40 million in career winnings.

THE FUTURE

Can Tiger ever pass Sam Snead for the all-time lead in PGA victories? And can he break Jack Nicklaus's record of winning 18 majors? Many people believe that both of these records are untouchable, but Tiger's numbers say something else.

• Snead had 82 victories over his career and was winning tournaments in his 50s. But as of March 2005, Tiger already had 42—at the age of 29. That gives him the most wins ever by a player in his 20s (Jack Nicklaus is second, with 30.) If he keeps on his current pace, averaging about four wins a year, Tiger will easily break the record before he's 40. If he does better—and most golfers play their best golf in their thirties—he'll do it sooner.

• As for Nicklaus's 18 majors, that's one of the most impressive records in all sports. The next closest is Walter Hagen with 11. But Tiger already has eight. Nicklaus won 11 of his after turning 30, and won his last one at age 46 (the 1986 Masters). If Tiger continues to play golf the way he's been playing all his life and doesn't suffer any injuries, who knows? But no matter what, it's sure going to be fun to watch. Enjoy the show.

*   *   *

THE TIGER SPEAKS

"Everyone gives me advice. I go into the grocery store and someone tells me what I did wrong with the 4-iron I hit on the 15th."

"I get to play golf for a living. What more can you ask for—getting paid for doing what you love."

THE GREATS OF THE GAME

Comments on the best players to ever swing a club.

BOBBY JONES

"Golf without Bobby Jones would be like France without Paris—leaderless, lightless and lonely."

  —Herbert Warren Wind

WALTER HAGEN

"When the Haig died in 1969, Junior called me from Detroit to tell me there would be no funeral. Instead, a bunch of his cronies were going to throw a party at the Detroit Athletic Club. They thought the Haig would prefer that. I didn't go. Like Hamlet, golf's sweet prince, I thought, he deserved a grander exit than that. He was splendid. They should have carried him out on a shield."

  —Charles Price

JACK NICKLAUS

"When Jack Nicklaus plays well, he wins. When he plays badly, he finishes second. When he plays terrible, he finishes third."

  —Johnny Miller

ARNOLD PALMER

"Arnold Palmer is the biggest crowd pleaser since the invention of the portable sanitary facility."

  —Bob Hope

"When you hear someone shout, 'You da man!' if he ain't shouting at Arnold Palmer, then he ain't da man."

  —Ron Green

JOHN DALY

"My Sunday best is a Wednesday afternoon compared to him."

  —Nick Faldo

TIGER WOODS

"Until Tiger Woods came along, I thought Jack Nicklaus was the greatest player ever. But Tiger Woods, he is the complete package. He has the intelligence of Nicklaus, the guts of Arnold Palmer, the beauty of Sam Snead's swing, the shot-making ability of Ben Hogan, and the patience and temperament of Gandhi."

  —Chi Chi Rodriguez

First mention of golf in the U.S.: when it was banned from Albany, NY, streets in 1659.

JOIN THE CLUB

The history of the club is an interesting one. No one is quite sure who the first person was to put turkey and bacon between three pieces of bread, but...oh, wait—wrong club.

THE UPPER CRUST

By the 1500s, Scottish golfers were already using different kinds of clubs for different shots. In those days, most players carved their own clubs out of wood, but the job was soon taken over by skilled craftsmen. And because making those early handmade instruments was time-consuming and expensive, only the wealthy could afford them, which means that golf—almost from its onset—was a game primarily enjoyed by the upper classes of society. In fact, the earliest known custom-made clubs were crafted in 1502 for King James IV of Scotland.

The shafts of early golf clubs were carved from either hazel or ash, and the heads were made of even harder lumber such as beech, blackthorn, pear, or apple. The shaft and head were connected and held together by a splint and twine. And they had strange names: early wedges were *niblicks* or *blasters*; 4-woods were *baffies*; and 2-woods were *brassies*. And when the golfer finally got to the green, he took out his *putting cleek*.

By the 1700s, golf balls had become more dense (see page 243), so harder wood was needed for the heads. Hickory was the lumber of choice, but even those needed to be reinforced with bone or ivory—a major drawback of the early game was dealing with shattered clubheads. Something even stronger was needed.

THE IRON AGE

In the mid-1800s, forged metal was introduced to golf—and changed the game dramatically: the clubs were stronger, so the ball went farther. Some of these early irons were known as *mashies*, *jiggers*, and *sammys*. But they proved to be *too* strong; instead of the clubhead shattering, now it was the "featherie" ball that was getting demolished. So most players utilized a combination of wood heads and iron heads.

Worse shot than usual: Al Capone once accidentally shot himself in the foot while golfing.

In the 19th century, some of the biggest innovations in club making came from the sport's premier players. Both Old Tom Morris and Allan Robertson were golf club makers, experimenting with different materials and angles of the clubhead to make the ball go farther and straighter. But the days of handcrafted golf clubs were coming to an end—by the end of the century, they were being replaced more and more by mass-produced ones.

So anyone could own golf clubs, right? Wrong. They were still very expensive. Whereas a baseball player could get by with one ball, one bat, and one glove, a golfer needed to buy an entire set of clubs. It was still primarily a game for the rich (another reason: golf took all day, so a golfer had to be wealthy enough to be able to take a day off), but its popularity was growing.

TWENTIETH-CENTURY CLUBS

The next big breakthrough in club technology came in 1908 when heads changed from smooth faces to grooved faces. This gave the ball more backspin, which led to greater distance, as well as more control. And now, not only were more golf clubs being churned out by factories than ever before, but with the advent of "drop-forging," the quality was more consistent. The days of an entire bag of matching clubs had arrived. But that didn't stop adventurous golfers from experimenting with every part of the club.

• Walter Hagen was one of the best at getting out of the rough and sand traps (where many of his tee shots landed). He had a special sand wedge made with an extended flange and concave face that could be adjusted to different lofts.

• Putters had also made the transition from wood to iron heads (although the shafts were still made of wood), and some of those heads were quite…strange. One had mirrors attached so the golfer could "line up the reflection with the real to achieve a clean stroke on every putt." Others had little wheels on the soles.

WHOA!

By the 1930s, it had become apparent to the governing bodies of golf that club technology needed to be reeled back in. Solely because of their equipment, many players had an unfair advantage. Courses were also at risk; formerly difficult par-5s could now be reached in two shots because some golfers were using drivers with heads six inches long. To even out the playing field, the USGA, in conjunction with the Royal and Ancient Golf Club at St. Andrews, set standards for clubhead size, face grooves, and shaft length. Hagen's adjustable-loft sand wedge, for instance, was outlawed in 1931, and the 14-club limit was initiated in 1938. The USGA also standardized the names—mashies, niblicks, and cleeks gave way to woods, irons, and putters.

INTO THE SPACE AGE

Steel was the primary material for clubs in the mid-20th century. And although they retained their name, most woods were made of metal. As technology advanced after World War II, so did the tools in the golfer's arsenal.

• Aluminum clubs were introduced in the 1960s. They were lighter than steel, which gave golfers better swing speed, but aluminum is soft, which made it prone to bending.

• The next big change: graphite, introduced in 1968. It is a stronger, lighter compound that gives the shaft more resilience and flexibility.

• Titanium clubs became available in the 1980s. They're even lighter (and stronger) than graphite…but they're also considerably more expensive.

• Steel clubs haven't completely vanished—they're still used by many amateurs because of their affordability.

DIGITAL DRIVERS

Golf equipment has become a multibillion-dollar industry, and the major manufacturers have pulled out all the stops to maintain a competitive edge. Now they're using complex computer models and simulations in equipment design. The latest breakthrough: peripherally weighted irons, which expand the sweet spot on the clubface.

But as most of us have found out, swinging with the same driver that Tiger Woods uses does not enable us to hit the ball like Tiger Woods. No matter how advanced the technology gets, the best tool the golfer has will always be the one between his ears.

STAYING A GOLF PRO

*Once you've made it to the PGA Tour, the trick
is to stay on the tour. Here's how you do it.*

WHAT'S YOUR RANK?

So you read "How to Become a Golf Pro" on page 91
and now you've got your Tour Card and you're a bona
fide member of the PGA Tour. Congratulations! But don't relax
yet—getting your card is no guarantee of anything. A new Tour
Card is only good for one year. Many golfers lose them at the end
of that one year and then have to start the difficult reentry process
all over again.

The trick to keeping your card is getting a good ranking. Since
1983, the PGA Tour has had what's called the "All-Exempt Tour
Priority Rankings" list. It's from this list that every tournament's
participants (usually 156 players) are chosen. There are 34 different categories on the rankings list, and a roster is filled from the
top down—top-ranked golfers first—until all the spots are filled.
The higher you get on the list, the more tournaments you can
enter, the more chance you have to improve your ranking, and the
more you can relax about keeping your card.

The highest ranking category on the list: Winners of the PGA
Championship or U.S. Open prior to 1970 or in the last 10 calendar years. If you win one of those two major tournaments, you are
set for a long time. The rules have changed a few times over the
years to accommodate the growing number of professional golfers:
players in this category used to get a lifetime pass, then it changed
to a 10-year pass, then in 1998 to a five-year pass. Going into the
2005 season, the All-Exempt list had 30 golfers in the top category,
and for that year they get to play in any PGA tournament they
choose. Some of those top-ranked golfers: Rich Beem, Ernie Els,
Jim Furyk, Gary Player, Davis Love III, Jack Nicklaus (lifetime
pass), Corey Pavin, Vijay Singh, and Tiger Woods.

DOWN THE LIST

The second category on the tour is for winners of the Players
Championship; the third category is for winners of the Masters

tournament, and fourth is for British Open winners. All players in the first four groups get to play on the PGA Tour, guaranteed, for five years after winning these tournaments.

In 2003 PGA Tour rookie Ben Curtis, the 396th-ranked golfer in the world and a complete unknown, shocked the golfing world when he won the British Open…and got a free pass for five years on the PGA Tour.

STAYIN' ALIVE

Some other ranking categories and some of the golfers in them:

• There are 36 golfers in the ninth category, which you get to by winning a PGA tournament. That earns you a two-year exemption. Bonus: for every additional win during those two years, you get a another year added onto your exemption (maximum five years). Some of the niners: K. J. Choi, Fred Funk, Sergio Garcia, Peter Jacobsen, and Craig Stadler.

• There are 58 golfers in the 20th group on the list, which is for the top 125 players on the previous year's official money list. Why only 58 if it's the top 125? Because many golfers from the top 125 are in higher-ranked positions for other accomplishments (such as winning a major). Some names in this group in 2005: Jesper Parnevik, Jeff Maggert, Duffy Waldorf, Justin Rose, Dudley Hart, Hank Kuehne, and Aaron Baddeley.

• Group 25 on the list is the top 30 from the previous year's PGA Qualifying School. For 2005, that includes Jason Allred, a pro golfer from right here in Uncle John's hometown of Ashland, Oregon. (Go Jason!)

• There are many notable golf names in the 28th group, which is for positions 126 to 150 on the tour's money list, and there's a good chance a tournament's roster will be filled by this point. But if they're needed to fill out the field, then Paul Azinger, Olin Browne, Glen Day, Matt Kuchar, and Jose Maria Olazabal can get into a tournament.

• The 34th—and the very last—rank on the All-Exempt list is for PGA Tour veterans who have made at least 150 cuts in their careers. If they're not otherwise eligible, veterans in this position can be used to fill a tournament's field as needed. As of 2005, however, there was nobody on the list.

Charles Boswell never golfed before he was blinded in World War II, but blind, shot an 81.

FALL FROM GRACE

But as we said, there are only 156 spots for any event. There are a
lot of Tour Card holders who will be ranked too low too often,
then fall off the list altogether and lose their cards. Case in point:
Mike Weir. In 1997 the Canadian pro qualified for the 1998 PGA
Tour by finishing in the top 30 in Q School. Weir played in 27
events, but didn't do very well. He only made the cut in 13 of
those tournaments, didn't win any, and he didn't win enough
money. Result: he got bumped right out of the PGA Tour.

But Weir didn't give up. At the end of that disappointing first
season he went back to Q School...and took first place. He was
back in the PGA for 1999, and by winning tournaments and making enough money, he's been able to keep his card ever since. In
2003 he got his best bump in the rankings to date by winning the
Masters. That put him in the third category and guaranteed him a
spot on the PGA Tour until 2008.

*   *   *

AMAZING GOLF ANAGRAMS

UNITED STATES OPEN
GOLF CHAMPIONSHIPS
  becomes...
**SEEING MEN FLOP
CHIPS AND PUTTS IS
A HOOT**

PHIL MICKELSON
  becomes...
HELP! I'M IN LOCKS!

FRED COUPLES
  becomes...
RESCUED FLOP

ERNIE ELS
  becomes...
SNEER LIE

THE HONOURABLE
COMPANY OF
EDINBURGH GOLFERS
  becomes...
**A GREATER BUNCH
OF UNEMPLOYED
HIGHBORN FOOLS**

THE IRISH GOLFER
PADRAIG HARRINGTON
  becomes...
**A HERO ARISING—LEFT
OR RIGHT HAND GRIP?**

ELDRICK "TIGER" WOODS
  becomes...
**STICK WIELDER,
OR GOD?**

Steve Elkington was once penalized two strokes for plucking a blade of grass to chew on.

LET'S PLAY GORUFU!

*Golf isn't just popular in England, Scotland, and the
United States—it's loved all over the world.*

DOMO ARIGATO
Before World War II, there were 23 courses in all of Japan.
Today, the number exceeds 3,000—in a country slightly
smaller than California. Despite the volume of courses and their
distance from urban centers (most are an hour's drive or more), the
courses are almost always busy. Although available tee times are
scarce, the clubs compete so fiercely that all kinds of specials
abound, such as free caddies, or, more commonly, half-price greens
fees on Monday. And that's a generous discount, as Japanese golf
(or *gorufu*) is very expensive—18 holes might cost $400. Even the
driving ranges are expensive: it can cost 50 cents to hit a *single ball*.

Only the very wealthy can afford country club memberships.
The price of joining a club costs the equivalent of about five years
of a middle-class worker's salary. The most prestigious clubs cost several million dollars. However, Japanese golfers view a membership as
an investment as well as a status symbol—they can be bought, sold,
transferred, and passed down. At the peak of the Japanese inflation
crisis in the late 1980s, country club memberships accounted for
roughly 10 percent of Japan's gross domestic product.

LAND OF THE RISING GREENS FEES

It's pricey, but Japanese golfers get a lot for their money. Courses
are so meticulously manicured that it's virtually impossible to lose
a ball, even in the rough. Clubhouses are lavishly decorated with
marble. Even daily fee-paying golfers are treated well, with access
to saunas, baths, and high-end restaurants. Refreshing hot towels
are provided at the 7th and 16th holes, and you can get a robot
caddie to carry your gear.

Links are so crowded that playing nine holes can take up to
three hours, but golfers are given a 45-minute lunch break after
the front nine (in Japan, you're assigned a tee time for each set of
nine holes). And after the round, there is a traditional bath followed by drinks and coffee, while clothes and shoes are left to dry
in special heated lockers.

Japanese slang for nice shot: "Nice-su shot-o." (Really.)

Some other notable golf hot spots (and cold spots) around the world:

- **ICELAND:** There are only 15 golf clubs in this tiny island nation, but the population is so small, the number of golf courses per capita is comparable to that of the United States. The Akureyri Golf Club is the northernmost course in the world. Each June it hosts the Arctic Open Golf Championship. The sun doesn't completely set for six months of the year in arctic regions, so tee off is at midnight and play continues until 6 a.m. On the other side of the country, the Westman Island Golf Club is set inside a volcanic crater adjacent to the Atlantic Ocean. The bumpy lava formations and unrelenting ocean winds make for a challenging round of golf.

- **INDIA:** One of the first golf clubs outside of the British Isles—the Royal Calcutta—was established in India in 1829. The first national competition, the All-India Amateur Championship, was established in 1892, making it the world's second-oldest open championship after the British Open. British golfers dominated the All-India until 1949, when Mohinder Bal became the first native-born Indian to win it.

- **AUSTRALIA:** Australians have golfed since the mid-1800s, when it was still a British colony. Today, there are plenty of elegant, highly manicured courses near the cities along the coast, but Australia also has huge expanses of largely uninhabited land in its interior. The Outback is mostly grass-free, hot desert, but that doesn't stop course developers from building nine-hole courses of oiled sand. Natural hazards: grazing kangaroos, wombat holes, and snakes.

- **MALAYSIA:** Summer temperatures hover around 90 degrees. Golf is popular there, but how do golfers avoid the extreme heat and humidity? Night golf under high-powered floodlights.

- **IRAN:** In 1979 Iran's pro-Western government was overthrown and replaced by a strict Muslim theocracy that viewed golf as a useless and decadent Western activity. Teheran's once prestigious Imperial Golf Club quickly fell into disrepair; five holes have even been confiscated by the government for their real estate value. Golf is now starting to regain popularity, though. Iran's vice president heads a program that provides funds and equipment to schools with golf programs. Golf is most popular among Iranian women, despite the requirement that on the course they be covered from head to toe and cannot play at the same time as men.

Trick shot artist Joe Kirkwood made the 1st hole in one ever captured on film...on his 1st try.

CADDIE LORE

Facts, figures, follies, and fortunes
from the ancient art of caddying.

JOB DESCRIPTION

In his book *The History of Golf*, Robert Browning writes that a good caddie must be "his patron's guide, philosopher, and his friend, his instructor when he is off his game, and co-arbiter with the opposition caddie in all disputes." (A more common description of the caddie's job: "Show up, shut up, and keep up!")

But out on the course, the caddie has many responsibilities: keeping track of tee times, keeping time on the course, counting the clubs, keeping the clubs and all equipment clean, making sure equipment is in good working order, knowing the yardage on every shot, and carrying a 50-pound bag around the course all day (an average of five to seven miles on the PGA Tour).

BABY, YOU'RE A RICH MAN

Although there are fewer caddies on the links today, those that land a job carrying for a pro can make a pretty decent living. The typical pay: a base salary, anywhere from a few hundred to a thousand dollars per week, plus 6 to 8 percent of the winnings. That's often bumped up to 10 percent if the golfer places first. At a big PGA event, that could mean $100,000 or more for a week's work. But on the other hand, if the golfer fails to make the cut… it's zero. The big lottery winner of caddies is Steve Williams. Since he started carrying for Tiger Woods in 1999, he's pulled in more than $3 million.

Golf pro Jeff Maggert elaborates: "The prize money has gotten so high that you have to take this much more seriously. The caddies now, the young guys you've seen coming up the last 10 years or so, take this *way* more seriously. It isn't like the old days when it seemed like they were a band of gypsies."

SERVING THEIR MASTERS

For many years, when a golfer came to Augusta National to play in the Masters, he wasn't allowed to bring his own caddie. Augusta National had a long-standing tradition of providing their own, all

---

Lori Garbacz once ordered a pizza while waiting to tee off at the U.S. Women's Open.

of them black men (they wore white jumpsuits), and they knew every inch of the course—some having more than a half-century of experience. And most of them had colorful nicknames:

• Gene Sarazen's bag was carried by a tall, thin black man known as "Stovepipe" because he always wore a stovepipe hat.

• Arnold Palmer's bag was toted by Nathaniel "Iron Man" Avery.

• Others were Tommy "Burnt Biscuits" Bennett and Willie "Cemetery" Poteat, who always carried for President Eisenhower when he came to play.

In 1983 Augusta allowed golfers to bring their own caddies.

A SHOULDER TO CRY ON

The duties of the caddie are many. On the Wednesday before the start of the 1995 Masters, Ben Crenshaw was a pallbearer at the funeral of his lifelong friend and mentor, Harvey Penick. On Thursday, the grieving Crenshaw teed off with his Augusta caddie of 20 years, Carl "Skillet" Jackson (so named, the story goes, because as a kid he couldn't throw hard enough to break an egg). Four days later, in one of golf's most memorable moments, after holing out his final putt and winning the tournament, Crenshaw broke down in uncontrollable sobs. The 6'4", 225-pound Jackson calmly walked over to Crenshaw, put his arm around him, and quietly comforted him.

IS IT "CADDY" OR "CADDIE?"

Both spellings are acceptable, but in this book, we've gone with "caddie" because that's what most dictionaries lead with. (Note from Uncle John to the people at *Webster's*: the movie is called *Caddyshack*—not *Caddieshack*.)

QUOTES ABOUT CADDIES

"Real golfers, no matter what the provocation, never strike a caddie with the driver. The sand wedge is far more effective."

—Huxtable Pippey

"A caddie is almost like a jockey. He has to know when to pull the reins and know when to give it some whip, when to give the horse a bit of stick."

—Nick Price

Eddie Lowery is the only caddie to have appeared on a U.S. postage stamp.

RECORD BOOK

The longest, strongest, fastest, and smartest (through the 2004 season).

LOWEST SCORE IN A ROUND

Al Geiberger, **59** (1977 Memphis Classic)

Chip Beck, **59** (1991 Las Vegas Invitational)

David Duval, **59** (1999 Bob Hope Chrysler Classic)

MOST CONSECUTIVE ROUNDS AT PAR OR BETTER

Tiger Woods, **52**

David Toms, **33**

Larry Nelson, **32**

Charles Howell III, **26**

MOST VICTORIES IN A SINGLE EVENT

Sam Snead, **8** (Greensboro Open)

Harry Vardon, **6** (British Open)

Alex Ross, **6** (North and South Open)

Sam Snead, **6** (Miami Open)

Jack Nicklaus, **6** (Masters)

WIDEST WINNING MARGINS

J. D. Edgar, **16** (1919 Canadian Open)

Joe Kirkwood, Sr., **16** (1924 Corpus Christi Open)

Bobby Locke, **16** (1948 Chicago Victory National Championship)

Tiger Woods, **15** (2000 U.S. Open)

MOST CONSECUTIVE BIRDIES

Bob Goalby, **8** (1961 St. Petersburg Open)

Fuzzy Zoeller, **8** (1976 Quad Cities Open)

Dewey Arnette, **8** (1987 Buick Open)

Edward Fryatt, **8** (2000 Doral-Ryder Open)

J.P. Hayes, **8** (2002 Bob Hope Chrysler Classic)

Jerry Kelly, **8** (2003 Las Vegas Invitational)

MOST CONSECUTIVE CUTS MADE

Tiger Woods, **133**

Byron Nelson, **113**

Jack Nicklaus, **105**

Hale Irwin, **86**

Dow Finsterwald, **72**

BIGGEST COME FROM BEHIND VICTORIES (STROKES DOWN)

Paul Lawrie, **10** (1999 British Open)

Stewart Cink, **9** (2004 MCI Heritage Classic)

(Seven tied at **8**)

OLDEST TOURNAMENT WINNERS

Sam Snead, **52** (1965 Greater Greensboro Open)

Art Wall, **51** (1975 Greater Milwaukee Open)

Jim Barnes, **51** (1937 Long Island Open)

John Barnum, **51** (1962 Cajun Classic)

Bzzzzz! Jack Nicklaus and Gary Player were once attacked by killer bees on the green.

THE COLOR BARRIER, PART II

*Here's the second installment of our look at how pro
golf became integrated. (Part I is on page 39.)*

GOING PUBLIC

When Joe Louis heard from the president of the PGA that he and Bill Spiller couldn't golf in the 1952 San Diego Open because they were black, he decided he was going anyway. So he called up Walter Winchell, then one of the most popular radio personalities in the country. Winchell raised a stink on his national show, and suddenly the eyes of the country were on San Diego. Louis turned the heat up even further when he gave an interview to the *San Diego Union*. He told them that even if his invitation were withdrawn, he'd be on the course the next morning at 7 a.m. to qualify for the tournament on his own.

"I want to bring this thing out into the light," he told the newspaper. "I want the people to know what the PGA is. The PGA will have to tell me personally that I can't play." He insisted that Bill Spiller be allowed to play as well.

BACKING DOWN

PGA president Horton Smith had a problem on his hands. Joe Louis was a World War II vet and one of the most popular athletes in the country, admired by blacks and whites alike. And here he was, challenging the PGA to a public fight over its policy of discrimination—a fight that Louis told reporters was the biggest of his life.

Smith tried to diffuse the controversy. When he arrived in San Diego, he met with Louis and told him he'd arrived at a decision: since Louis was playing as an amateur, he was not subject to the PGA's rules. The tournament's sponsors were free to invite him, and he was free to accept. Bill Spiller was another matter—he was a professional golfer. Since he was black, he couldn't become a member of the PGA. And since he wasn't a member of the PGA, he wasn't eligible to play in the tournament, either.

Rules were rules, Smith explained.

Only 22% of golfers regularly break 90 for 18 holes.

DOWN TO THE WIRE

The tournament was about to begin. Horton Smith had offered Louis some of what he wanted, but not all of it, and Louis had to decide whether "some" was enough. He and Smith continued to negotiate right up until tee time. In the end Louis agreed to play after Smith promised he would work with Louis to find some kind of compromise to accommodate black professional golfers.

For *this* tournament, though, Bill Spiller was out. Spiller was so mad at the PGA—and with Louis for letting him down—that he went and stood on the first tee box and tried to stop the tournament from getting underway. Louis eventually talked him into ending his protest. After that, the tournament went off without another hitch.

Louis and Smith met after the tournament and hashed out a plan by which *some* black professional golfers would be allowed to participate in *some* PGA tournaments: A committee of five black golfers—Louis, Spiller, Teddy Rhodes, Eural Clark, and Howard Wheeler—would come up with a list of "approved" black golfers. The list would have to be approved by the PGA; then, if a tournament's sponsor and the hosting golf club both approved, blacks on the approved list could be invited to play. But black golfers still could not *join* the PGA—its Caucasians-only clause stayed on the books. Tournaments and golf clubs that wanted to discriminate against blacks could do so with the PGA's blessing.

The new deal wasn't much, but it was better than nothing, and even Bill Spiller reluctantly agreed to put up with it for the time being. The new rules would be tested at the Phoenix Open, less than one week away.

SOME WELCOME

Seven blacks made the trip to Phoenix: Louis, his secretary Leonard Reed, Eural Clark, and Joe Roach entered as amateurs; Bill Spiller, Teddy Rhodes, and a third golfer, a UGA champion named Charlie Sifford, entered as pros. Just how little Louis had accomplished in San Diego became apparent when the men arrived at the Phoenix Country Club. The tournament had been opened to blacks, but the clubhouse had not. Louis and the others learned this at the first tee of the first round, when a club official told them to remove their belongings from the locker room and

Tennis star Althea Gibson was the first African-American member of the LPGA in 1964.

put them in the caddie shack. The showers were off limits, too, and eating in the dining room (which was staffed by black waiters) was out of the question.

Louis and the others could have made a fuss about the way they were being treated, but they decided to grit their teeth and see the tournament through. Things got worse: They were the first group to tee off at the tournament, and when they got to the first green they discovered that someone had defecated into the cup just moments earlier. Then, when they came up to the scoreboard, they noticed that one of the radio announcers was wearing a Confederate cap. All of the golfers kept their cool except Spiller. He decided he'd had enough and told the others he was going to the locker room to shower; then he stormed off. Ten minutes later, a tournament official asked Louis to get Spiller out of the showers before someone killed him. Louis went and got him.

The next three rounds of the tournament passed fairly smoothly; then the golfers went on to Tucson and played another event. No other PGA tournaments invited blacks that winter.

STRIKING THE CLAUSE

By the late 1950s, fewer than 15 of the more than 40 tournaments on the PGA Tour had opened themselves to black golfers. Like a lot of his peers, Bill Spiller dreamed of making his living on the pro circuit, but the purses were smaller then and he was shut out of so many tournaments that he couldn't make ends meet. He ended up running a doughnut store with his wife in Los Angeles and caddying at the Hillcrest Country Club on the side.

One day in 1960, Spiller was carrying the bags of a club member named Harry Braverman. When Braverman asked him why he wasn't trying out for the PGA Tour, Spiller told him about the PGA's Caucasians-only clause. Braverman repeated the story to his friend, California Attorney General Stanley Mosk, and Mosk decided to do something about it. He contacted the PGA and told them that holding segregated tournaments on public golf courses was illegal in California, and he threatened to sue the organization if they continued the whites-only policy. That fall the PGA's national convention entertained a motion to remove the Caucasians-only clause from their constitution. The motion was voted down 67-17; the clause stayed in place.

In 1961 Mosk contacted the PGA again. This time he told them that holding a segregated tournament on a *private* golf course would also be illegal, and he threatened to block the 1962 PGA Championship, which was scheduled to be held at the Brentwood Country Club in Southern California. The PGA responded by moving the tournament to Pennsylvania, but then at the fall 1961 national convention it brought the Caucasians-only clause up for another vote. This time the PGA's executive committee recommended that the clause be removed—the resolution passed unanimously and the Caucasians-only clause was stricken from the constitution.

The door to the PGA Tour had finally swung open, and the pace of progress gradually began to quicken. In 1962 Charlie Sifford became the first black golfer to play on the PGA Tour full-time. He went on to win the Greater Hartford Open in 1967 and then the Los Angeles Open in 1969. In 1975, after qualifying for the third year in a row, Lee Elder finally received an invitation to Augusta National and became the first black golfer to play in the Masters.

MISSED THE CUT

For Bill Spiller, the change in the PGA's constitution and all the progress that followed came too late. By the time the vote was taken in 1961, he was in his late 40s and well past his prime. But he still played golf whenever he could get away from his doughnut store, and for the next several years he continued to dream of playing on the PGA Tour.

In 1967 he went to the PGA's qualifying school in Florida but failed to score well enough to make the Tour. The following year Spiller tried again. In the end it came down to eight rounds of golf—144 holes. If Spiller scored well enough, he'd qualify for the Tour. If he didn't, he might never get another chance.

Now 55 and suffering from so many ailments that friends nicknamed him the "Medicine Man" for all the pills he took, Spiller had swing problems and had a shaky putting game. Still, he did well in the first seven rounds and had a good chance of making the Tour. But in the eighth round, his luck ran out. On one of the last holes, he shanked three shots and missed qualifying by a single stroke.

BITTER END

Bill Spiller fought for 25 years to make it into the PGA, but never succeeded and never got over the defeat. When he died in 1988 at the age of 75, his wife sold his golf clubs. His son Bill Jr. remembers that when he called the newspapers to give them his father's obituary, nobody ran it. "I see my father as forgotten, overlooked, and unappreciated, never getting credit for what he actually did."

Spiller *was* underappreciated, but his contribution to the game is undeniable, having paved the way for a generation of minority golf pros to play on the PGA Tour. The same year that Lee Elder became the first black golfer to play in the Masters tournament—1975—was the year that Tiger Woods was born. In 2000 Woods became the first black golfer to win it.

*   *   *

AHEAD OF HIS TIME

In 1896 John Shippen played in the second U.S. Open, held at Shinnecock Hills in New York. What's so special about that? Shippen was black. The 16-year-old Shippen and several other local kids had been taught to play by the club's Scottish pro, Willie Dunn. Dunn recognized that Shippen was a very talented golfer and entered him in the tournament, along with Shippen's friend, Oscar Bunn—a Shinnecock Indian.

The British pros who had come to play complained to USGA president Theodore Havemeyer, telling him he had to get "the black boys" out of the tournament...or *they* wouldn't play. Havemeyer responded that if they didn't want to play in the tournament, they could go home and the event would be played with just the two boys in it—and one of them would be declared champion. At that, the Brits relented, and the second U.S. Open in history was played with an African American golfer and a Native American golfer in the field.

Bunn's score is lost to history, but Shippen finished fifth and won $10, making him one of the first—if not *the* first—American-born golfer to earn money in a pro golf tournament. He would play in five more U.S. Opens, although none as well as his first, the last one being in 1913. But had Havemeyer's example been followed, American golf might have been integrated from its outset.

BIG SHOTS

More of the best golf shots in history.

DATE: 1982
EVENT: The U.S. Open at Pebble Beach, California
THE SHOT: Tom Watson was at the 71st hole of the tournament. At four under, he was tied with Jack Nicklaus for the lead, but he was in trouble. His tee shot at the 209-yard par-3 had drifted left, into deep rough. Even worse: he'd have to chip it onto a downhill green. To this day, golf experts say that getting the ball near the hole without going past it was close enough to impossible to *be* impossible. Nicklaus was already in the clubhouse and watching Watson on TV. "There was no way in the world he could save par," Nicklaus said later. "So I figured it was over. I thought I had won the tournament."

Even Watson's caddie, Bruce Edwards, knew how hard it would be to even get the ball anywhere near the hole. "Get it close," he whispered to Watson.

And in what has now become one of golf's most famous lines, Watson replied, "I'm not gonna get it close, I'm gonna make it."

Then he hit the shot. It landed just on the edge of the green...started rolling...broke left...and almost 20 feet later dropped into the hole. Watson exploded like a cannon onto the green and danced around while the crowd went berserk around him. "At that moment," he recalls, "I could have long-jumped all the way to Tokyo Harbor." He went on to sink another birdie—a 20-footer—on the 18th to claim his one and only U.S. Open title by two strokes.

DATE: 1960
EVENT: The U.S. Open at Cherry Hills Golf Club, near Denver
THE SHOT: After Sunday morning's third round, Arnold Palmer was seven shots off the lead and tied for 15th place. Sitting in the locker room with two sportswriters, Bob Drum of the *Pittsburgh Press* and Dan Jenkins of *Sports Illustrated*, Arnie was thinking about starting off the afternoon's fourth round by driving his first shot all the way to the first green—a distance of 346 yards. "If I

During WWII, materials were in such short supply that many golfers used wooden balls.

drive the green and get a birdie or an eagle, I might shoot a 65. What'll that do?" he asked the men.

"Nothing," said Drum. "You're too far back." He was wrong.

Palmer drove the first green, all 346 yards of it, and two-putted for birdie. And that began a *run* of supershots. He went on to birdie six of the first seven holes, finishing with 65 and winning the tournament. The seven-stroke comeback is still the biggest in U.S. Open history.

BONUS: The 1960 U.S. Open was also significant for another reason. The players that Palmer had to beat? Forty-eight-year-old Ben Hogan, trying to win a fifth U.S. Open title, and a 20-year-old amateur named Jack Nicklaus, who had started the day tied for the lead. He finished just two shots behind Palmer. "On that afternoon," said writer Dan Jenkins, "in the span of just 18 holes, we witnessed the arrival of Nicklaus, the coronation of Palmer, and the end of Hogan."

DATE: 1953

EVENT: The Tam O'Shanter World Championship in Long Island, New York

THE SHOT: It was one of modern golf's biggest moments. Why? It was the first time a golf tournament was nationally televised. The broadcast was only an hour long, and showed only the 18th green on the last day, but it was there that Lew Worsham helped make golf's TV debut a great one.

Coming to that last hole of the tournament, a par-4, Worsham needed a birdie to tie Chandler Harper for the lead and force a playoff for the then-huge first prize of $25,000. He hit a good tee shot and had just 121 yards to the hole—but first he'd have to clear the creek that fronted the green. Worsham hit a high wedge shot that landed right at the front edge of the green, ran more than 50 feet...and fell into the hole for an eagle. He didn't need a playoff; he had won the tournament. The crowd went crazy...and so did announcer Jimmy Demaret. To the more than 600,000 people who were watching at home, Demaret yelled, "The son of a bitch went in!" Indeed it did, and golf had become a national sport.

Only golfer to shoot a triple-triple-triple-triple bogey in the U.S. Open: Ray Ainsley (1938).

TEED OFF

*Safety tip from Uncle John: if the people behind
you on the links think you're golfing too slowly,
don't argue—just let them play through.*

GOLFERS: Robert Borkowski, 50, and Robert Jacobs, 62
INCIDENT: In May 2001, Borkowski and his wife were
on the 2nd green at the University Park Country Club in
East Manatee, Florida. Jacobs was behind them on the fairway,
waiting for them to finish. He thought the Borkowskis were golfing too slowly, so he hit a shot onto the green.
TEED OFF: Borkowski took offense at that and hit Jacobs' ball
into a nearby water hazard. According to Jacobs, the fight started
when he reached into Borkowski's golf bag to get a new ball and
Borkowski shoved him; Borkowski says Jacobs started it. But however it started, Jacobs punched Borkowski several times, knocking
him down. Borkowski ended up with a swollen ear; Jacobs ended
up in the county jail and was charged with two counts of battery.
AFTERMATH: Jacobs was later released on $1,500 bail, and the
charges were eventually dropped after he agreed to perform community service, attend an anger-management class, and write
Borkowski a letter of apology. "It probably sounds kind of funny,"
Jacobs said. "If I opened up the paper and read about this, I'd
probably laugh at it, too...but it happened to me."

GOLFERS: Warren Franke, 41, and David Holly, 63
INCIDENT: Both men were golfing at the Lakeside Golf Course
in Fort Wayne, Indiana, on May 23, 2002. Franke was part of a
slow-moving threesome; Holly's impatient foursome was right
behind them. Franke made things even worse by talking on his
cell phone when he should have been focusing on the game.
Someone in Holly's group even yelled "Hurry up!" to move them
along. After his round was over, Franke realized he'd left his
seven-iron back on the 17th green. He hopped in his cart to get
it, and as he passed Holly on the 18th green, he yelled "Hey" just
as Holly was putting the ball, causing him to blow the shot.
TEED OFF: Holly was furious. He went to the clubhouse to

complain, then went to the parking lot to get his car. That's when he spotted Franke. What happened next depends on who you believe: Holly claims Franke punched him in the head and then pulled out a Walther PPK handgun and threatened to shoot him; Franke says that it was Holly who started the fight, punching him repeatedly until he finally drew his weapon in self-defense. "I pulled my gun to *stop* the fight," Franke says.

AFTERMATH: Franke was charged with misdemeanor battery and one felony count of pointing a firearm, which could have landed him in jail for four years. But his self-defense story worked: the jury deliberated just three hours—less time than it takes to play a round of golf—before finding him not guilty on both counts.

GOLFERS: Hugo Torres, 33, John Tennyson, 30, and Howard Polley, 36

INCIDENT: Is this story starting to sound familiar? In June 1993, Torres was golfing with two friends at the Sabal Palm Golf Club in Florida. Tennyson and Polley were right behind them and became frustrated at the slow play of Torres's threesome. According to Torres, when they got to the 7th hole, Tennyson and Polley tried to play through without asking permission. One of their balls nearly hit Torres on the head.

TEED OFF: Polley tells a different story—he says that they *did* ask, but that Torres swore at them and told them no. However the argument started, it quickly turned physical. When Tennyson got out of his golf cart "in an aggressive manner," Torres swung his putter at him, hitting him in the back. Then Polley swung his driver at Torres, who fended off the blow with his putter, causing the head of the putter to snap off. Torres then attacked Polley with the jagged end of the putter, stabbing him in the neck. Polley had to be airlifted to a nearby hospital; Torres was jailed on two counts of aggravated battery.

AFTERMATH: The case went to trial in early 1994. After watching a reenactment of the fight with the broken golf clubs, the jury deliberated for 45 minutes and found that Torres had acted in self-defense and was not guilty on both counts. Torres celebrated the verdict by playing a round of golf...at a different golf course.

Clifford Ann Creed won 3 events a year from 1964 to 1967. She never won before...or again.

MORE CHAMPS

More amazing golfers from the all-time best list.

GARY PLAYER

Player was born on November 1, 1935, in Johannesburg, South Africa. "The Black Knight," as he was known because he almost always wore black on the course, was one of the greatest international players of all time. He always had his family in tow—his wife Vivienne and their six children—as he traveled the world to play in tournaments. He estimates he traveled more than 14 million miles in his career.

Player won only 24 tournaments on the American PGA circuit (and 19 more on the Champions Tour), but when you add his international wins the total comes to 163 wins worldwide. That includes 13 South African Opens, seven Australian Opens, and five World Match Play Championships. He won nine majors, the third-most all time, and is one of only five to win the career Grand Slam. (He won three Masters, three British Opens, two PGA Championships, and one U.S. Open.)

Because he was from South Africa and played during the time of that country's oppressive apartheid policy, he was the target of protests—and even death threats—in the United States. "I didn't believe in apartheid," he later said, "and I surely wasn't responsible for it, but I was a ripe target." In fact, he worked to help provide education to underprivileged youth throughout rural South Africa through his Gary Player Foundation.

Player was inducted into the World Golf Hall of Fame in 1974. In 2000 he was voted South African Sportsman of the Century, and that year was also voted by *Golf Digest* the eighth-best player in the history of the game.

> "Golf is a puzzle without an answer. I've played the game for 40 years and I still haven't the slightest idea how to play."
>
> —Gary Player

BYRON NELSON

Nelson was born in 1912 near Fort Worth, Texas, and started golfing as a young boy at a local country club, along with his friend Ben Hogan. And like Hogan, Nelson became one of the dominant golfers of his era. He won 54 PGA tournaments over his career, including five majors (the 1937 and 1942 Masters, the 1939 U.S. Open, and the 1940 and 1945 PGA Championships), and recorded some of the best stretches of golf in history. From 1942 to 1946, Nelson finished in the top 10 in 65 straight tournaments. In 1945 alone he won 11 tournaments in a row and 18 overall.

Nelson retired at the age of 34 and lived the rest of his life at the Texas ranch he'd always dreamed of owning. His golf swing, which he developed for the change to steel-shafted clubs in the 1930s, is called the first "modern swing." It was so precise that it was the model for the PGA's testing robot, known as "Iron Byron." One of his protégés, Ken Venturi, said of him: "You can always argue who was the greatest player, but Byron is the finest gentleman the game has ever known." Nelson was inducted into the World Golf Hall of Fame in 1974.

> "The only shots you can be dead sure of are those you've already made."
> —**Byron Nelson**

TOM WATSON

Watson was born on September 4, 1949, in Kansas City, Missouri. As a freckle-faced (and very competitive) kid, he got the nickname "Huckleberry Dillinger." Records indicate he wasn't a great golfer as a youth, and not even when he was on the golf team at Stanford University. But that changed when he joined the PGA in 1971. By 1975 Watson and Jack Nicklaus were the two best golfers in the world, and after Nicklaus's dominance began to decline in the late 1970s, Watson took over. He finished as the leading money winner for four straight years (1977 to 1980), a record he shares with Tiger Woods, and was voted PGA Tour Player of the Year in six different seasons. He won 39 PGA events, eight of them majors, including two Masters, one U.S. Open, and five British Opens. His last win came in 1998 at the age of 49, and he has gone on to win six more times on the Champions Tour. Watson was inducted into the World Golf Hall of Fame in 1988,

A perfect shot or scoring 10 on a hole are both called a "Bo Derek" (star of the movie 10).

and in 1999 was made an honorary member of the Royal &
Ancient Golf Club of St. Andrews, one of only five Americans to
ever receive the honor. He still plays on the Champions
Tour…and occasionally even on the PGA Tour.

> "A putt cannot go in the hole if it's short. I'd rather face a
> four-footer coming back than leave the ball on the front lip."
> —**Tom Watson**

*   *   *

GREG NORMAN'S AUGUSTA HEARTBREAK

It was 1996. Tiger hadn't yet hit the scene and Jack and Arnie
were past their prime. Greg Norman was poised to take over; he'd
won two British Opens titles in the early 1990s, and was 1995
Player of the Year. A Masters win would solidify his place as one of
the all-time greats. And it looked good: Norman was heading into
the final round with a five stroke lead. Then it all fell apart.

He pulled his first drive into the woods, missed a two-foot putt
for par on 11 and an eagle putt fell an inch short on 15. Then his
tee shot on 16 landed in the lake. One of the largest final round
leads in Masters history was gone.

Meanwhile, his playing partner, Nick Faldo, cleared every hazard that Norman hit and hit every green that Norman missed.
Faldo shot a nearly flawless 67, the lowest round of the tournament. He walked up to a sullen Norman on 18, gave him a hug,
and whispered in his ear, "Don't let the b*stards get you down."

Good Sports, Bad Press

The "b*stards" Faldo was speaking of were the reporters who were
more interested in battering Norman about his meltdown than congratulating Faldo for his win. To his credit, Norman faced the
onslaught, answering all of the hard questions directly and keeping
his cool. "I screwed up. I know that. But losing this Masters is not
the end of the world. I'll wake up tomorrow, still breathing, I hope."

And the fans responded with thousands of letters of support.
"That whole experience helped change my life," Norman said
later. "I don't think I could have ever gotten the reaction, the letters, the outpouring if I had won."

No dough! The Masters prohibits TV announcers from ever mentioning prize money.

HOW'D YOU GET YOUR NICKNAME?

Some more nicknames for some legendary linksters.

Golden Bear: In his early days, Jack Nicklaus was known as "Ohio Fats" (he's from Columbus). In 1964 Australian golf writer Don Lawrence saw the upstart 24-year-old and thought Nicklaus looked more "like a cuddly golden bear." The name stuck.

• **Skeech:** LPGA legend Nancy Lopez got the name, said a friend, "from laying strips of rubber with her car."

• **El Niño:** Sergio Garcia got the name from golfer José Mañuel Lara because "he was rushing around the course like a hurricane."

• **Lumpy:** Portly Tim Herron says he got the name as a kid on his first day on the job at a golf course in Minnesota.

• **Dresses:** Australian star Aaron Baddeley was so nicknamed for his clothing style, as in "he dresses baddeley."

• **Boss of the Moss:** The "moss" is the green, and Loren Roberts got the name for his great putting game.

• **The Smilin' Assassin:** Japanese star Shigeki Maruyama is always smiling—and always a threat to beat you.

• **Wild Thing:** John Daly got the name for his on- and off-the-links lifestyle (including trashing hotel rooms and losing $2 million in Vegas… in two days).

• **Tank:** K. J. Choi, the first Korean-born golfer to earn a PGA Tour Card, was a power-lifter before he was a golfer. (He could squat 350 pounds—when he was 13 years old.)

• **Doc:** Cary Middlecoff, one of the best players of the 1950s, was a dentist before he was a golfer.

• **The Desert Fox:** Johnny Miller got the name after winning the Tucson Open three years in a row (1974–1976).

• **The Walrus:** Craig Stadler was so named, writes golf historian Dan Jenkins, "because he is built like a freezer and he has a mustache that is only slightly smaller than the forest around Lake Tahoe."

Jack Nicklaus once filled John Montgomerie's car with horse manure as a "friendly" prank.

THE 20th HOLE

*Golfers talk about "dying" on the 14th hole, but few of
them mean it literally. Be careful, though—even out on
the golf course, Death might want to play through.*

DER BINGLE

In 1977 a doctor told 74-year-old Bing Crosby that
because of his ill health, he should restrict his game to
nine holes. That was a tall order for the famous singer, who for
many years kept his handicap in single digits. On October 14,
Crosby and a friend were playing two Spanish pros at La Moraleja
golf course near Madrid. Crosby was shooting a great game—
prancing around the links and singing out loud. There was no way
he was stopping after nine holes.

Somewhere around the 15th, Crosby's partner noticed he was
favoring his left arm, but the crooner said he was okay and played
the last three holes. The good news: Crosby won, shooting an 85
for the day. The bad news: shortly after proclaiming, "That was a
great game of golf, fellas!" he collapsed. His friends thought he'd
slipped and they carried him back to the clubhouse. But Crosby
hadn't slipped, he suffered a major heart attack and died right
there on the links. His wife Kathryn issued a statement, saying: "I
can't think of any better way for a golfer who sings for a living to
finish his round."

HOGG HEAVEN

Jimmy Hogg, 77, was on the first hole at his Fife, Scotland, golf
club in 1996 when he suffered a major heart attack and died. Out
of respect, Hogg's partners waited for the ambulance to come and
take their friend away…then they resumed their round. "I'm sure
Jimmy would have wanted us to do that," said one.

WHAT WAS HE DOING THERE?

China has more than a billion people, but very few of them play
golf—it's a game for the superwealthy. When a civil servant
named Li Zhen'e was killed in a golf cart accident in 2003 (the
cart tumbled 30 feet down a slope onto a paved road), it created

an uproar about official corruption in the Hunan province. How could a modestly paid civil servant afford to play golf? In response to the public indignation, an official inquiry determined that Li Zhen'e was on the links only because he was conducting official government business, and not having fun.

DON'T GREVE FOR ME
A 65-year-old man named Donald DeGreve was golfing near his home in Winter Haven, Florida, in 1992. He died of a heart attack on the 16th green. But it was league day at the club, and dozens of golfers were still playing behind him. Solution: course officials left DeGreve's body on the 16th green, covered with a sheet. The rest of the field continued playing, going straight from the 15th green to the 17th tee to avoid disturbing the body while the club's management tried to contact the dead man's wife so she could make arrangements to "retrieve" her husband. "Life goes on," said one of the other players, "so we had to keep going."

HIGH-RISK SPORT?
Some fascinating facts about death and the links:
• A study in 1999 found that people who walked instead of rode in a cart had improved cholesterol levels and better overall health. (Ironically, however, many golfers spend their recreational time the way they spend their daily commute time—driving.)

• According to an insurance company that sells golf liability insurance, in 1999 alone a total of 9,291 British golfers were injured by golf clubs or balls, including 3,530 head injuries and 677 bone fractures.

• The most likely place to suffer an alligator attack in the United States is not in some swamp…but on a golf course. Still, your odds are pretty good. Of 365 reported alligator attacks on humans in recent years, only 3.6 percent (13 cases) were fatal.

THE FINAL LIE
Many die-hard players have had their ashes scattered on the greens. And if you can afford it, your remains can be set inside the shaft of a driver, so you can slice balls into the water long after you're gone.

THE RYDER CUP

Who the heck is Ryder and why do they want his cup?

BRITS AND YANKS

The Ryder Cup is the biennial competition between the best professional American and European golfers. They play for no prize money, but simply for the chance to win the cup, which they then get to keep for two years. Its popularity has gone up and down through the decades, but reached a new high in the 1990s, thanks to some excellent play—and a growing rivalry between the two teams.

The tournament began in the 1920s as an exclusive competition between American and British players. Professional golf was gaining popularity in the United States at the time, and some great players were beginning to emerge. Many golfers were regularly traveling back and forth between the U.S. and Great Britain to play in various tournaments. The Walker Cup had been established in 1922 as an international competition for amateur golfers, and some people thought it was time to make an official match for the pros.

PLANTING THE SEED

In 1925 Samuel Ryder, an English businessman (and amateur golfer) who had made a fortune selling penny-packets of seeds, decided to do something about it. He proposed an official tournament between American and British professional golfers—and he backed up his proposal. He donated a 16-inch-high, 14-carat gold trophy topped by the figure of a golfer. (Pop quiz: Which golfer inspired it? Answer at the end of the article.) That got the attention of the PGA of America, which had recently been formed in 1916, as well as the British PGA, founded in 1901. They agreed to sponsor a tournament to be played the following year at Wentworth Golf Club, just outside of London. The British team would be captained by Ted Ray, winner of the 1912 British Open and the 1920 U.S. Open, and the American team by Walter Hagen.

It was also agreed that a match play format would be used. Most PGA tournaments today are stroke play. In match play, golfers play for the lowest number of strokes on each hole, collecting one point for each hole they win. The first day would be four "foursome" matches—two players on a team, each team playing with one ball and alternating shots; the next day would be ten singles—or one-on-one matches. That year there were 14 total matches with 14 total points.

A TRADITION LAUNCHED

The British team trounced the Americans that year with a score of 13½ to 1½. (The Brits won 13 matches, the Yanks won one, and one was tied.) But Ryder refused to award a trophy to the Brits— four of the ten "Americans" were British-born and one was Australian-born. So they decided that the 1926 match would be called "unofficial" and that the first official match would be played the next year, in 1927. From then on it would be played every two years with the location alternating between the United States and Great Britain. And every player on a country's team had to be native-born.

The 1927 match was held at the Worcester Country Club in Worcester, Massachusetts. Some of the names on the first U.S. Ryder Cup team: Walter Hagen, who would be the captain of the first six teams; Joe Turnesa, of the seven golfing Turnesa brothers; and Gene Sarazen. The British team consisted of such golfing greats as Ted Ray, Archie Compston, and Arthur Havers. More than 8,000 people showed up to watch the matches over the two days, and saw the Americans make up for the previous year's loss with a 9½ to 2½ win. The Ryder Cup was off and running.

RYDER CUP HIGHLIGHTS

• **1931:** During a match in Columbus, Ohio, Gene Sarazen hit a tee shot on the par-3 4th into a shack. He chipped the ball off the concrete floor through an open window and the ball landed 10 feet from the pin. The Americans won the cup, 9 to 3.

• **1937:** In England, Sarazen sent a shot at a par-3 hole into a woman's lap behind the green. She reflexively knocked it off— onto the green—and Sarazen made birdie. He won the match by one hole and the United States won the cup, 8 to 4.

• **1947:** The first competition in 10 years (because of World War II) was almost canceled when the Brits couldn't afford the trip. But wealthy Oregonian Robert Hudson offered his course, the Portland Country Club, for the matches, and paid the way for the British

---

Smokin': English golfer Archie Compston had a second caddie just for his tobacco and pipes.

team. All good feelings vanished, though, when Britain's Henry Cotton accused Ben Hogan of having illegal grooves in the faces of his clubs. Officials disagreed—and the United States won 11 to 1, one of the biggest whippings in the cup's history.

• **1949:** At the Ganton Golf Club in England, U.S. captain Ben Hogan turned the tables on the Brits and accused them of having illegal grooves in *their* clubs…before the matches even began. A Royal and Ancient official inspected the clubs—and agreed. The Brits were forced to send the clubs away to be filed down. The Americans won again, 7 to 5.

• **1957:** The Brits won for the first time since 1933. They wouldn't win again until the 1980s.

• **1963:** A new game is added to the event: fourball. Day one now has eight alternate-shot foursomes matches; day two has eight four-ball matches (two teams of two, each man with their own ball and the best one being scored); and day three has 16 singles matches.

1969: The Ryder Cup sees one of its more sportsmanlike moments at Royal Birkdale in England when Jack Nicklaus concedes Tony Jacklin's final putt in the final match, ending the event in a tie for the first time.

1973: Ireland is added to the British team, with the team now being known as GB&I—Great Britain and Ireland.

1979: To bolster waning interest in the event (from lack of competition—the British had won only one Ryder Cup since 1933), a change was made. Henceforth, the matches would be between the United States and Europe, bringing such stars as Spaniard Seve Ballesteros and German Bernhard Langer to the competition.

1981: The last format change was made: four foursomes and four fourballs on days one and two, and 12 singles matches on day three, making 28 total points.

1985: The American team is beaten for the first time since 1957.

1989: Europe kept the cup (they won in 1987 also) with the second tie in history.

1999: The United States made the biggest comeback in cup history, fighting back from a 6 to 10 deficit to a 14½ to 13½ win. The highlight was Justin Leonard's 45-foot putt at the 17th, after which

Playing through: At the Jinja Golf Course in Uganda, elephants have the right of way.

the American team roared onto the green in celebration...before Spain's Jose Maria Olazabal attempted a 25-footer that could have tied the match (it didn't). The Americans were roundly ripped in the British press and some individual golfers, including Tiger Woods, were criticized after suggesting that since the PGA makes millions on the event, the players should be paid for playing.

2001: The Ryder Cup was interrupted for the second time in its history after the attacks of September 11, 2001. It was held in 2002 instead, and henceforth would be played in even-numbered years.

2004: The format change that made the Brit team into Team Europe has proven successful in terms of equalizing the teams and improving the cup's popularity. In the 13 matches since the change, the United States has won six, Team Europe has won six, and the teams have tied once. In 2004 Team Europe beat the United States by a score of 18½ to 9½, the biggest American loss in the cup's history.

POP QUIZ ANSWER: Samuel Ryder honored his own professional instructor (and original captain of the first British Ryder Cup team), Abe Mitchell, by putting Mitchell's likeness on top of the trophy. Unfortunately, Mitchell got appendicitis right before the match and couldn't compete for the cup. He chose Ted Ray to take his place.

*　　*　　*

ON THE COURSE AGAIN, JUST CAN'T WAIT TO GET ON THE COURSE AGAIN...

Country singer Willie Nelson owns his own golf course, where the rules include:

• No more than 12 to a foursome.

• Change-jingling or wind-letting on the greens is forbidden.

• If you land in rocks, you can take the "Pedernales Stroll" option: picking up your ball and walking it onto the grass.

• USGA rules apply except where you can think of something better.

GOLF AND GOD

*We've noticed that when talking about golf, a lot
of people like to mention the man upstairs.
Coincidence? Hmmmm…*

"Some of us worship in churches, some in synagogues, some on golf courses."
—**Adlai Stevenson**

"There are two things you can do with your head down—play golf and pray."
—**Lee Trevino**

"If I'm on the course and lightning starts, I get inside fast. If God wants to play through, let him."
—**Bob Hope**

"Watching the Masters on CBS is like attending a church service. Announcers speak in hushed, pious tones, as if to convince us that something of great meaning and historical importance is taking place. What we are actually seeing is grown men hitting little balls with sticks."
—**Tom Gilmore**

"If you are caught on a golf course during a storm and are afraid of lightning, hold up a one-iron. Not even God can hit a one-iron."
—**Lee Trevino**

"The only time my prayers go unanswered is on the golf course."
—**Billy Graham**

"I never pray to God to make a putt. I pray to God to help me react good if I miss a putt."
—**Chi Chi Rodriguez**

"I'm gambling that when we get to the next life, St. Peter will look at us and ask, 'Golfer?' And when we nod, he'll step aside and say, 'Go right in; you've suffered enough.' One warning: if you go in and the first thing you see is a par-3 surrounded by water, it ain't heaven."
—**Jim Murray**

"I just hope I don't have to explain all the times I've used His name in vain."
—**Bob Hope**

"If you call on God to improve the results of a shot while it is still in motion, you are using an 'outside agency' and subject to appropriate penalties under the rules of golf."
—**Henry Longhurst**

75% of professional golfers admit to praying on the course.

#$-%&*@!
(FLUBBED IT!)

More stories about some of golf's most famous goofs.

BLUE BIRDIE

Sam Snead won more tournaments than anyone in the history of the PGA (82), but he never won a U.S. Open. One of the great disappointments in his career came at the 1939 U.S. Open at Philadelphia Country Club, which he almost certainly would have won were it not for a mental error. Snead came to the final hole, a par-5, knowing he needed a birdie to win. That induced him to take the risk of going for the green in two shots—but it didn't pay off. He ended up in the bunker and finished with a triple-bogey 8. The worst part: he was wrong about the birdie—a simple par would have won him the tournament.

CRYBABY

At the 2001 Royal Caribbean Classic, Isao Aoki got distracted by a crying baby in the gallery and missed a five-foot putt for par. Miffed, he took a one-handed swing at the tap-in for bogey, whiffed it, and ended up with a double bogey. The tournament was using Stableford scoring, in which players receive points based on how well they do on each hole. The flub cost Aoki two points. Even worse: he lost the tournament by one point.

TRAIN WRECK

Arnold Palmer had a five-stroke lead at the 1966 U.S. Open with four holes to go. In very un-Palmerlike fashion, he lost the seemingly insurmountable lead and finished the round in a tie with Billy Casper. "I doubt if I have ever felt as alone or as devastated on the golf course," he said years later. "I know what a train wreck the world was witnessing." The next day, he lost the playoff. What he did after the tournament, however, was very Palmerlike. A USGA official discreetly offered to sneak Palmer out the back door of the clubhouse so he could avoid the press. He refused. "I deserve everything they want to give me."

Golf lingo: caddying for a player who has an awful round is called a "safari."

RANGE BALLS AND SHAG BAGS

Our guide to golfspeak, Q–S.

Q School: PGA Tour Qualifying School. (For more info, see page 91.)

Quarter shot: A shot hit with a greatly reduced swing (presumably 25% of a normal swing).

R & A: The Royal and Ancient Golf Club of St. Andrews, golf's governing body worldwide (except in the United States and Mexico).

Range balls: Golf balls specifically made to be used on a driving range.

Ranger: An on-course official who keeps play moving at a proper pace (in other words, not too slowly).

Rating marker: A permanent marker next to the tee from which the yardage to the green is measured.

Reading the green: Determining how a ball will roll on the green, i.e., its speed and path.

Recovery shot: A shot taken to get out of an undesirable position, such as in the woods.

Release: When a ball releases on the green, it lands and then rolls forward, rather than stopping on impact.

Relief: Moving the ball before taking a shot. A golfer is entitled to relief without penalty in some situations, such as when a ball lands in a gopher hole.

Rough: The high grass adjacent to the fairway and green.

Routing: The path an entire golf course takes from the 1st hole to the 18th.

Run: The distance the ball travels after it hits the ground.

Sandbagger: A golfer who pretends to be worse than he actually is, usually to gain an unfair advantage for gambling.

Sand wedge: A highly lofted iron designed to lift balls out of sand traps.

Sclaff: Onomatopoetic Scottish word for when a club hits or scrapes the ground well behind the ball.

Scoop: An improper swing that attempts to lift the ball into the air rather than letting the club loft it.

Scratch player: A golfer who has a zero handicap or better.

Semiprivate course: A club with members that also allows the public to pay and play.

Shag bag: A bag for carrying practice balls.

Shagging: Picking up balls from a practice range.

Shank: To hit the ball on the hosel, making it fly way off to the right (for a right-hander).

Short game: The parts of the game that comprise the shorter shots—chipping, pitching, and putting.

Shotgun start: When players in a tournament start from different holes at the same time.

Skull: To hit the ball above its center, making it fly low to the ground. ("Skulled it!")

Sky: To hit only the bottom of the ball, making it fly straight up. ("Skied it!")

Slice: A shot that curves sharply to the right (for a right-hander) due to sidespin. (The opposite of hook.)

Smile: A cut in a golf ball. (It looks like a smile.)

Snake: A long, winding putt.

Snap hook: An especially sharp hook.

Snipe: A ball that hooks but also drops very quickly.

Sole: The bottom of the clubhead.

Spade-mashie: Old term for a six-iron.

Speed (or green speed): How fast or slow a ball will roll on a green, given its condition (dry, wet, etc.).

Spike wrench: Tool used to remove spikes from shoes.

Spoon: A three-wood.

Spot putting: Aiming at a spot other than the hole to account for a green's break.

Square stance: When both feet are parallel and at right angles to the ball.

Stance: The position of your feet as you prepare to swing.

Starter: The official who introduces players and oversees play at the first tee.

Stick: The flagstick.

Stimpmeter: An instrument used to accurately measure the speed of a green. (Named for its inventor, Edward Stimpson.)

Straightaway: A hole with a straight fairway.

Stroke: A completed swing, whether it hits the ball or not.

Stymie: When a ball's path to the hole is blocked by an object such as a bush or tree.

Swale: A depression in the ground.

Sweet spot: The preferred spot on the clubface with which to hit the ball.

"Divorce court" is golfer slang for couples who play together.

Golf in the Year 2000

*More wacky predictions about the future of golf from
the 1892 book* Golf in the Year 2000, or, What We
Are Coming To *by Scottish golfer, J. McCullough.
He came close on some, but was way off on others.*
(For the first part of the story, see page 138.)

(For the first part of the story, see page 138.)

A **man's place is on the course:** "[Adams told me that] all we men have got to do is to play golf, while the women do all the work.

"'What?' I cried, slapping my knee, 'the dream of my former existence come true! I am, indeed, a lucky man to see it. The women working while the men play golf! Splendid!…Oh, how I would like to wake up some of my old chums! I know a few who would appreciate the arrangement.'"

Televised golf: "'This will give you some idea to what lengths we have brought golf. You observe there is a double row of poles, one on each side of the course. Between those two rows a mirror is suspended horizontally at the height of four hundred and fifty feet, covering the whole length of the green. Of course it does not require to be the breadth of the course; a strip down the centre serves the purpose. The glass is only put up when an important match is in progress. Everything going on on the green is then reflected overhead; in the club-house, at the first hole, there is a small mirror, so placed that it reflects what is in the large mirror overhead, at any point you choose. Thus, when a match starts, the small mirror is almost horizontal, the players being so close, and being first reflected to the mirror above and then back again on to the small one.'

"'As the players get further off—of course we are only following one couple or foursome, as the case may be—the small mirror gradually tilts up, till, when the players are at the furthest distance from the start, it is at an angle of about eighty degrees. Then gradually, as the players return, the angle gets smaller, till the glass resumes its former almost horizontal position. You observe it has been following the reflection of the players all this time. It is worked by a female, who has full charge of it, and has to be very careful in the following of the match.'"

The clubhead of a driver stays in contact with the ball for half a thousandth of a second.

Following the action: "'This small mirror is connected by a wire, specially prepared, as in the case of the theatre wires, to a mirror in London, we will say, though of course it can be, and sometimes is, connected with a thousand different mirrors....The figures are seen life-size, walking along and taking their shots; indeed, you see them from the first drive off, till they hole out the last putt; and people in London and all the large towns can watch a golf match going on here. They pay two shillings, take a seat as if they were at a theatre, and watch the reflection on their own special mirrors, wherever they may be. Of course they don't hear anything. But you mustn't think every golfing green has this contrivance; it is confined to only a very few, I think about fifty or so, and they play the big matches only on those.'

"'By Jove!' I said, 'that seems almost a fable; but I would like to be in London and watch a match played here.'"

Make Golf, Not War: "I should mention, by the way, that wars had ceased in Europe. They had come to be too much of a farce. Guns and rifles were out of date altogether. They had invented some kind of gas which, encased in a bomb, could be projected any distance up to one hundred miles, and then made to burst. When it burst it turned everybody within a radius of ten miles insensible, and they remained so for about two days. Thus one shot would render a whole army *hors de combat.*

"An agreement was therefore come to among the powers of Europe that wars should cease, and disputes should instead be settled by—by what do you think? Why, golf matches. There is a triumph for golf. Fancy the fate of an empire hanging on a putt—the hopes of a country shattered by a bad lying ball!

"These matches were, however, very rare. They were played by a hundred men a-side—fifty playing in the one country and fifty in the other, and each couple on a separate green. You may judge the excitement such matches caused in the country—or the world, for the matter of that. They were watched eagerly by crowds in every large town, and the position of the whole match was known at every hole. If a Frenchman missed a short putt at Pau, it was seen, and chuckled over, throughout the whole of Great Britain."

The April Foolish Open in Florida poses temporary hazards such as clotheslines of laundry.

SCOTLAND'S GAME: A TIMELINE

*How golf was first played in Scotland, and
how it developed into the game we know today.*

THE FIFTEENTH CENTURY

1420s: "Gowf" is being played on Scotland's east coast, in the county of Fife. Handmade wooden clubs and balls are used.

1457: The earliest known official mention of golf is made by Scotland's King James II, when he makes playing golf illegal. Reason: the game had become so popular that it was taking away from the men's military training (mostly archery), and James was expecting an attack by the English. The ban on the game was upheld in 1470 and 1491…but research says most people ignored it.

THE SIXTEENTH CENTURY

1502: Golf gets its first official boost. With the signing of the Treaty of Glasgow between England and Scotland, King James IV lifts the ban on golf. The probable reason for the move shows up in his official accounts: a 1502 purchase of golf clubs and balls. Apparently, James IV loved the game, and his royal endorsement led to its spread among royalty all across Scotland. Although where James played is unknown, the town of Perth claims to have hosted the first royal golfer.

1504: Official court records show that on February 3, history's first documented golf match is played between King James IV and the Earl of Bothwell.

1513: In a letter to a friend, Queen Catherine of England mentions the growing popularity of the sport in her realm.

1527: The first "commoner" recorded to be a golfer is Sir Robert Maule. A town register says he liked to "exercisit the gowf" near the now-legendary golfing town of Carnoustie.

1553: The archbishop of St. Andrews gives approval for local people to play "golff" (and other sports) on public land.

A ball that lands on a road or path is called a "Willie," as in Willie Nelson.

1567: Mary, Queen of Scots is criticized when she plays golf just days after the murder of her husband (to which some historians believe she was a party).

1589: Golf is banned in the Blackfriars Yard, Glasgow, marking the earliest reference to the game in the west of Scotland.

1592: The City of Edinburgh bans golfing at Leith on Sundays.

THE SEVENTEENTH CENTURY

1618: King James VI of Scotland (and I of England) makes Sunday golf legal again.

1620: A new ball—leather-stitched and stuffed with feathers—is introduced in Scotland. The "featherie" improves ball flight, which helps make the game more popular. It is also expensive, which helps to keep the game a "gentleman's" sport.

1641: King Charles I of England is playing golf at Leith Links when he learns of the Irish Rebellion, an event that led to the English Civil War the following year.

1691: St. Andrews is already known as "the metropolis of golfing."

THE EIGHTEENTH CENTURY

1735: The Edinburgh Burgess Golfing Society claims this as the year of their founding, which would make them the world's oldest golf club. However, their claim is questionable—there's no official record of their existence until 1770.

1744: The Gentlemen Golfers of Leith (they will later become the Honourable Company of Edinburgh Golfers) form what *they* insist is the first golf club. They also organize the first known annual golf competition, played at Leith Links, and for the event they write up the first recorded rules of golf (see page 118).

1754: The St. Andrews Society of Fife, later the Royal and Ancient Golf Club of St. Andrews, adopts a version of Leith's 13 rules. They also buy a silver club trophy for their own championship. Their competition is the first with the stroke play scoring format.

1764: The St. Andrews golfers reduce the number of holes from 22 to 18 for a match. (Their course had ten holes, eight of which were played twice.) As they become the premier golf club over the years, 18 becomes the standard number of holes.

That's a hazard: Tony Lema once fell off a cliff during a tournament. (He lived.)

1766: The Royal Blackheath Club, near London, becomes the first golf club outside of Scotland.

1767: James Durham's winning score of 94 for the 18 holes of the St. Andrews silver cup competition sets a record that will stand for 86 years.

1768: The Golf House at Leith is built, becoming the first known golf clubhouse.

1770: The first recorded yelling of "Fore!" by Scottish reformer John Knox.

THE NINETEENTH CENTURY

1820: The Bangalore Club in India becomes the first golf club outside the British Isles. The Royal Calcutta Golf Club will follow in 1829. As the British Empire continues to grow, the game spreads around the world.

1826: Hickory from America is first imported by Scottish craftsmen to make golf club shafts. It will be the standard wood for shafts for about 100 years, until steel replaces it in the 1930s.

1833: King William IV gives the title "Royal" to the Perth Golfing Society, making it the first club so endowed. A year later, he will make St. Andrews "Royal and Ancient."

1836: Samuel Messieux hits what is the longest drive ever recorded with a featherie ball, 361 yards, at Elysian Fields, St. Andrews.

1848: The gutta-percha golf ball, or "gutty," is invented in St. Andrews by Robert Adams Paterson. It is much less expensive than the "featherie" and the game now becomes more accessible to the general public.

1850: Iron starts to be used for clubheads.

1857: The first book on golf, *The Golfer's Manual*, is published in Scotland by H. B. Farnie.

1858: Allan Robertson, the world's first professional golfer, becomes the first to break 80 at the Old Course at St. Andrews. That same year, the R&A issues new rules for its members with Rule 1 being: "...one round of the Links or 18 holes is reckoned a match unless otherwise stipulated."

1860: The first Open Championship, better known as the British

Open, is played at Prestwick Golf Club in Ayrshire, Scotland. Willie Park wins.

1867: The first golf club for women, the Ladies' Golf Club at St. Andrews, is founded.

1870: The first mention of "par" is written. English writer A. H. Doleman asked pros Davie Strath and Jamie Anderson what score would be needed to win the Open at Prestwick. They said that playing perfectly would result in a score of 49 over the 12-hole course. Doleman called it "par," from the Latin word for "equal."

1880: The next great improvement in golf technology occurs when gutta-percha balls, invented in 1848, are made with molds that put dimples on the surface, greatly improving the ball's aerodynamics.

1890: Hugh Rotherham introduces the concept of "ground score," a hypothetical "perfect" golfer's score on every hole. Dr. Thomas Brown of the Great Yarmouth Golf Club calls that hypothetical golfer a "bogey man" after a popular song about an elusive man who hides in the shadows. The "bogey man" was equated with the elusive perfect golf game and "bogey" came to mean that perfect score. Years later, as equipment and scores improved, it changed to one over the perfect score, which became "par."

1892: Gate receipts are used as prize money for the first time in Cambridge, England.

1893: The first international golf tournament—the Amateur Golf Championship of India and the East—is held at the Royal Calcutta Club. It is still played and is one of the world's oldest golf tournaments after the British Open.

1897: The Royal and Ancient Golf Club of St. Andrews is given sole control of the Rules of Golf Committee.

By 1900 golf had become a popular and well-organized international sport, with courses in France, India, South Africa, the United States, Canada, and Australia. Despite a few changes (mostly due to technology), golf remains the same game developed over centuries by the Scots, and Scotland will always be considered golf's homeland.

Biodegradable tees were introduced in the 1980s. Early models dissolved in golfers' pockets.

NEW RULES

In 2004 the Royal and Ancient Golf Club of St. Andrews and the USGA, the two leading rule-making bodies in the world of golf, made the biggest rewrite of the rules of golf in 20 years. Here are some of the new rules.

S TUDY UP
• If you fail to yell "Fore!" when you hit an errant shot or if you smash your club into the ground in a fit of golfing fury, you can be disqualified.

• You can now use a towel or rag to remove loose impediments from the line of a putt. Before 2004, you could only use your hand or your club.

• If you're in a water hazard and you touch the water or the ground with your hand or club to stabilize yourself, it's a two-stroke penalty. (In match play it's the loss of a hole.)

• Maximum tee height is 4 inches, and all tees must be specifically designed for the purpose of holding a golf ball off the ground—no more pencils to raise a ball up. Penalty: disqualification.

• Before 2004, if you moved a leaf, twig, or other "loose impediment" within a club's length (three feet) of your ball, and then the ball happened to roll because it was blown by a gust of wind or because it was on a slope, you were penalized. Not anymore—the rule was eliminated.

• Golfers may accept prizes with a maximum value of $750, up from $500, without losing their amateur status.

• Using two caddies at the same time used to be an automatic disqualification. That rule was changed because of an incident in 2003. Mark Johnson was playing in the Arizona Mid-Amateur Championship on Father's Day. He had his 14-year-old son, Seth, caddying for him, and Seth had brought a friend along. During the final round, Seth handed a putter to his friend, who then handed it to Johnson. Johnson was disqualified for using two caddies—and he was leading by eleven strokes. The USGA received so many complaints that they changed it to a two-stroke penalty.

Andy Bean once had to grab a six-foot gator by the tail and flip it over to play his shot.

DRESSED TO KILL

"Golf and fashion go together like politics and honesty." —Uncle John

"The golf course is the only place I can go dressed like a pimp and fit in perfectly. Anywhere else, lime-green pants and alligator shoes, I got a cop on my ass."
—**Samuel L. Jackson**

"'Play it as it lies' is one of the fundamental dictates of golf. The other is 'Wear it if it clashes.'"
—**Henry Beard**

"Although golf was originally restricted to wealthy, overweight Protestants, today it's open to anybody who owns hideous clothing."
—**Dave Barry**

"The one thing in this world dumber than playing golf is watching someone else playing golf. What do you actually get to see? Thirty-seven guys in polyester slacks squinting at the sun. Doesn't that set your blood racing?"
—**Peter Andrews**

"Baffling late-life discovery: Golfers wear those awful clothes on purpose!"
—**Herb Caen**

"You can't call it a sport. You don't run, jump, you don't shoot, you don't pass. All you have to do is buy some clothes that don't match."
—**Steve Sax**

"Golf is not a sport. Golf is men in ugly pants walking."
—**Rosie O'Donnell**

"Hockey is a sport for white men. Basketball is a sport for black men. Golf is a sport for white men dressed like black pimps."
—**Tiger Woods**

"I'd give up golf if I didn't have so many sweaters."
—**Bob Hope**

"To play golf you need goofy pants and a fat ass."
—**Adam Sandler,**
Happy Gilmore

"I figured it out,
The thing my game lacks:
I'll never be a pro
'Cause I can't stand the slacks."
—**John Prince**

"Nobody asked how you looked, just what you shot."
—**Sam Snead**

Tammie Green participated in the 1998 Solheim Cup...while six months pregnant.

VARIATIONS ON A GAME

Here are some of golf's grandkids.

GAME: XTreme Golf
RULES: It's just like regular golf, except the players run instead of walk. The final score is the number of shots added to the number of minutes it takes to complete 18 holes. So if a player shoots a 75 in 35 minutes, his score is 110.

HISTORY: Steve Scott made a name for himself in the 1970s and '80s for breaking the American record for running the mile (his 3:47.69 is still the U.S. record). In 1979 he wanted to see how fast he could play a round of golf. So he went to the Dad Miller Golf Course in Anaheim, California, and after completing the course in 29 minutes, 30 seconds (shooting a 95), he had set a new world record for the fastest round of golf. The new sport didn't catch on, but Scott's round quickly became legendary.

Fifteen years later, John Bell, the head pro at the Ram's Hill Golf Course in Borrego Springs, California, wanted to prove to his members that if golfers played faster, they'd play better. So in 1994 he invited Scott, along with a few other world-class runners, to play an exhibition round. The event was a success. A few months later, ESPN aired the PowerBar Speed Golf Challenge, making XTreme golf an official sport.

Interested in trying this intense workout? Check with your local course for an XTreme Golf club in your area. Players usually start at dawn so as not to disturb the slower golfers.

GAME: Disc Golf
RULES: First of all, it's not Frisbee golf—it's disc golf. In disc golf, instead of hitting a ball into a hole in the ground, a player throws his disc—a smaller, heavier type of Frisbee—into a specially made chain basket suspended on a pole. For the most part, disc golf plays like regular golf, i.e., the player who is away throws first. One variation is that the thrower gets a running start for long throws. And just as a golfer has differently lofted clubs for different shots, the disc golfer has specially weighted discs for driving, approaching, and putting.

Augusta's minor league baseball team is known as the Green Jackets.

HISTORY: Disc golf was unofficially born in the 1960s when Frisbee throwers became bored with just throwing Frisbees to each other. Early courses were usually neighborhoods—the "holes" being trees, fire hydrants, telephone poles, etc. In the 1970s, Ed Headrick, the man who had earlier patented the modern Frisbee at Wham-O, wanted to make disc golf a legitimate sport. He founded the Disc Golf Association in 1976 and set up the first course in Pasadena, California.

Today, there are an estimated three million recreational players and 20,000 professionals in the PDGA (Professional Disc Golf Association). The United States alone has more than 1,000 courses—200 of them designed by Headrick. The Disc Golf World Championship is held on a different course each year.

Uncle John's warning: DO NOT try to catch a thrown disc. They are not Frisbees—they hurt. (How was he supposed to know?)

GAME: Shotgun Golf

RULES: It's a two-player combination of golf and skeet shooting. One player stands at the tee with a golf club, the other stands 10 feet away with a "finely tuned 12-gauge shotgun." The golfer hits a drive toward the green and the shooter tries to blow it out of the air. If the shooter hits the ball, he gets two points. If he misses and the golfer gets his ball to stay on the green, that's two for the golfer. Then the players switch equipment and head to round two.

HISTORY: It was invented in 2004 by gonzo journalist, golfer, and gun aficionado Hunter S. Thompson at his Owl Farm in Colorado. He described it in his "Hey Rube" column on espn.com. "Shotgun golf will take America by storm," he wrote. "It will bring a whole new meaning to the words 'driving range.'...And given the mood of this country, being that a lot of people in the mood to play golf are also in the mood to shoot something, I think it would take off like a gigantic fad. I see it as the first truly violent leisure sport." Sadly, Thompson took his own life before the official launching of his new sport. Perhaps his legions of fans will keep his dream alive by setting up their own shotgun golf courses. Listen for one near you.

"It's good sportsmanship to not pick up golf balls while they are still rolling." —Mark Twain

THE SQUIRE

The shooter of the "Shot Heard 'Round the World," and so much more.

CHAMPION: Gene Sarazen

BACKGROUND: Born Eugenio Saraceni to Italian immigrant parents in Harrison, New York, on February 2, 1902.

HIS STORY: He was introduced to golf at the age of nine when he was given a golf club for a birthday present. The Saracenis were very poor, so Gene had to drop out of school in the sixth grade to do odd jobs and help support the family, including working as a caddie at a nearby golf course. By the time he was 13, he had shot his first round under 70. But his father soon made him go to work in his carpentry shop and wouldn't allow him to go to the course. Then, at age 15, Gene became very sick and the family doctor told his parents that he needed an outdoor job. The outdoor job: assistant pro at the golf club. At 16 he changed his name to Gene Sarazen because he thought the name "sounded like a golfer." He turned pro at 18 and just two years later, in 1922, won both the U.S. Open and the PGA Championship, and then won the PGA Championship again the next year.

CAREER HIGHLIGHTS

• He won 39 tournaments in his career, seven of them majors.

• He played in the first Ryder Cup in 1927, helping the Americans to a 9 ½ to 2 ½ win.

• In 1931, with the airplane as inspiration (some historians say he got the inspiration from his friend Howard Hughes), he invented the sand wedge by soldering extra metal on the back of an iron. "When a pilot wants to take off, he doesn't raise the tail of his plane," he said, "he lowers it. Accordingly, I was lowering the tail or sole of my niblick to produce a club whose face would come up from the sand as the sole made contact with the sand." He started using it professionally in 1932...and won the British Open and the U.S. Open that year. In 1933 he won his third PGA Championship—and then everybody started using the sand wedge.

Oldest golf club in North America: Canada's Royal Montreal Golf Club (1873).

- In 1932 he was named Associated Press Male Athlete of the Year.

- Until Ian Woosnam won in 1991, he was the shortest Masters winner ever. (Sarazen was 5'5", Woosnam was 5'4½")

- On April 7, 1935, he hit one of the most famous golf shots in history at the second Masters, helping to launch that tournament into its fame. (Read about the "Shot Heard 'Round the World" on page 170.) "The aspect I cherish most," he said about his amazing double eagle, "is that both Walter Hagen and Bobby Jones witnessed the shot."

- With his 1935 Masters win, "the Squire" became the first golfer to win the professional Grand Slam (the Masters, the U.S. Open, the British Open, and the PGA Championship). He is also one of only two (Fuzzy Zoeller, 1979) to win the Masters on his first attempt.

- He played competitively until 1973—when he was 71 years old. In 1973 he played the 50th anniversary of his British Open win. At Royal Troon's famous "Postage Stamp" hole, Sarazen made a hole in one.

- In 1996 he won the PGA Tour's first Lifetime Achievement Award.

- A bridge by the 15th green at Augusta National is called "Sarazen Bridge."

- He was inducted into the World Golf Hall of Fame in its first year, 1974.

- From 1981 until 1999, Sarazen joined Byron Nelson and Sam Snead in hitting a ceremonial tee shot before each Masters. A month after teeing off in 1999, Sarazen died at the age of 97.

*   *   *

"I don't care what you say about me. Just spell the name right."

—Gene Sarazen

Members of Augusta National may not wear their green jackets off the club grounds.

A DIMPLED HISTORY OF THE GOLF BALL

The evolution of the little white ball.

THE WOOD ERA

The first golf balls—from golf's early years in Scotland—were made of wood. No examples survive, but historians believe the original balls were made of hardwoods such as beech or yew. Each was made individually by hand, which meant that each one was a different shape, size, and weight—making it nearly impossible to keep an even playing field. Wooden balls would dominate golf from the 15th century until the 17th century, when the "featherie" came along. These were leather balls stuffed with feathers, so you might assume that they were soft and lightweight, but they weren't. Featheries were made with *wet* leather and feathers; when they dried, the feathers expanded and the leather shrank, making them very hard.

Here's a description of the featherie-making process from H. Thomas Peters's *Reminiscences of Golf and Golfer* (1890):

> The leather was of untanned bull's hide, two round pieces for the ends and a piece for the middle, being cut to suit the weight wanted. These were properly shaped, after being sufficiently softened, and then were firmly sewn together. A small hole was left through which the feathers would be afterwards inserted. But before stuffing, it was through this little hole that the leather itself had to be turned outside in. This was a very difficult operation that resulted in only smooth seams showing on the exterior of the ball.
>
> The skin was then placed in a cup-shaped stand and the worker placed the appropriate amount of feathers in the pocket of his apron. The actual stuffing was done with a crutch-handled steel rod, which the maker placed under his arm. And very hard work, I may add, it was. After the ball was tightly packed, the aperture was closed and firmly sewed up. The resultant ball was smooth and only the outside seam was visible.

The featheries were then given three coats of paint. Result: the end product was as hard as a rock...and fairly round. Making them was a time-consuming process, which made them very expensive, helping maintain golf's status as a game played mostly by the wealthy. That would change with the advent of the "gutty."

THE GUTTY

In 1848 Reverend Robert Paterson invented the gutty. It was so named because it was made from gutta-percha, a tough substance made from the resin of the Isonandra Gutta tree in Malaysia. Gutta-percha was first seen in Europe in 1843, when Dr. William Montgomerie, a surgeon in the British army, sent samples from Singapore to the Royal Society of Arts in London. They found that they could heat it and shape it, and when it cooled it would retain that shape in a hard, plasticlike texture. For golf balls, it meant that for the first time they could make something very close to a sphere that would roll straight and true.

And more than that:

• They were more durable and water-resistant and flew better than featheries.

• They could be made fairly quickly in presses, so they were cheap (which—along with the fact that golf clubs were also now being mass-produced—made golf much more accessible to middle-class players).

• They could be repaired by heating them up and reshaping them.

• And golfers noticed something else about guttys: old ones flew farther than new ones. Why? All the nicks and scars on the ball's surface reduced drag as it flew and allowed the ball to travel farther. So manufacturers began to make the balls with rough surfaces. The "bramble" design, which resembled a brambleberry, became the most popular type of gutty, and was the first textured golf ball.

THE HASKELL

The gutty reached the end of its days in 1898 when Coburn Haskell, in association with the BF Goodrich Company, invented the Haskell. It had a solid rubber core wrapped with rubber thread, and a gutta-percha cover. It took a while for golfers to accept them, but when Walter Travis won the 1901 U.S. Amateur using a Haskell ball (it gave him an average of 20 more yards per drive), American players got interested. When Alex Herd won the British Open with a Haskell in 1902, they became accepted in Europe as well.

Hole in one (tooth): Gutta-percha rubber was used for dental fillings in the 18th century.

In 1905 inventor William Taylor took the process a step further and gave the balls a dimple pattern. The modern golf ball was born.

The basic design hasn't changed much since, but the manufacturing process and materials have. Over the years, different substances have been tried for cores—steel, glass, silicone, water, iodine, mercury, dry ice, arsenic, and even tapioca. In 1906 Goodrich even tried using compressed air. Unfortunately for the "pneumatic" balls (and their owners), heat caused the air to expand and they would sometimes explode.

Another change in the early 1900s was the use of *balata*, a rubbery material once made from tree resin, but today made synthetically, for the cover. It made for a softer, springier ball that golfers liked because it gave the ball more "feel" and better spin control. Balata remained the basic golf ball cover for much of the 20th century.

THE MODERN ERA
The golf ball had come a long way since the days of wooden balls, but there was still no standard size and weight, which gave some golfers an unfair advantage. That changed in 1920 when the USGA and R&A agreed to a standard ball size: not less than 1.62 inches in diameter and no more than 1.62 ounces. In 1932 the USGA changed it, increasing the maximum diameter to 1.68 inches. It would take until 1990 for the USGA's dimensions to be accepted as the worldwide standard.

But standard doesn't mean that all golf balls are the same—as new technologies and materials fuel the quest for the perfect golf ball, hundreds of variations have been produced. As long as they fit the rule book's standards for size and weight, they can pretty much be made of anything. Yet for all the different brands out there, until very recently there were just two main types of balls: two-piece (or wound) and three-piece.

• Three-piece is the old style of ball construction: a small liquid or solid core surrounded first by tightly-wound rubber thread and then a cover.

• Two-piece balls, which were introduced by Spalding in 1972, have a large solid core and a cover.

Titleist once advertised that no one was ever paid to use their equipment.

For many years, the better players—including the pros—preferred the wound ball, which was softer and therefore had better feel and spin control. Less-talented golfers liked the two-piece because they went farther and lasted longer.

Cover Me

In the 1980s, DuPont developed a new synthetic material for the cover, Surlyn. It was an extremely hard and durable plastic that suited the amateur-friendly two-piece balls in both their hardness and longer lifespan. Because there are a lot more bad players than good ones, Surlyn-covered balls soon became the most popular type of ball in the world. But the two-piece ball kept improving. New cover materials, such as Elastomer and Urethane, were introduced to provide the softness and feel of balata with the durability of Surlyn. In the 1990s, Nick Price became the first notable PGA Tour pro to use one—and he was the winningest golfer of the decade.

GOLF BALLS GO ONION

The latest golf ball breakthrough: the multilayered ball. These balls have a fairly large inner core, then an inner cover, then an outer cover. Mark O'Meara made this new style famous in 1998 when he won the British Open with a Spalding Strata multilayered ball.

By 2000 nine of the first eleven events of the season were won with mutilayered balls. That year they got another boost: Tiger Woods, who had played wound balls his entire life, switched to a Nike multilayered ball two weeks before the U.S. Open. He not only won that major tournament, he won with the lowest score and by the largest margin in history.

*   *   *

IT STANDS FOR "GOT TOWED"

After Craig Parry sank his amazing eagle to win the 2004 Doral Open, he was awarded $1.2 million and a 2005 Ford GT. "I'm going to have a lot of fun with it," he grinned. Wrong. The $140,000 sports car was recalled due to a suspension problem. "I didn't even get to drive it," Parry said. "I did get to start it, though. Once."

In the rough: Nils Lied drove a golf ball 2,640 yards...on a sheet of ice in Antarctica.

THE MASTERS

The "Super Bowl of Golf"—as it's been called in recent years—has had a storied and often tumultuous history.

GRAND DESIGN

Bobby Jones was one of the best golfers ever to play the game. A refined gentleman from a wealthy Southern family, Jones never turned pro—he considered playing golf for money beneath his social station. Yet, despite his amateur status, he dominated golf throughout the 1920s. In 1930 he won what was then considered golf's Grand Slam, with victories in the U.S. Open, British Open, U.S. Amateur, and British Amateur.

With the Grand Slam under his belt, that same year Jones decided—at the ripe old age of 28—to retire from competitive golf and turn his sights toward building his dream golf course. With a handful of rich cronies, he purchased 365 acres outside of Augusta, Georgia, and formed one of the most exclusive country clubs in America: the Augusta National Golf Club.

MAGNOLIA LANE

From the beginning, Augusta National, as it is now known, was dedicated to an upper-class vision of the golfing life. Only the richest and most influential businessmen (emphasis on *men*—no women have ever been members of the club) were invited to apply for membership. The club's most famous member: Dwight D. Eisenhower, who visited Augusta regularly before, during, and after his presidency.

Jones and his buddies wanted the grounds of their new club to reflect its high-class membership. With that in mind, they hired acclaimed English golf course architect Dr. Alister Mackenzie to design it. And under his hand, landscaping at Augusta National became an art form. Magnolia trees and azaleas planted back in the 1850s—when the property belonged to a Belgian baron with a taste for expensive horticulture—gave them a head start. By the time the course opened in 1932, the clubhouse, grounds, and the links themselves looked like a museum replica of plantation days in the Old South.

Youngest player ever to qualify for the PGA Tour: Ty Tryon, at age 17.

THE AUGUSTA NATIONAL INVITATIONAL

With the best golf course money could buy, it was only natural that the club members would want to host a major tournament. After a deal to host the 1933 U.S. Open fell through, they decided to inaugurate their own annual tournament. The first one was held in the spring of 1934 and was called the Augusta National Invitational Tournament (the name wouldn't be changed to the Masters until 1939).

Bobby Jones was such an important figure in the golfing world that he had no trouble convincing the game's greatest players to come play at Augusta. Horton Smith was the tournament's first winner in 1934, and the next year Gene Sarazen took the title with his famous "Shot Heard 'Round the World." Byron Nelson, Jimmy Demaret, Ben Hogan, and Sam Snead were among the legendary players who won early Masters tournaments and helped give the event the credibility it now enjoys.

Both Arnold Palmer and Jack Nicklaus mastered the course—they hold ten Masters titles between them. Their rivalry during the 1960s focused world attention on Augusta National and added to its legend. In recent years, Tiger Woods has dazzled the galleries at Augusta, winning three times since becoming its youngest champion in 1997 at the age of 21.

THE GREEN JACKET

The membership of Augusta National has always been obsessed with tradition. In 1937 club members began wearing green jackets that bore the club crest to distinguish themselves from common fans. When Sam Snead won the first of his three Masters titles in 1949, he was presented with his own honorary club jacket—and a new tradition was born.

Every year since then, the new champion has been given a green jacket by the previous year's winner. Having won the Masters, the champion gets to take his green jacket home with him for a year. After that, he is given a locker in the exclusive Champions Locker Room, where his jacket will be waiting for him whenever he returns to Augusta.

Along with the green jacket, Masters winners receive a lifetime exemption from qualifying for future tournaments. In other words, once a golfer has won the Masters, he is welcome to come back and play every year for the rest of his life—he has a permanent invitation. Many golfing legends have taken advantage of this clause, returning to Augusta every spring, even long after their game has passed its prime. Arnold Palmer played his 50th consecutive Masters in 2004 (he hadn't made the cut since 1983). Older past champions traditionally start off the tournament by ceremonially hitting the first ball.

THE GALLERY

Another tradition holds that the Masters is the "toughest ticket in sports." Augusta National hasn't offered tickets for sale to the general public since 1972 and the "preferred" waiting list was cut off in 1978. Today, tickets are available only from scalpers or outside dealers—and they aren't cheap. Although the face value of a ticket to the four-day event is fixed at $125, they often go for as much as $12,000.

The eccentricities of Augusta National's leadership are as legendary as the golfers who play there. They make a point of placing their own refined tastes above profits, and have maintained absolute control of their tournament through the years. Nowhere is this more apparent than in their relationship with CBS Television.

MASTERS OF THE AIRWAYS

The network that has cornered the market on golf has televised the event every year since 1956, but Augusta officials still require them to renegotiate their contract every year. These one-year contracts allow only three commercial sponsors and limit commercial time to four minutes per hour of coverage. And until 2002 they restricted television coverage of the first nine holes so that part of the course would remain a mystery to anyone who hadn't seen it in person.

There are even unofficial rules that CBS commentators must follow when covering the Masters. They are to refer to "patrons" rather than "fans." Bobby Jones is to be referred to by his full name, not simply "Jones." Two different commentators have found out the hard way that the club is serious about these rules.

Jack Whitaker covered the event for CBS in the 1960s...until he referred to the crowd around the 18th hole as a "mob." The following year's contract stipulated that he not be in the booth. The same thing happened in 1994 when Gary McCord commented that the notoriously fast greens of Augusta National were behaving as though they had been "bikini waxed." That, apparently, was not in keeping with the dignity of the event. McCord was out.

CONTROVERSY BENEATH THE PINES

The Old South traditions that have been so key to the tournament's prestige have also been the source of much of its negative publicity. Some of Augusta National's traditions are of the sort that antidiscrimination laws were designed to stop.

The darkest chapter of the PGA's history was the organization's failure to issue tour cards to black golfers until 1961. Even then, the Masters lagged behind the rest of the golf world. Any player who wins a Tour event is supposed to receive an automatic invitation to the next year's Masters. But black golfers like Charlie Sifford found that their wins didn't count with the Masters invitation committee. They were not invited. In 1973, 18 members of Congress wrote to Augusta National to express concern over their policies, but the club ignored them. Finally, in 1975 Lee Elder became the first black golfer to play at Augusta after winning the Monsanto Open.

Elder may have integrated the tournament, but no African American was invited to apply for membership in the club itself until 1990. And there are still no women members—a fact that continues to dog the club's reputation. In 2002 attorney Martha Burke publicly challenged Augusta National to admit a female member and threatened a boycott of the tournament's television sponsors. The club responded by underwriting a commercial-free Masters in 2003.

A GENTLEMAN'S GAME

Although the Masters is, to many golfers, the most important professional tournament on the PGA Tour, Augusta National still honors the principles of amateurism as exemplified by the life and career of Bobby Jones.

Five spots in the tournament are held aside for the best amateur players: the winner and runner-up of the U.S. Amateur; the winner of the British Amateur; the winner of the U.S. Amateur Public Links tournament; and the champion of the U.S. Mid-

---

A golf ball that would normally fly 230 yards would only fly 160 yards in a vacuum.

Amateur tournament. The top floor of the Augusta National clubhouse is called the Crow's Nest and is used to provide housing for amateur players during the tournament. In the old days, when amateur events were a more important part of big-time golf, they needed bunk beds to house all of the young players staying in the Crow's Nest. These days, there are only five beds.

MASTERFUL FACTS

• Jack Nicklaus has won the Masters six times—more than any other player.

• To ensure that Augusta National looks its best for television, the waters of Raes Creek, which winds through the course, and several water hazards at "TV holes" are dyed blue every April for the event.

• The Masters was not played from 1943 to 1945. During World War II, the tournament was suspended and the grounds of Augusta National were used to raise turkey and cattle for the war effort.

• How many people attend the Masters? No one knows. Augusta National refuses to release attendance numbers or gate receipts.

* * *

UNCLE JOHN'S TEN BEST TIPS

1. Back straight, knees bent, feet shoulder width apart.

2. Form a loose grip.

3. Keep your head down.

4. Avoid a quick backswing.

5. Stay out of the water.

6. Try not to hit anyone.

7. If you are taking too long, please let others go ahead of you.

8. Don't stand directly in front of others.

9. Quiet, please…while others are preparing to go.

10. Don't take extra strokes.

Well done! Now flush the urinal, wash your hands, go outside, and tee off!

In his dozen Masters, Bobby Jones never once broke par.

THE AMATEURS SPEAK

We've heard enough from the pros. Now for the "ams."

"It took me 17 years to get 3,000 hits in baseball. I did it in one afternoon on the golf course."
—**Hank Aaron**

"I've done as much for golf as Truman Capote has done for sumo wrestling."
—**Bob Hope**

"Sometimes when I look down at that little white golf ball, I just wish it was moving."
—**Dusty Baker**

"I was three over: one over a house, one over a patio, and one over a swimming pool."
—**George Brett**

"In baseball you hit your home run over the right-field fence, the left-field fence, the center-field fence. Nobody cares. In golf everything has got to be right over second base."
—**Ken Harrelson**

"The safest place would be in the fairway."
—**Joe Garagiola, on where spectators should stand during celebrity golf tournaments**

"If you think it's hard to meet new people, try picking up the wrong golf ball."
—**Jack Lemmon**

"Anything I want it to be. For instance, the hole right here is a par 47, and yesterday I birdied the sucker."
—**Willie Nelson, on what's par on his Texas golf course**

"Every rock and roll band I know—guys with long hair and tattoos—plays golf now."
—**Alice Cooper**

"The reason the pro tells you to keep your head down is so you can't see him laughing."
—**Phyllis Diller**

"If I can hit a curveball, why can't I hit a ball that is standing still on a course?"
—**Larry Nelson**

"I had a wonderful experience on the golf course today. I had a hole in nothing. Missed the ball and sank the divot."
—**Don Adams**

"Swing hard in case you hit it."
—**Dan Marino**

Odds against an amateur scoring a hole in one: About 12,000 to 1. For a pro: 3,708 to 1.

OFF COURSE

From a weird world comes the weirdest golf stories.

GIVING NEW MEANING TO "TAKING A SHOT"

"Two California inventors have patented a golf club that detonates an explosive charge to fire the ball across the fairway so golfers don't have to swing at all. Roy Taylor and James Duncalf are not the first to use spring-loaded or ballistic charges in golf clubs to help the ball along. But in earlier inventions, the player still had to swing the club and smack the head against the ball to trigger the firing mechanism. No longer. Their invention rockets the ball into the sky from a standstill. While the club will not win approval for use in tournaments, the inventors said it would help slam a golf ball up to 250 yards, its ejecting face plate slamming the ball down the fairway at 180 miles an hour. 'At first, we took a .22-caliber firing system off a rifle and coupled it to the appliance we made, so you just pulled the trigger and it would go off,' Duncalf said. The inventors also thought the original model would use a six-round rotating cartridge but quickly realized that would mean a golfer would be carrying around a 'loaded' golf club."

—*The New York Times*

B-A-A-A-D SHOT

"Peter Croke was playing in Porthcawl, Wales, when his tee shot on the 17th ended up wedged under the tail of a sheep that was grazing near the fairway. 'The sheep looked mildly surprised by the whole thing, but we were in hysterics,' Croke said. The ball still wedged in, the sheep meandered 30 yards closer to the hole, 'then shook the ball free, like it was laying an egg.' Croke won the match."

—**Reuters**

DREDGING FOR DOLLARS

"John Collinson was caught by police late at night in 2001 dredging Whetstone Golf Club's pond in Leicestershire for lost balls. Officers found two sacks nearby containing 1,158 balls. He was found guilty of theft by a jury last month, but released on bail after nine days in jail. His six month prison sentence was later overturned; he was given a two-year conditional discharge instead. Collinson, 36, regarded retrieving and reselling the balls as his career—not a crime—and had even declared it on a tax return. He earned approximately $32,000 a year selling salvaged balls to small companies which washed, graded, and resold them. Now he plans to work for a company legally retrieving balls."

—*The Guardian*

GUM AND GET IT

"Gay Brewer was playing the 1978 Hartford Open with Barry Jaeckel. 'On a par-4, Gay was over the green and in some fluffy grass in two,' says Jaeckel. 'While he was taking his last practice swing with a wedge, a piece of freshly chewed bubblegum got stuck to the face of his club.' Brewer hit what he thought was the perfect shot, and it started towards the green. But then, as if connected to a bungee cord, it came back at him, landing three feet away. 'Brewer, nicknamed Hound Dog for the unusually dour expression on his face, flashed an incredulous look at the ball,' says Jaeckel. 'Then, like everyone else, he fell to his knees, laughing at his incredible bad luck.'"

—*The Virginian-Pilot*

GOOD SHOT, BAD COP

"With crime surging as hard times hit Thailand, Bangkok police have been ordered to take a drastic measure to combat mayhem on the streets. The directive: Stop golfing while on duty. Police Gen. Wannarat Katcharak said no officer will be allowed to hit the links unless their neighborhood is absolutely crime free, the *Bangkok Post* reported. The general said policemen caught driving in the rough instead of driving around town will be transferred to an inactive post. What's the significance of that? Losing one's job in the Thai civil service, police or military for wrongdoing is extremely rare. Instead, wrongdoers are shifted to jobs with no responsibilities, where they still pick up a government paycheck but have less opportunity to pocket bribes."

—**WhiteBoard News Service**

* * *

"The biggest liar in the world is the golfer who claims he plays the game merely for exercise." —Tommy Bolt

---

One bunker at the Oakmont Country Club in Pennsylvania is called the "church pew."

GOLF 101: THE CLUBS

If you were just out in the garage adjusting the lie angle on your utility woods and your GW…then you probably don't need to read this article.

T HE CLUB
Knowing which club to use in any given situation is a fundamental part of the game of golf. The best way to learn: just get out there and hit the ball—a lot—and experiment with all the clubs in many different situations. But there are some basics.

Professional golfers are allowed to carry 14 clubs in their bag during a tournament. They don't all carry the same 14 and they might change them for different courses, conditions, or just because they want to, but all clubs fall into one of four main types: woods, irons, wedges, and putters. The woods and irons are the numbered clubs, the numbers differentiating the clubs according to length and, more importantly, *loft*. Loft is the angle of the face of the club, measured in degrees from vertical when it's held as if it were about to strike the ball. How much loft a club has affects how the ball travels: the lower the number and the loft, the lower the trajectory of the ball and the greater the distance it will travel. The higher the number, the higher the trajectory and the shorter the distance. It's the same for wedges, but they are differentiated by names, not numbers.

WOODS

Woods get their name from the days when they were actually made of wood. Today, however, nearly all woods are made out of metal. The average size of a clubhead was about 200 cc, until Callaway introduced the "Big Bertha" in the 1990s. Many are now more than 500 cc, but the largest allowed by the USGA is 485. There are three different types of woods:

The driver: The one-wood (also called the "Big Dog"). It is the longest club, averaging 44.5 inches, has a very large head and the least loft, varying from seven to eleven degrees. It's used for very long, low shots off the tee that are meant to roll when they land.

Fairway woods: Fairway woods range from two-wood up to five-wood, the most popular being the three and the five. For many

---

Cue ball, golf ball: there is a tournament just for bald men in Clarkston, Washington.

years, pro golfers used only three-woods and drivers, but today many carry the five-wood, too.

Utility woods: The more lofted woods, numbered above five. They're often used in lieu of longer irons. Balls hit with seven- and nine-woods travel about the same distance as balls hit by three- or four-irons, but woods are easier to use because they have larger heads. They also put the ball higher into the air, which makes it stop rolling when it hits the green. Utility woods are more common among recreational golfers than pros, but some pros do use them: Rich Beem uses a seven-wood regularly on tour; and Vijay Singh often uses a nine-wood instead of a two-iron. (They're rare, but you can get utility woods all the way up to a nineteen-wood, which would be the equivalent of a pitching wedge.)

IRONS

Irons are numbered from one to nine. They range from 35 to 40 inches long and fall into three different categories:

Long irons: Numbers one through three. They are long, low-lofted clubs, used off the tee or on the fairway for long, low shots. The one-iron, also called the "driving iron," is known as the hardest club to master because it's so long and doesn't have the forgiving head size of a wood. A standard set of clubs doesn't include a one- or two-iron, and many pros don't even carry them.

Mid-irons: The four- through six-irons. They are, as you might assume, used for mid-range shots.

Short irons: Seven, eight, and nine make up the short irons. The loft is really getting up there now, with the nine-iron angled to 44 degrees from vertical. They're used for high, relatively short shots with a lot of backspin, in situations where accuracy and control of the ball's roll are important.

WEDGES

Wedges are technically irons but are most often grouped into their own category. These are highly lofted clubs used for pitching and chipping onto the green, and for getting out of bunkers or other trouble. The clubheads of wedges are often made of softer metals, such as copper or beryllium alloy, to increase the "feel" of the club.

The pitching wedge: The PW has from 45 to 50 degrees of loft.

It's used in situations similar to a nine-iron—just for shorter shots.

The gap wedge: The GW is a relatively new invention, made to cover the "gap" in loft between the pitching wedge and sand wedge. It has from 49 to 54 degrees of loft.

The sand wedge: The SW is highly lofted—from 54 to 57 degrees —with a head specifically designed to get the club through sand without digging in. It is also used for short shots from the fairway and rough.

The lob wedge: The LW goes all the way to 60 degrees (it's almost like sliding a spatula under the ball). Use it for *really* high shots in the 40- to 60- yard range—with a lot of backspin. Lob shots are meant to land softly on the green and stop immediately, or, for more accomplished players, to roll backward once they hit.

PUTTERS

Putters were once considered just another kind of iron, but now get their own category. There are three main types:

• **Short putter:** The traditional putter, used for centuries. It's the smallest club in the bag, ranging from 33 to 36 inches long.

• **Belly putter:** About 45 inches long. The end of the shaft is jabbed into the golfer's belly, which is used as a fulcrum for the swing of the club.

• **Long putter:** Also known as a "broomstick putter," it can be as long as 55 inches and the shaft's end is held against the golfer's chest or under the chin. The belly putter and the long putter were first introduced on the Senior Tour (now the Champions Tour), because they helped with the "yips" (bouts of erratic, unconfident golfing, not uncommon to older players) and because they required less bending. By 2002, many PGA pros were using them, too—although some, like Ernie Els, called for them to be banned, claiming they give golfers that use them an unfair advantage.

There are countless shapes, weights, sizes, and materials for putter heads. And there are inserts for putter faces that come in metal, rubber, ceramic, plastic, wood, and even glass. Experts say: try a variety of them and play the one that feels the best.

Arnold Palmer started the trend of placing the glove in the back pocket before putting.

EXTRAS

Getting the right lie angle: The lie angle is the angle of the sole of the clubhead, from heel to toe, in relation to the ground. It should be parallel to the ground when you hit the ball. Different golfers need clubs with different lie angles, depending on height, arm length, body style, and stance. To test whether you have the right lie angle, hold an iron as if you're about to swing, with the clubhead on the ground. Make sure you're on a flat surface. Now have a friend check whether the grooves on the face of the iron are parallel to the ground. If the toe of the club is jutting up, then your lie angle is too upright. This will cause a tendency to pull or hook your shots. If the toe is pointed toward the ground and the heel is up in the air, then your lie angle is too flat, which will cause you to push or slice. You can adjust your lie angle by bending the hosel—the part of the head where the shaft is inserted—or by getting a different-length club.

CLUB DISTANCE GUIDE

Here's a handy reference guide for the average distance attained from different clubs depending on whether you're a pro, a recreational golfer…or Uncle John. These distances are all based on taking a full swing at full speed.

Club	Pro	Recreational	Uncle John
Driver	260 yards	200 yards	3 yards
3-wood	235 yards	190 yards	3 feet
5-wood	220 yards	180 yards	3 inches
2-iron	210 yards	170 yards	3 centimeters
3-iron	200 yards	160 yards	3 millimeters
4-iron	185 yards	150 yards	0 anythings
5-iron	170 yards	140 yards	1 toe length
6-iron	160 yards	130 yards	Oops!
7-iron	150 yards	120 yards	Off shin
8-iron	140 yards	110 yards	Off knee
9-iron	130 yards	95 yards	Off head
P. wedge	120 yards	80 yards	"Pee" wedge?
S. wedge	100 yards	60 yards	Forget it.

The 12th hole at Meadows Farms in Virginia is the longest in the U.S., a par-6 of 841 yards.

HOLLYWOOD HACKS

Want to compare your game to those of the stars? Here's a list of celebrity handicaps. (Okay, so they're not all hacks, but it's fun to say.)

Craig T. Nelson: 5.6	Michael Douglas: 15.5
Bruce Willis: 6	Tom Smothers: 15.5
Chris O'Donnell: 6.6	Alan Thicke: 16
William Devane: 7.4	Martin Sheen: 16
Matt Lauer: 8	Mikhail Baryshnikov: 16
Tea Leoni: 8	Steve Van Zandt: 16.2
Bob Newhart: 8.2	Cheryl Ladd: 16.4
Jim Brown: 9	James Woods: 16.9
James Garner: 9.4	Leslie Nielsen: 17.8
Sylvester Stallone: 10	Kevin James: 18
Samuel L. Jackson: 10.1	Ray Romano: 18
Clint Eastwood: 11	Cheech Marin: 18
Andy Garcia: 11	Catherine Zeta-Jones: 20
Kyle MacLachlan: 13	Matt Damon: 20
Aidan Quinn: 14	Judd Nelson: 20
Will Smith: 14	Dennis Hopper: 21
Joe Pesci: 14.1	Warren Buffett: 21.4
Rob Lowe: 14.5	Tom Cruise: 23
Dennis Franz: 14.6	Arnold Schwarzenegger: 24
Sidney Poitier: 14.6	Tom Selleck: 24.7
Richard Roundtree: 14.6	Joe Mantegna: 25
Sean Connery: 15	Mel Gibson: 26.7
Frankie Muniz: 15	Richard Dreyfuss: 31.3

Q: Who was the last major winner with facial hair? A: Corey Pavin, 1995 U.S. Open.

FAIRWAY FUNNIES

Is that a putter in your pocket or are you just happy to see me?

A bum asks a man on the street for ten dollars. "Will you use it to buy booze?" the man asks. The bum says no.

"Will you gamble it away?" Once again the bum says no.

"Will you waste it on the golf course?"

The bum says, "No, I don't play golf."

"Really? Wow. Would you like to come to my house for dinner?"

The man takes the bum home, introduces him to his wife, and says, "You see what happens to a man who doesn't drink, gamble, or play golf?"

Golfer: "Why do you keep looking at your watch?"
Caddie: "This isn't a watch, sir. It's a compass."

One day, Thom decided that for once in his life, he wanted to win a golf match and make back a bit of the money he'd lost over the years. So he walked up to the club pro and said, "I'll bet you $1,000 that I can get a lower score than you in nine holes of golf. But since you're so much better than me, I get two 'gotchas'."

"What's a gotcha?" asked the pro.

"Nothing too bad," replied Thom. "I'll do the first one on the first tee."

The pro figured that whatever gotchas were, giving up only two of them was no big deal—especially if Thom used up one on the first tee. "You've got yourself a bet, my friend."

An hour later, club members were amazed to see the pro writing Thom a check for $1,000. "How did you get beat by Thom of all people?" they asked the pro at the clubhouse.

He sighed, "Well, on the first tee, I was in the middle of my backswing when old Thom ran up from behind, grabbed my crotch, and yelled, 'Gotcha!'" The pro then paused for a moment, shook his head, and continued, "Have you ever tried to play nine holes of golf waiting for the second 'gotcha'?"

"**I'd move heaven** and Earth to be able to break 100 on this course," sighed Jeff, the golfer.

"Try heaven," advised his caddie. "You've already moved most of the earth."

A man and his wife were playing golf with another couple. They came to a par-4, dogleg left. The man pulled his drive and landed his ball behind a storage barn. The other man said, "If you open the front and back doors of the barn, you'll have a clear shot to the green." So they opened the doors and the man took his shot. The ball rattled through the rafters, shot out through a window, hit his wife on the head, and killed her!

It took the man ten years to get over the horrible event, but eventually he remarried, started golfing again, and one day found himself at the very same course. Sure enough, they got to the same hole, he pulled his drive again, and ended up behind the same barn. The man he was playing with this time said, "If you open the front and back doors, you'll have a clear shot to the green."

"I don't think so," the man said. "The last time I tried that,

something terrible happened."

"What?" asked his partner.

The man replied, "I got a seven!"

Jay and Brian were out golfing when Jay hit a terrible slice on the 2nd hole...and hit a guy on the 17th fairway. They ran over to him—but he was out cold.

"Oh no," said Jay, "what should I do?"

"Don't touch him!" said Brian. "If he's unconscious, then he's an immovable obstruction and you can either play the ball as it lies or drop it two club lengths away."

An extremely cocky golfer teed up at the 1st hole at St. Andrews. "Looks like I'll need one long drive and one short putt," he said to his caddie. He then took a mighty swing, after which the ball came to rest about three feet from the tee.

The caddie handed him a club and said, "And now for one hell of a putt."

Overheard at the 19th hole: "The other day I was out playing golf and I hit two of my best balls...I stepped on a rake"

SIR WALTER

Walter Hagen was an important figure not only in
golf history, but in all of professional sports.

THE HAIG

Walter Hagen is consistently cited as one of the top 10 golfers to ever play the game. In a career that lasted from 1914 until the 1930s, he was golf's most prolific winner, taking a total of 44 PGA tournaments, still seventh on the all-time victory list. In 1922 he became the first American to win the British Open, and went go on to win it three more times. He won four PGA Championships—consecutively—from 1924 to 1927, and a total of five. In the era of such golfing legends as Bobby Jones and Gene Sarazen, "the Haig" won a total of 11 majors. That's second only to Jack Nicklaus for the most in history. (Some count his major wins at 16 because he won five Western Opens—there was no Masters during those years and at the time, the Western Open was considered a major tournament.)

But Hagen wasn't just a great golfer—he was a great show.

LIVING THE GOOD LIFE

Hagen brought glamour and character to a game that, up until then, had little of either. He wore fancy clothes, traveled with an entourage, and threw expensive parties after tournaments (sometimes *during* tournaments). After he won the U.S. Open in 1914 at the age of 21, he started charging appearance fees to play exhibition matches. He became the first golfer to sign an endorsement deal, getting $500 a year for every club he carried in his bag (which may be why he carried 22 instead of the normal 14).

Even his style of play was flamboyant. Hagen is not known as one the great ball-strikers in the game's history—he'd often be in trouble after a wild tee shot—but was one of the best at getting *out* of trouble. His bunker shots and his putting are ranked among the best ever. Bobby Jones once said of Hagen: "When a man misses his drive, and then misses his second shot, and then wins the hole with a birdie, it really gets my goat!"

THE SERVANTS

Hagen's flamboyant lifestyle and unpredictable game became a big draw at tournaments. The crowds—many of whom weren't even that interested in the game—came to see what Sir Walter would do next. But although he was bringing people—and money—to the clubs and to the game of golf itself—this was a time when professionals were considered a lower class of player. Amateurs were the "real" golfers, and the country clubs still treated the pros as servants who were there primarily to teach their gentlemen patrons how to play. Pros weren't even allowed inside the clubhouses—not even to use the bathroom. Hagen, who was the son of a blacksmith and had left school at age 12, hated it.

At the 1920 British Open, Hagen showed up in a rented Rolls-Royce. He parked the car right in front of the clubhouse and used it as his locker room. He even had dinners and champagne delivered to the car. At another British tournament, he refused to enter the clubhouse for the trophy presentation because he hadn't been allowed inside previously. Later that year, Hagen and another golfer, George Duncan, threatened to boycott the French Open unless the professionals were allowed in the locker room. Fearing a low turnout without the game's biggest star, the French relented.

HIS LEGACY

Hagen is believed to be the first sportsman in the world to have earned more than $1 million in his career. He is known as the golfer who put the "green" into golf. And his influence wasn't limited just to golf—following Hagen's lead, professional baseball players and prizefighters also began demanding more money...and getting it.

Gene Sarazen once said of Sir Walter, "All the professionals who have a chance to go after the big money today should say a silent thanks to Walter Hagen each time they stretch a check between their fingers. It was Walter who made professional golf what it is." Hagen died in 1969 at the age of 76, and was inducted into the World Golf Hall of Fame in 1974.

*　　*　　*

"I don't want to be a millionaire—I just want to live like one."
—**Walter Hagen**

Walter Hagen was the first pro athlete to be named to the list of "Best-Dressed Americans."

RANDOM THOUGHTS

More observations on the game of golf.

"To be truthful, I think golfers are overpaid. It's unreal, and I have trouble dealing with the guilt sometimes."
—Colin Montgomerie

"Golf and sex are about the only things you can enjoy without being good at it."
—Jimmy Demaret

"The trouble that most of us find with the modern matched sets of clubs is that they don't really seem to know any more about the game than the old ones did!"
—Robert Browning,
A History of Golf

"That little white ball won't move 'til you hit it…and there's nothing you can do after it's gone."
—Babe Zaharias

"I miss. I miss. I miss. I make."
—Seve Ballesteros,
describing his four-putt at Augusta's 16th hole in 1988

"If you watch a game, it's fun. If you play it, it's recreation. If you work at it, it's golf."
—Bob Hope

"A hole in one is amazing when you think of the different universes this white mass of molecules has to pass through on its way to the hole."
—Mac O'Grady

"Swinging at daisies is like playing electric guitar with a tennis racket: if it were that easy, we could all be Jerry Garcia. The ball changes everything."
—Michael Bamberger

"The fundamental problem with golf is that every so often, no matter how lacking you may be in the essential virtues required of a steady player, the odds are that one day you will hit the ball straight, hard, and out of sight. This is the essential frustration of this excruciating sport. For when you've done it once, you make the fundamental error of asking yourself why you can't do it all the time. The answer to this question is simple: the first time was a fluke."
—Colin Bowles

"Live…Laugh…Golf!"
—Kathryn Schaefer Plaum

When putting, the ball actually skids about 20% of the distance before it starts rolling.

WOMEN'S GOLF

*This is the story of their struggle to be taken seriously
and compete to the best of their ability.*

GIRLS IN THE CLUBHOUSE

The history of women in golf is a long one—nearly as long as the history of golf itself. But the women's game wasn't taken seriously for centuries, right up until 1900, and it still had an uphill battle after that. The earliest known woman golfer was Mary, Queen of Scots. An avid player, she was reportedly rebuked in 1567 for being out on the course within days of the murder of her husband, Lord Darnley. And Queen Mary is the reason golf first became an "international" sport—she introduced the game to France during her education there.

THE FISHWIVES

The history then jumps all the way to the late 1700s at the Royal Musselburgh Golf Club, one of Scotland's oldest. The Reverend Alexander "Jupiter" Carlyle, a golfing legend in Scotland, noted that women at Musselburgh "do the work of men" and were regularly out on the links playing golf. In 1810, the club proposed the world's first formal competition for women:

Musselburgh, 14th Dec. 1810

The Club resolve to present by subscription a new Creel & Skull to the best female golfer who plays in on the annual occasion on 1st Jan. next, to be intimated to the Fish Ladies by the Officer of the Club.

Being the wives of the town's fishermen, these women were known as "fishwives." A creel and skull was a wicker basket used to hold freshly caught fish, carried on the back and held by a strap around the forehead. The fact that these commoners were playing in a formal tournament shows that golf was not just for royalty—and not just for men.

By the mid-1800s, women were playing regularly at clubs all over Scotland, and what is thought to be the first official women's golf club was opened at St. Andrews in 1867. More would soon follow.

The women's game wasn't quite the same as the men's. Because

When not golfing, 17-time LPGA winner Amy Alcott has a part-time job: short-order cook.

it was thought that women couldn't handle the rigors of a full course, they were relegated to short "ladies courses," consisting of just three or five holes, with only 80- or 90-yard fairways. But if they couldn't play the same game as the men, it may have been because of the bulky, unathletic clothing women were required to wear. Victorian dress codes all but ruled out any possibility of an effective swing. Women were permitted to play the game, but were never encouraged to take it seriously.

TAKING IT SERIOUSLY

As more women took up the sport toward the end of the 19th century, the level of play began to improve and more regular "ladies" golf tournaments began to take place. The Ladies' Golf Union of Great Britain was formed in 1893 and held the first British Women's Amateur Championship. In 1895 the USGA began the U.S. Ladies' Amateur. Women's amateur golf was even played at the 1900 Olympic Games in Paris. An American, Margaret Abbott, won the gold medal, the first woman ever to win an Olympic medal. More notably, at least in terms of golf, she was also the very first American, man or woman, to win an international golf tournament.

In 1907 British Ladies' Amateur Champion May Hezlet wrote, "It is now generally acknowledged that golf is a game—par excellence—for women. It is essentially a game for women: the exercise is splendid without being unduly violent, as is sometimes the case in hockey or tennis."

Not everybody agreed. British Men's Amateur Champion Sir Ernest Holderness expressed the feelings of many when he objected to organized competition for lady golfers, saying: "Who could expect a married woman with young children to win championships? It would be enough ground for divorce!"

THE CURTIS CUP

In 1905 Margaret and Harriot Curtis, sisters from a prominent Boston family, sailed to England with six other American women to compete in the British Ladies' Amateur. After the tournament, the American and British women played a friendly team competition in which the Americans were badly beaten. The experience convinced the Curtis sisters that international competition would

Because featherie balls floated, it was possible to play off the surface of a water hazard.

elevate the quality of women's golf on both sides of the Atlantic, so they drew up plans for a formal women's tournament. It took a long time for that dream to come true. Lack of support from the men who ran the USGA, lack of finances, and World War I put the idea off for decades. But they kept trying.

In 1927 the Curtis sisters commissioned a trophy inscribed with the words "to stimulate friendly rivalry among the women golfers of many lands." But they still lacked the finances to pay for the trip. Finally, after 27 years of trying, the USGA got on board and in 1932 financed the trip and the competition. The tournament, which is held every two years, and the trophy are still called the Curtis Cup.

THE WPGA

Throughout the 1930s, the game of golf became more popular—and more profitable. It was during this time that men's professional golf gained favor over the amateur game...and the women weren't far behind. In 1934 Helen Hicks signed a contract to promote Wilson Sporting Goods, and other women golfers followed her lead. In the late 1930s and early 1940s, professional women golfers started playing at the few American tournaments that were set up specifically for women.

The struggle for acceptance came to fruition in 1944 with the formation of the Women's Professional Golf Association. Players like Babe Zaharias, Patty Berg, and Louise Suggs added legitimacy to the women's game. Zaharias, a two-time Olympic gold medalist, was hugely popular at the time. When she took up pro golf, it lent credibility—and a lot of new fans—to women's golf. When she qualified for a PGA event in 1945, the first woman to do so, she raised their status even higher. Within six years, the WPGA would fail due to a lack of revenue, but the precedent had been set. These golf legends would soon be among the original 13 members of a new organization that would not fail—the LPGA.

THE LPGA

The early years of the Ladies' Professional Golf Association were a labor of love. Formed in 1950, the organization was run by the players. They administered the tournaments and still found time to play top-notch golf—all for very little money. In its inaugural year, the tour gave out just $50,000 in prize money (the men's tour

---

LPGA winner Jan Stephenson was offered $150,000 to pose for *Playboy*. (She refused.)

gave out ten times as much), spread over 14 tournaments. But the hard work of these early LPGA members paid off, and by 1959 they were putting on 26 events per year and giving out more than $200,000.

In 1963 the LPGA made another big breakthrough when the final round of the U.S. Women's Open was televised for the first time. In the 1970s, players such as Nancy Lopez and JoAnne "Big Momma" Carner (who was still hitting 250-yard drives in her 60s) would give the sport another boost, and by the end of the 1970s the prize money increased more than $4 million. Today, the LPGA Tour has grown to more than 30 events with purses totalling in excess of $40 million. And like the PGA, it is a nonprofit organization, generating over $160 million for charities since 1981.

WOMEN IN THE PGA

LPGA courses are generally shorter than their PGA counterparts, requiring less powerful drives, and the grass of the rough is cut shorter. Because their courses have been designed and built for less powerful swings, women have not traditionally practiced the same shots or styles of play as men—but that's changing.

In the spring of 2003, Annika Sorenstam became the first woman to tee up alongside the men at a PGA tournament since Babe Zaharias in 1945. And at least five other women golfers have followed her example, including Michelle Wie, who, in January 2004 shocked the golf world when she played against the men in the Sony Open in Hawaii…at the age of 14. She is the youngest person—male or female—ever to play in a PGA event.

How did the men feel about that? Some liked it, some didn't. Scott Hoch, winner of eleven PGA events, said, "She doesn't have a chance in hell of making the cut. She doesn't have a prayer." Wie shot a 72 on the first day and a 68 on the second— and missed the cut by one stroke. Her score was better than 48 professional men (and one stroke better than Scott Hoch). She returned in 2005, but didn't do as well, shooting 75 and 74 to miss the cut again. But she'll be back, and who knows, someday— maybe not that far in the future—she may become the first woman to win an event on the PGA Tour.

Hey, Mom! Nancy Lopez won the Uniden LPGA Invitational four months after giving birth.

TIME FOR TEE

Golf tees are cheap and practical. Besides propping up your ball, they can clean mud from your shoes or pick crud from your teeth (hopefully not the same tee). But even though tees are so perfect for what they do, they were one of the last additions to the game of golf.

IT AIN'T EASY BEING GREEN

In the early days of golf, there was no formalized, separate teeing area at the beginning of each hole. Instead, after a player holed out, the rules dictated that he begin the next hole from within no more than one club length from the cup. This created two problems: players loitering around the cups, creating bottlenecks and slowing down the play behind them; and too many divots on the carefully groomed greens.

To decrease the damage, golf courses provided buckets full of wet sand at each green—the idea being that golfers would build a little mound on which to place the ball. Result: the greens were perpetually soggy and sandy. Furthermore, golfers needed a supply of towels and water to wash off their hands.

It would take until the late 1800s for officials at St. Andrews to try a new approach. And it was Old Tom Morris who first created a separate teeing area at the beginning of each hole. The condition of the greens improved, but wet sand was still the tee of choice.

GOING UP

Looking at a golf tee today, you'd think that such a simple design would be easy to come by. It wasn't—the process would take more than three decades. The first try came in 1889, when two Scottish inventors named William Bloxsom and Andrew Douglas created a rubber slab with vertical rubber prongs to hold the ball in place.

Although it was a step forward, most golfers still preferred to use wet sand. Other inventors experimented with similar contraptions made of paper, rubber, cork, and wood. The first device to penetrate the ground was patented in 1892 by Percy Ellis, also from Scotland. He called it the "Perfectum" and it consisted of a rubber circle (to hold the ball) attached to a metal spike (to anchor the rubber to the ground). An improvement to this design

---

Q: Which talk-show host mimed a golf swing at the start of every show? A: Johnny Carson.

came in 1897 from another Scotsman, P. M. Matthews, who designed a cup-shaped piece of rubber that was nailed into the ground. The modern tee was taking shape.

Meanwhile, across the ocean, the United States Patent Office issued David Dalziel (yet another Scot) the first American golf tee patent in 1897. Dalziel's design was a throwback to earlier non-spike tees—a one-piece rubber tee with a flat base that simply sat on the ground. But it was the first to feature the most important part of the modern tee: a slightly concave top.

DOWN IN THE MOUTH

The final chapter of the tee's development would be spurred on by two American dentists.

First came Dr. George Grant, who was one of the first African-Americans to graduate from Harvard. While he wasn't cleaning his patients' teeth, he was either practicing his golf swing or designing new golf equipment. In 1899 Dr. Grant's rubber-topped peg design received America's first indigenous golf tee patent. It stuck into the ground, but it lacked a concave head to cradle the ball, and Grant soon lost interest in marketing it.

Combinations of all of these various designs would be tested for 20 more years until another American dentist, Dr. William Lowell, put it all together in 1921. He created a golf tee that was as simple and elegant as a well-crafted dental bridge. Dr. Lowell marketed his "Reddy Tees" in the familiar shape we know today, crafted from wood and painted white with a red top—possibly for visibility (or because they resembled a freshly extracted tooth).

The Reddy Tee was a huge success and became the model for all modern golf tees. And today more than two billion of them are stuck into the ground every year.

*   *   *

LOWEST ROUNDS EVER SHOT (NON-PGA EVENTS)

- Amateur Homero Blancas, 55, 1962 Premier Invitational, Texas
- Larry Nelson, 58, pro-am at 2000 Kroger Senior Classic
- Shigeki Maruyama, 58, qualifier for 2000 U.S. Open
- Jason Bohn, 58, 2000 Bayer Championship on Canadian Tour

Richard Boxall broke his leg teeing off at the 1991 British Open.

TEXAS WEDGES AND ZOYSIA

Our guide to golfspeak continued, T–Z.

Takeaway: The start of the backswing.

Tap-in: A very short putt.

Tee blocks: Two markers that designate the front boundary of the teeing ground. You must tee up behind them.

Tee box (or teeing ground): Designated area from which a golfer is permitted to tee off.

Texas wedge: A putter, when it's used to take a shot from off the green.

Three-putt: To take three putts to hole out. Also called a three-jack.

Three-quarter shot: A shot made with a slightly reduced swing (presumably 75% of a normal swing).

Tiger tees (or back tees): The tee boxes set farthest from the holes. (PGA pros use the tiger tees.)

Tight lie: When the ball is on bare dirt or very short grass. (Considered a bad lie.)

Toe hook: A hook caused by hitting the ball with the toe (end) of the club.

Top: To hit the top of the ball, causing it to roll or bounce.

Track iron (or rut iron): An old-style club that was used to hit the ball from cart tracks.

Trap: Another term for a bunker.

Triple bogey: Three over par on one hole.

Turn: To "make the turn" is to finish the first nine and start the back nine holes.

Underclub: To use a club that can't hit the ball all the way to the target, intentionally or not.

Undue delay (or slow play): Play deemed by an official to be too slow. It can cause a two-stroke penalty.

Unplayable lie: When the ball cannot be played from where it lands (like under low tree branches). Usually results in taking relief and a one-stroke penalty.

Up and down: Missing the green in regulation, but then saving par by getting onto the green (up) and into the hole (down) in two shots.

The spot on the moon where Alan Shepard played golf is now called the "Fra Mauro Country Club."

Uphill lie: When the ball is on a slope and above the golfer's feet at address.

Vertical roll: An integral part of club design—the curve of the face of a wood from top to bottom, which aids shot accuracy.

Waste bunker: An unmaintained area of a golf course, usually filled with sand, pebbles, and rocks, that is not considered a hazard.

Water club: A club designed to hit the ball out of water, used in the early 1900s.

Water hazard: Any creeks, ponds, lakes, ditches, etc. on a golf course—whether they contain water or not.

Water hole: A hole where the ball must be hit over a water hazard to get onto the green.

Wedge: A highly lofted iron used for short, high shots.

Whiff: To miss the ball completely during a swing.

Whins: Scottish term for heavy rough.

Whippy: A golf club that has a very flexible shaft.

Winter green: A temporary green used in the winter (so the permanent green won't be damaged).

Winter rules (also preferred rules or improved lies): Local rules that allow a player to improve a ball's lie without penalty in some weather-related (e.g., wet or muddy) conditions.

Wormburner: A shot that doesn't rise but rolls quickly along the ground.

X: Mark put on a scorecard to indicate the golfer has taken more strokes on a hole than he'd care to admit.

X-outs: Name brand golf balls that have had the name covered with a row of X's because of a production flaw...and are sold for much less than normal.

Yardage book: A notebook kept by a golfer or caddie to record yardages, landmarks, and notes about a course.

Yardage marker: A landmark, such as a sprinkler head or stake, used to note yardage.

Yips: A case of nerves that makes golfers miss simple putts.

Zoysia: A low-growing grass species from Asia, popular on golf courses in warm, dry regions.

THE HISTORY OF MINIATURE GOLF

We tried to keep this short, but it's such a BIG story...

THE HIMALAYAS

The Ladies' Putting Club in St. Andrews, Scotland, is considered by some to be the "world's oldest miniature golf course." The club was founded in 1867 by some members of the Royal & Ancient Golf Club who wanted a place their daughters could play. At the height of the Victorian era, girls and women weren't allowed to lift the club past their shoulder (it was considered vulgar), which meant they couldn't hit the ball very far. So a very hilly and lumpy 18-hole putting green, known as "the Himalayas," was built on the sand dunes next to St. Andrews's famous Old Course. It was an entire 18-hole course designed in miniature size. It became—and remains to this day—hugely popular. (Tom Watson, Craig Stadler, and many other pros have played the Himalayas.)

GOFSTACLE

The earliest mention of a miniature golf game that resembles the one we play today comes from a 1912 article entitled "Bridge, Stick, Tunnel and Box: A Golf Game for Putters." It appeared in the *Illustrated London News* and featured an illustration with the caption, "At the Garden Party: An Exciting Moment of Gofstacle." The picture showed a group of young men playing a game that looked like a mix between miniature golf and croquet. Here's how the game was described:

> Gofstacle is played with golf balls and putter. The obstacles to be negotiated include hoops, rings, a tunnel, a bridge, and a box which has to be entered up an incline. It is played like golf croquet, and may also be played as is golf, the obstacles taking the place of holes. It is claimed for it that it is calculated to improve putting. Its popularity is undoubted.

Iced tee: the Chili Open ice golf tournament is held annually in Crystal Lake, Illinois.

OTHER MINI COURSES

In the early 1900s, small private courses began to be built at the homes of wealthy golfers in North America and Europe. Here are a few examples:

Thistle Dhu: The best known—and possibly the first—miniature course in the United States was built in 1916 at the winter cottage of James Barber in Pinehurst, North Carolina, not far from Pinehurst Golf Club. Barber hired amateur architect Edward H. Wiswell to build an elaborate, tiny course in a garden setting, complete with walkways, benches, flower beds, and a fountain. When it was finished, the story goes, Barber gazed upon his tiny course and exclaimed, "This'll do!" So the course was named "Thistle Dhu," which he thought had a Scottish ring to it. The game didn't catch on with the public, but the concept of a "garden course" did pique the interest of other wealthy golfers.

Astro-Green: In 1922 Scottish-born Thomas McCulloch Fairbairn gave miniature golf an unexpected boost when he constructed a small golf course on his cotton plantation in Mexico. He soon discovered that the dry climate wouldn't allow him to grow decent greens, so he started experimenting with artificial surfaces. He finally came up with a surface made of cottonseed hulls, sand, oil, and green dye. It worked so well that he patented it, and his invention would soon help put miniature golf on the map.

Fairyland: A successful Tennessee businessman named Garnet Carter opened a 700-acre holiday resort on top of Lookout Mountain near the Georgia border in 1924. He called it "Fairyland" because of his wife Frieda's interest in European folklore. One of its promised features: a golf course. But it was taking much longer than expected to be built. As John Wilson writes in *Lookout: The Story of an Amazing Mountain*:

> Before the Fairyland Golf Course was opened, one impatient guest at the Fairyland Inn suggested to Garnet Carter that he construct a putting green in front of the Inn. Carter readily agreed to this idea and, as he was designing the green, he noticed some extra tile and sewer pipe lying nearby. Experimenting, he found that a golf ball could be hit so as to roll through the pipes. So Carter decided to add the pipes as part of the green and thus the worldwide sport of miniature golf was born.

This time, miniature golf caught on. The mini-links soon became so popular that he had to charge a "greens fee" to keep the huge crowds down.

BOOM!

Carter was an astute businessman—he immediately recognized the potential profits in miniature golf. So he founded the Fairyland Manufacturing Company and began constructing "Tom Thumb" courses all over Tennessee, and eventually the entire South.

By the fall of 1929, the pygmy links invaded California and New York, and soon the rest of the nation. For only $4,500, Carter's company would lay down a course that could be operational in less than a week, and they proved to be so popular (and profitable) that many courses would earn back their initial investment in only a few weeks. The game was the first of many recreational fads of the Great Depression, successful mainly because it was so inexpensive to play.

Within a year, mini-golf courses were everywhere—from highway filling stations to vacant city lots. By the middle of 1930, 20 million Americans were regular players. On any given night, there were close to four million people flooding over 40,000 courses nationwide. People joked that the only industry still hiring during those early years of the Great Depression was miniature golf, which in 1930 employed 200,000 workers and generated profits of more than $225 million. Not only that, the fad helped bolster the flagging cotton and steel industries because of Fairbairn's turf recipe.

THOU SHALT NOT PUTT-PUTT

Even a pastime as harmless as miniature golf was not without controversy. The courses were banned within 50 feet of churches, hospitals, and public schools. The nongolfing element of the population complained that the late-night revelry of reckless young golfers—who would spike their sodas with bootleg liquor—disturbed their sleep. The game also sparked a debate between physicians and pastors. Doctors liked it—miniature golf took young folks out of stuffy movie theaters at night and put them in the fresh outdoor air for some healthy activity. But church officials claimed that playing on the Sabbath—the most popular day for recreation—was a sin. Ironically, a few churches around the coun-

---

Moo: the first golf course in the United States was a cow pasture in Yonkers, New York.

try saw a chance to help pay off their debts and went over to the dark side, encouraging one and all to come and play (but never on the Sabbath).

BUST!

The great mini-golf craze didn't last long. Too many entrepreneurs saw a cheap, profitable Tom Thumb course as their road out of financial hardship. The fatal combination of market saturation and dwindling interest in the game brought about its swift end. In 1931 *Miniature Golf Management*, a year-old publication, noted that every California course was in the red financially. By the mid-1930s, nearly all of the courses were abandoned and many were destroyed. But Garnet Carter survived the fall. In 1929 he had the foresight to sell out to a Pennsylvania pipe manufacturer and settle for royalties from future miniature courses. At the end of the tiny sport's three-year heyday, he emerged unscathed. But that wasn't the end of the craze.

THE RETURN

The postwar boom of the early 1950s saw a rise in wealth, leisure time, cars, and roadside attractions—a perfect recipe for the return of miniature golf. In 1953 an insurance salesman from Fayetteville, North Carolina, named Don Clayton was ordered to take a month off work due to stress. One of the activities he took up was miniature golf. But he hated it—by that time the designs had become even more trick-filled and were less about golf than they were about goofy gadgets. Clayton was more interested in actual golf, so he decided to build his own course…and Putt-Putt miniature golf was born. (They still don't allow windmills.) Other companies, such as Lomma Miniature Golf and Goofy Golf, soon followed and tiny courses started showing up again. And not just in the United States:

• In 1953 Swiss architect Paul Bongni invented his own course and patented the name "Minigolf." Minigolf would become (and still remains) hugely popular all over Europe. Unlike his American counterparts, Bongni saw the game as a true sport and wanted to create standardized courses and rules. His *Beton* ("concrete" in German) courses had smooth—and very fast—concrete putting surfaces and simple, standardized obstacles.

• In 1958 German designer Albert Hess invented *Eternit* courses, which were small, transportable courses similar to the Betons, with fiberglass obstacles.

• Swedish Felt courses came next, using wood designs with felt surfaces and obstacles such as ramps and holes to shoot through.

While one-of-a-kind, theme-oriented courses (like Goofy Golf's Easter Island) are the norm in the United States, standardized courses like the Beton, Eternit, and Swedish Felts are more common in Europe.

PROFESSIONAL MINIATURE GOLF?

Yes, you read that correctly. In 1955 a local Putt-Putt tournament event was held in Fayetteville, North Carolina. First prize: a free vacation to Miami Beach. In 1957 the first national putting championship was held. Warren Gaines won the prize—a brand-new Cadillac. Then in 1959, the Putt-Putt Professional Golfers Association was formed. The name was changed a year later to the more businesslike Professional Putters Association (PPA). But if the pro Putt-Putters are embarrassed, they're embarrassed all the way to the bank: the PPA has given out more than $7.6 million in prize money since it began.

The PPA, however, is not to be confused with the USPMGA— the U.S. Pro Minigolf Association, just one part of the WMF—the World Minigolf Federation, the worldwide governing body of the sport of minigolf. Every year, international competitions are held (several countries even subsidize players so they can take time off work to practice) and one of the biggest events is the Masters—the Minigolf Masters—held every year in Myrtle Beach, South Carolina, the U.S. minigolf capital with more than 100 courses.

WMF players from around the world come to compete for the grand prize of $4,000 (the *other* Masters has a grand prize of more than $1 million). But that doesn't mean that you can't make a living on the Minigolf Tour. David McCaslin, winner of the 2002 Minigolf U.S. Open, has made more than $250,000 as a professional minigolfer. And the International Olympic Committee has sanctioned miniature golf as a provisional sport for the 2008 games.

Only brothers to win PGA Championships: Lionel (1957) and Jay Herbert (1960).

INCREDIBLE COMEBACK

Tommy Armour golf clubs are one of the most popular brands in the business. They're named after an amazing golfer—and man.

WARTIME

Tommy Armour was born in 1894 in Edinburgh, Scotland, the world headquarters of golf. He was a good amateur golfer in his teens, but hadn't yet had the opportunity to make a career out of it when World War I broke out in 1914. Armour immediately enlisted in the British Tank Corps, a move that would have a major effect on his golf career. Late in the war, Armour suffered casualties, first in an explosion that left him needing a metal plate in his head and then in a mustard gas attack that left him blinded. But while recovering from his wounds, Armour regained the vision in his right eye and decided to take up golf again, just to get back into shape. The game soon became an obsession, and although he probably didn't expect it at the time, he did a lot more than just get back into shape.

THE SILVER SCOT

In 1920 Armour entered and won the French Amateur Championship. In 1924, by that time living in the United States, the 29-year-old Armour decided his game was good enough to join the PGA. Over the next 11 years, the one-eyed guy with the metal plates in his head won 25 PGA tournaments, still 21st on the all-time victory list. In 1935 Armour retired from touring and started teaching full time for the then-outrageous sum of $50 for a half-hour lesson. "He was legendary," wrote *Golf* magazine, "both for his fee and the large sun umbrella he sat under, drink in one hand, golf club in the other....Folks from Bobby Jones to Richard Nixon spent time next to Armour's umbrella."

The "Silver Scot," as he became known for his prematurely gray hair, was inducted into the World Golf Hall of Fame in 1976. Golf historian Ross Goodner wrote of him: "At one time or another, Tommy Armour was known as the greatest iron player, the greatest raconteur, the greatest drinker, and the greatest teacher in golf." Armour died at his home in Boca Raton, Florida, in 1968.

According to the rules, technically speaking, you could play golf with a beach ball.

THE GOLFER-IN-CHIEF

Presidents and golf go together like Congress and kickbacks.

ULYSSES S. GRANT (1869–1877): Grant is believed to be the first U.S. president to hold a golf club and (attempt) to hit a golf ball. After his presidency, Grant made a two-and-a-half-year trip around the world, which included a stop in his ancestral home, Scotland. In his *Personal Recollections of General Ulysses S. Grant*, one of Grant's biographers, Gen. John C. Smith wrote: "Induced to enter the game and being given a club by the caddy, the General looked earnestly at the ball, then at his club, and having measured the distance, carefully made a strike, his club going six inches above the ball." Grant tried several more times, Smith says, but was never able to hit the ball. And he never touched a golf club again.
Presidential Golf Quote: "I have always understood the game of golf was good outdoor exercise and especially for the arms. I fail, however, to see what use there is for a ball."

WILLIAM MCKINLEY (1897–1901): McKinley was the first sitting president to try the game. Although golf was relatively new in the United States (the first American golf club opened in 1888), Vice President Garret Hobart was already an avid player and got the president to play a round in 1897. McKinley's score was never officially recorded, but some accounts put it well above 200. After that, McKinley played a few more times, but never improved and didn't seem to like the game that much, anyway. That doesn't mean that McKinley's wasn't a golf *presidency*, though. Many of his cabinet members were enthusiastic golfers—and were among the first politicians to wheel and deal on the links.

THEODORE ROOSEVELT (1901–1909): Roosevelt was a man's man who hunted big game in Africa, rode horses, and loved athletics, including boxing…but he refused to play golf. He even tried to get his handpicked successor, William Howard Taft, to stop playing the game, telling him most people saw it as a rich man's game.

Southpaw presidents Reagan, Bush Sr., and Clinton play (or played) golf left-handed.

Presidential Golf Quote: "You never saw a photograph of me playing tennis," Roosevelt wrote to Taft. "Photographs on horseback, yes; tennis, no. And golf is fatal."

WILLIAM HOWARD TAFT (1909–1913): Taft ignored Roosevelt's advice and became the first president to regularly play golf. Result: the popularity of the game soared—the number of golfers in the United States doubled during Taft's presidency. He wasn't good at the game, shooting regularly above 100, but he loved to play. (Many people complained that he liked being on the links more than being in the White House...and it was probably true.) Taft was also one of the heaviest U.S. presidents ever, peaking at about 350 pounds while in office. Some said that his caddies had to place the ball on the tee for him.

WOODROW WILSON (1913–1921): Wilson first started playing golf shortly after he was elected, but not by choice—he was ordered to play by his doctor as a way to relieve stress. It didn't take long for him to become addicted. He played six days a week, rain or shine, and even had golf balls painted black so he could play in the snow. But like Taft before him, Wilson never became very good, regularly shooting well above 100. His First Lady Edith Wilson, golfed with him nearly every morning. Reports indicate that she often won.

Making Golf History: Wilson was playing golf when he got word that the cruise ship *Lusitania* was sunk by a German sub. But he was back on the links a day after that event prompted him to ask Congress to declare war on Germany, marking the United States' entry into World War I.

WARREN G. HARDING (1921–1923): Harding was an avid golfer. He was also an avid gambler (his cabinet was known as the "Poker Cabinet" for their legendary all-night games) and took his gambling to the golf course. There he and his wealthy friends would bet on every swing and have a servant bring them scotch and sodas every four holes (during Prohibition). Harding once wrote to his friend Henry P. Fletcher, the American ambassador to Belgium: "I have a challenge out to play under ninety at Chevy Chase before the year is done. I am going to win it or make a bonfire of all the golf sticks I possess." The USGA honored Harding's contribution to the popularity of the game by naming the trophy for the U.S. Public Links Championship the Harding Trophy.

Presidential Golf Quote: Harding was interrupted during a golf game to sign the joint Congressional resolution that ended World War I. He is reported to have said, "That's all," and then returned to his game.

CALVIN COOLIDGE (1923–1929): Presidential historians call Coolidge the worst golfing president ever. They also point out that he ignored the rules of golf etiquette, often showing up to play in his street clothes. (Argyle vests and socks were a must in those days.) He didn't play often and did so only because the game had become so popular, especially among Washington politicians. On May 23, 1924, Coolidge presided over the opening of the Congressional Country Club in Washington, still one of the country's premier clubs...but never returned to actually play a round.

Extra Credit: In 1924 Coolidge proclaimed the first Father's Day, one of the most popular golfing days in history.

HERBERT HOOVER (1929–1933): Although he was the first president of the Congressional Country Club, Hoover didn't play golf.

Presidential Golf Quote: "I don't play golf."

FRANKLIN D. ROOSEVELT (1933–1945): True or false: President Roosevelt, who suffered from polio and was confined to a wheelchair, loved to play golf. Answer: True. FDR wasn't stricken with the disease until he was 39. Before that, he was a gifted athlete, and that included a passion for golf. He started playing when he was 12 on a small course on his family's summer home on Campobello Island in New Brunswick, Canada. By the time he was in college he had become very good and actually won the Club Championship in 1904. In 1921 he contracted polio, but even though he lost the ability to play, Roosevelt kept his heart in the game. In 1927 he founded the Roosevelt Warm Springs Institute for Rehabilitation in Georgia, a hospital for polio patients. On the grounds he ordered a nine-hole golf course built—with plenty of roadways so patients who could get around could at least play a little of their favorite game. Roosevelt was not one of them, but often watched people play on his course from his limousine.

Making Golf History: To help lift the country out of the Great Depression, FDR instituted massive public works programs in the 1930s, including the construction of more than 250 public golf courses.

HARRY S. TRUMAN (1945–1953): Truman saw the game as too elite for his liking and never played at all, although he was once accused of it. A newspaper in his hometown published an article saying that one of the president's tee shots hit a spectator in the head. Truman was incensed. "I have never played golf in my life," he wrote to the paper, "so I couldn't possibly have fired a ball on the Independence golf course and hit anybody on the head!"

DWIGHT D. EISENHOWER (1953–1961): The single most golfing president in history, Eisenhower played an estimated 800 rounds during his two terms. During that time he kept a cottage at Augusta National Golf Club (it became known as the "Little White House") and often played with his friend Arnold Palmer. He was also the first president to have a putting green built at the White House. How good was he? Pretty good, reportedly breaking 80 on numerous occasions.

Presidential Golf Quote: "How has retirement affected my golf game? A lot more people beat me now."

JOHN F. KENNEDY (1961–1963): During the 1960 presidential campaign Kennedy and his aides referred to the outgoing Republican Eisenhower as the "Duffer-in-Chief" and criticized him for playing the "elite" game so often. But it was a ruse—Kennedy actually loved the game, and made aides and Secret Service agents keep it a secret when he snuck out to play a round. That changed when rumors surfaced that the president was having extramarital affairs. His aides refuted the claims by saying, in effect, the president couldn't have been with that woman—he was golfing. Kennedy was a very good golfer who often shot in the 70s, and he could have been a lot better if not for his bad back.

Presidential Golf Quote: "It is true that my predecessor did not object, as I do, to pictures of one's golf skill in action. But neither, on the other hand, did he ever bean a Secret Service man."

LYNDON B. JOHNSON (1963–1969): He was terrible at

golf…and played as much as he could. Not caring for the rules, Johnson would openly cheat, redoing tee shots, fairway shots, and putts as often as he liked and not counting them. He is said to have taken 300 or more shots per round.

Presidential Golf Quote: "One lesson you better learn if you want to be in politics is that you never go out on a golf course and beat the president."

RICHARD M. NIXON (1969–1974): Nixon didn't take up the game until he was in his forties. And that was only because he was vice president to the golfing zealot Eisenhower. He couldn't hit the ball very far but supposedly developed a pretty good short game. It's said that he sometimes broke 90, but that claim is disputed by many historians because, like a lot of other presidents, he cheated. In 1978, at the age of 61, he reported that he had fulfilled his lifelong dream of breaking 80. "Who was keeping score?" asked humor columnist Lewis Grizzard, "G. Gordon Liddy?"

Making Golf History: Nixon might not have been a great golfer, but he was one of the only U.S. presidents to score golf's favorite shot: a hole in one. He did it on Labor Day 1961, at the Bel Air Country Club in Los Angeles.

GERALD R. FORD (1974–1977): Ford was often the butt of jokes for his famous clumsiness, but he was actually a great athlete (as a young man, he turned down an offer to play professional football). And he was an avid golfer, maintaining an official 12 handicap for many years. When he lost the White House after one term in 1976, he went straight to the golf course. Bob Hope joined in the joking, saying of the former president: "At least he can't cheat on his score—because all you have to do is look back down the fairway and count the wounded."

Presidential Golf Quote: "I deny allegations by Bob Hope that during my last game, I hit an eagle, a birdie, an elk, and a moose."

JAMES E. CARTER (1977–1981): Jimmy Carter did not play golf. He did, however, hire Tim Finchem as the national staff director for his 1980 presidential campaign. Carter lost to Ronald Reagan, but Finchem went on to become commissioner of the PGA Tour in 1994.

RONALD W. REAGAN (1981–1989): Reagan was a pretty good golfer as a young man, shooting regularly in the low- to mid-80s. He played less than 20 times in his eight years as president, but one of those times was when he was playing Augusta National in Georgia…and a gunman took over the pro shop. Charles R. Harris took seven hostages—two of them White House aides—and demanded to speak to the president. (He also demanded a bottle of whiskey.) Reagan actually tried to contact the man by phone several times, but Harris kept hanging up. He finally released all the hostages and surrendered without a fight, and Reagan never played Augusta as president again.

WILLIAM J. CLINTON (1993–2001): Bill Clinton started golfing when he was 12 and became a fair player. During his presidency Clinton claimed to be a 12 to 13 handicapper, but he was also known for his frequent use of mulligans (do-overs). The president denied this, but only a few people know for sure, because like nearly every commander-in-chief, his scores were kept secret from the public. According to political writer Thomas L. Friedman, if you played a round of golf with Clinton, "there were seven golf carts following you bearing Secret Service agents, a black-clad police sniper, an official White House photographer, a man carrying America's nuclear codes in case of a missile attack, assorted aides and a mobile secure telephone so the president can talk to any world leader he wants to between putts."

Presidential Golf Quote: "The great thing about this game: even the bad days are wonderful."

Wondering where the Bushes are? Shank over to page 141 for the story of the Bush family golfing dynasty.

*   *   *

KENNEDY COLLECTIBLES

A set of JFK's golf clubs—his MacGregor woods—was auctioned off in 1996 for $772,500. His Ben Hogan irons went for $387,500, and his putter for $65,750. Besides the clubs, three monogrammed head covers and a stroke counter were sold for a total of $63,250.

UNIQUELY GOLF

Golf ranks up there with baseball and football in popularity (and success), but it's the only major professional sport...

...**where** the scores are kept by fellow competitors, not by officials.

...**where** players penalize themselves.

...**where** aging players have their own "senior" league, in which they can still compete and make millions.

...**where** more than one ball is being played at the same time.

...**where** each player has a servant to carry their equipment.

...**that** cannot be played indoors (or in a stadium).

...**where** a 14-year-old girl can compete alongside a 54-year-old man in an official competition. (Michelle Wie and Tom Kite in the 2004 Sony Open.)

...**that** is sometimes played in the woods.

...**where** a fan can be ejected for taking a photo.

...**that** has been interrupted by an alligator.

...**that** has a pro-am format, allowing fans to play alongside the best professionals.

...**where** a player can play an entire season and make no money at all.

...**where** the lowest score wins.

...**whose** rule book includes the word "dung."

...**where** an equal playing field is not guaranteed. One player can play in sunshine with no wind, another in a howling rainstorm.

...**that** has no regulation-size playing field.

...**that** has a predetermined score (par) against which all players are measured.

...**where** fans are allowed on the playing field.

...**where** a fan watching the play at home can call and get a player disqualified. (See page 33.)

...**that** has been played on the moon.

Our favorite: a "toilet flusher" is a putt that swirls around the rim of the hole.

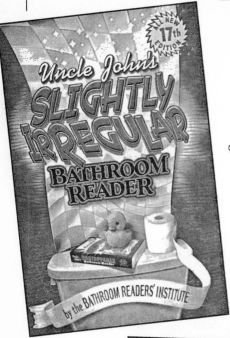

Find these other
great titles from
*Uncle John's
Bathroom Reader*
at your local bookstore
or order online at
www.bathroomreader.com

Coming Soon

Uncle John's
Fast-Acting Long-Lasting
Bathroom Reader

Uncle John's **Wild & Wooly**
Bathroom Reader For Kids Only

Uncle John's Bathroom Reader
Plunges into New Jersey

Uncle John's Bathroom Reader
Plunges into Michigan

Uncle John's
Slightly Irregular
Bathroom Reader (the Audio)

Uncle John's Bathroom Reader
Puzzle Book #3

Uncle John's Bathroom Reader
Christmas Collection

Uncle John's Bathroom Reader
Plunges into Hollywood

Uncle John's **Strange & Scary**
Bathroom Reader For Kids Only

For a complete listing of
Uncle John's Bathroom Reader
books and products, go to
www.bathroomreader.com

THE 19TH HOLE

FELLOW BATHROOM READERS:
The fight for good bathroom reading should never be taken loosely—we must do our duty and sit firmly for what we believe in, even while the rest of the world is taking pot shots at us.

We'll be brief: now that we've proven we're not simply a flush-in-the-pan, we invite you to take the plunge: Sit Down and Be Counted! Become a member of the Bathroom Readers' Institute. Log on to our Web site, www.bathroomreader.com, or send a self-addressed, stamped, business-sized envelope to: BRI, PO Box 1117, Ashland, Oregon 97520. You'll receive your free membership card, receive discounts when ordering directly through the BRI, and earn a permanent spot on the BRI honor roll!

If you like reading our books...
VISIT THE BRI'S WEBSITE!
www.bathroomreader.com

Well, we're out of space, and when you've gotta go, you've gotta go. Tanks for all your support. Hope to hear from you soon. Meanwhile, remember:

Keep on flushin'!